Pensions policy in Britain

Radical Social Policy

GENERAL EDITOR:

Vic George

*Professor of Social Policy and
Administration and Social Work
University of Kent*

The **Radical Social Policy Series** provides critical accounts of different aspects of social policy, to develop the body of knowledge in social policy and administration and to provide a forum for democratic socialist debates in social welfare.

Pensions policy in Britain

A socialist analysis

Eric Shragge
McGill University, Montreal

Routledge & Kegan Paul
London, Boston, Melbourne and Henley

First published in 1984
by Routledge & Kegan Paul plc

14 Leicester Square, London WC2H 7PH, England

9 Park Street, Boston, Mass. 02108, USA

464 St Kilda Road, Melbourne,
Victoria 3004, Australia and

Broadway House, Newtown Road,
Henley-on-Thames, Oxon RG9 1EN, England

Set in Press Roman 10/11
by Hope Services, Abingdon, Oxon
and printed in Great Britain
by Billing & Sons Ltd, Worcester

Library of Congress Cataloging in Publication Data

Shragge, Eric, 1948–

Pensions policy in Britain
(Radical social policy)
Bibliography: p.
Includes index.
1. Old age pensions–Great Britain–History.
I. Title.   II. Series.
HD7105.35.G7S47   1984   331.25'2'0941   84-3301

British Library CIP data also available

ISBN 0-7100-9842-1

Contents

Acknowledgments

The research for this book was undertaken while pursuing doctoral studies at the University of Kent in Canterbury. I am grateful to the many people who helped make this experience possible. On the Canadian side, Myer Katz arranged a two-year leave of absence from my job at the School of Social Work, McGill University. I received grants from Health and Welfare Canada, and the Quebec Department of Education to pursue my studies. In Britain Vic George acted as far more than a Ph.D. supervisor — he is a friend, and supportive critic. Thanks to those Canterbury comrades who listened, criticized and debated with me and to the CSE State Group for providing stimulating forums. In particular, the following people either read parts of my manuscript at various stages or were of particular assistance in other ways: Assaf Bayat, Henry Bernstein, Colin Barker, Richard Disney, Norman Ginsberg, John Holloway, Steve Jordan, John Macdonald, Chris Pickvance, Geoff Rayner, Gerry Rubin and Tony Skillen. The final product is, of course, my own.

The typing of the final draft was helped by a Social Science Research Grant from McGill University. Special thanks to Lillian Barclaay, Nicola Richards and Kathy Wilmott for the typing.

Special thanks to Davida, Joseph and Aaron for patience and time lost to them.

The author and publishers are grateful for permission to reproduce the tables from the following: (Table 2.1) G. D. Gilling-Smith, *The Complete Guide to Pensions and Superannuation*, Harmondsworth, Penguin, 1971 and the University of California Press; (Table 2.2) A. Peacock, *The Economics of National Insurance*, Glasgow, William

Hodge & Co., 1952; (Table 3.1) adapted from the Analysis of
Public Expenditures 1951-63, with permission of the Controller
of Her Majesty's Stationery Office; (Table 3.2) M. Pilch and V. Woods,
New Trends in Pensions, London, Hutchinson, 1964; (Table 3.3) *Oc-
cupational Pension Schemes: A New Survey by the Government
Actuary*, 1966, p. 7, Table Two, with additional data from 1956
and *Occupational Pension Schemes: A Survey by the Government
Actuary*, 1958, pp. 4-5, with permission of the Controller of Her
Majesty's Stationery Office; (Table 3.4) *Report of the Government
Actuary on the Fifth Quinquennial Review, National Insurance Act
1946, House of Commons Papers*, 30 November 1954, p. 15, with
permission of the Controller of Her Majesty's Stationery Office; (Table
3.5) J. C. R. Dow, *The Management of the British Economy
1945-1960*, Cambridge University Press, 1964, p. 188; (Table 4.1)
Hansard, 2 February 1976, column 453, and 8 July 1976, column 663,
cited in the *Campaign Guide*, Conservative Research Department,
March 1977, p. 56; (Table 4.2), I. Gough, *The Political Economy of
the Welfare State*, London, Macmillan, and Atlantic Highlands,
New Jersey, Humanities Press, 1979, p. 77; (Table 4.3) Peter
Townsend, 'Social Planning and the Treasury', in *Labour and Equality*,
ed. Nick Bosanquet and Peter Townsend, London, Heinemann, 1980,
p. 11; (Table 4.4) *Occupational Pension Schemes 1975: Fifth Survey
by the Government Actuary*, HMSO, 1978, p. 9, with permission of
the Controller of Her Majesty's Stationery Office; (Table 4.5) *Family
Expenditure Survey 1975*, cited in *Occupational Pension Schemes
1971: Fourth Survey by the Government Actuary*, DHSS, 1977,
with permission of the Controller of Her Majesty's Stationery Office;
(Table 5.1) Peter Townsend, *Poverty in the United Kingdom*,
Harmondsworth, Penguin, 1979.

Introduction

Capitalism is confronted by its production of enormous wealth and prosperity and at the same time incredible poverty and underdevelopment, on a world scale. In Britain, as in other advanced capitalist nations, even with the long period of post-war prosperity and social democratic welfare state reform this contradiction has not disappeared, particularly in relative terms. Since the Second World War, one group has been the most highly represented among the poor — the elderly. With forced retirement, more and more people turn to the state for their basic needs in the last years of life. Retirement has become almost synonymous with poverty. The key to this problem is the nature of state retirement pensions. This study will analyse their development in the context of British post-war capitalism.

It will be argued in this book that the failure of the welfare state and retirement pensions cannot be isolated from the development of post-war capitalism but the contradictions of its development not only impose limits to the growth of the welfare state but shape the social relations of welfare state and pension practice on a daily basis. As the present crisis continues, and attacks on workers increase, and provision by the welfare state is reorganized and cut back, the future of those dependent on the state is bleak. Capitalist class and social relations created during the war years are ending and new class strategies are emerging. These imply a profound change in welfare state provision. This book will study the development of pensions from the major post-war reforms of Beveridge to the present crisis, emphasizing the developments up to 1975. In this way major changes and development in the post-war period and the nature of capitalism itself can be examined, as to how they shape welfare state and particularly pension provision.

There will be several themes explored in this book. The major emphasis will be on explanations for the development of retirement pensions in the post-war period. The book will examine those forces that shape and limit the welfare state and pension development. These will be situated in the context of how class and broader capitalist social relations and domination change and how the state responds to changing conditions of accumulation and struggle. State strategies as a response to these changes will be examined and form the context for the discussion of the welfare state, and pension policy. Most of the book will examine these developments and how they shape retirement pensions. Another theme is the examination of the relations of class and patriarchy implicit in state pensions. Much of the discussion of the welfare state focuses on the question of distribution. Although this area will be explored, the forms of relations implicit in state pensions will be emphasized in relation to a theoretical framework. Next, the relation of state pensions to private occupational pensions will be examined. This is of particular importance both because of the rapid growth of private pensions, particularly among workers in the post-war period, and because of the present tendency to encourage market forms of provision. Private pension development has formed state pension policy in many ways, and its examination is a good example of the relationship between market and state forms of provision. Another theme explored is the relationship of the trade union movement to the development of state pensions. Their positions, during the post-war period, show a mixture of conservatism and progress. This is important for the left to understand so that historical and political errors are not repeated and the relation of the trade unions to the welfare state is not to be misunderstood. Along with this, changing positions of both political parties and parts of the capitalist class will be discussed. A final theme in the last chapter is the presentation of a libertarian socialist alternative to pension provision as part of a socialist orientation. The goal is not to present a blueprint, but much more to raise an alternative in a time when the choice seems to be to defend or attack the welfare state. The goal of the total project is to understand and to criticize one aspect of the welfare state — pensions — in a broader context and provoke a debate on socialist perspectives for the provision of human need.

The outline

This book will study the development of state retirement pensions from

1940 to 1975 — the post-war period. The war years were chosen as
the beginning of the study because of the significance of Beveridge,
his Report, and the reforms that followed. The Castle plan, passed
in 1975, will form the basis of state retirement pensions for the rest
of the century and is where the study ends. The book will be divided
into five chapters. The first will present a libertarian socialist critique
of welfare state provision. The focus of this chapter will be on explanations for the development of the welfare state. The next three
chapters will discuss the development of state pension plans. Chapter
2 will discuss the war, and the immediate post-war period; Chapter 3
will discuss the boom years; and Chapter 4 will discuss the crisis of
British capitalism and state pensions. In each of these chapters, state
pension reform will be situated in a broader historical context, and
analysed in relation to changing state policies. A final section will
briefly discuss Thatcher and implications for the welfare state and
pensions, and raise a libertarian socialist option to the welfare state.

1

The welfare state: A libertarian socialist critique

Introduction

This chapter will discuss the welfare state and state pensions in theoretical terms. The perspective will be based on recent Marxist theories of the state[1] and their application to the welfare state. As well, this analysis is influenced by a libertarian, anti-state, socialist orientation.[2] This analysis assumes that the goal of socialism is not the taking over of the state by the working class but the abolition of all forms of domination, which implies different forms of organization, and a self-managed society based on organization from the bottom up — factory and neighbourhood councils — and not from the top down — vanguard, party and state.[3]

This chapter will cover the following topics: a conception and definition of the welfare state, functions performed by the welfare state, tensions and limits faced by welfare state expansion, and explanations for the development and reform of the welfare state.

The welfare state: conception and definition

Ian Gough's conception of the welfare state provides a good starting point. As opposed to the social democratic or social administration views which see the state as a progressive force, Gough defines the welfare state in terms of contradictory tendencies. He writes:

The welfare state exhibits positive and negative features within a contradictory unity. . . . It simultaneously embodies tendencies to enhance social welfare to develop powers of individuals, to exert social control over the blind play of market forces; and tendencies to repress and control people, to adapt them to requirements of the capitalist economy.[4]

This viewpoint is extended in his 'Political Postscript,' where he writes:

Once the contradictory nature of the welfare state and its contradictory impact on capitalism is appreciated, then the political strategy of all who work in it, use it, or are concerned with it can be refined. The positive aspects of welfare policies need defending and extending, their negative aspects need exposing and attacking.[5]

The problem with this definition is in the separation of enhancing and repressive tendencies. Put another way, the welfare state has a good and a bad side,[6] and extending the good parts is the goal of socialists or Marxists. Can this distinction be made, or are the enhancing aspects also a form of domination and more specifically a form of capitalist social and class relations? Is it possible to separate these tendencies?

The welfare state does not only do things for people, but it performs these functions in a certain way. The way that the welfare state functions is inevitably a form of social relations. The welfare state provides services and benefits, but in doing so it imposes relations of domination. Central to this position is that it is not what the welfare state does that makes it a form of domination, but more important is how it functions on a daily basis. Further, the relations imposed by the welfare state are as much a part of the welfare state as the benefits and services given out by it. Because the relations of the welfare state are forms of domination this implies that these are relations of struggle, and that they are not fixed in one way more or less permanently. The welfare state changes with the ebb and flow of broader class forces and other struggles, but in the shifts, sometimes beneficial to the working class, it is able to maintain itself as a form of domination. What relations of domination are implicit in the welfare state? The welfare state and, to varying degrees, each program, are forms of class domination, patriarchy, individualization, and technocracy. Each of these will be explored and then applied to state pensions.

The central feature of capitalism is the relations of domination based on class. This domination is rooted in private ownership of productive property and the production of surplus value by the working class. Although these relations appear to be economic, they extend beyond what is commonly understood as the economy, and are social.[7] The development of capitalism is closely intertwined with the relations of wage labour. As capitalism develops more and more people become dependent on wage labour for their own reproduction. Individuals sell their labour power for a wage. In the process, they give up control of their labour time to the capitalist or the state. This is the basic relation of domination in capitalism–wage labour.[8] In this relation, struggles and tension exist concerning the conditions of wage labour including wage levels, conditions of work and the length of the work day. This is the basis of struggles between workers and capitalists, and struggles are usual. Further, the process of production and the reproduction of workers cannot easily be separated. The reproduction of labour power through the market, the welfare state and unwaged domestic labour is closely intertwined with relations of production. It is important *not* to reduce relations of wage labour only to the interface of capitalists and workers or workers and the state but these relations must be understood as extending into the total conditions allowing production of surplus value to occur.[9] The relations of wage labour form the basis of class domination in capitalism. They extend further than the point of production, and although having an economic expression, they are social, and these relations of domination are relations of struggle.

How are these relations expressed in welfare state provision? The central feature of the welfare state is the link between benefits and wage labour or work. Benefits in many programs are directly related to past performance in work or on future guarantees of seeking work. This is central in most social security programs, and specifically in programs related to unemployment. Unemployment benefits balance the demand for wage labour, and discipline those working by making sure the 'reserve army of labour' is ready and able to compete for existing jobs. This relation is a direct expression of class; that is, forcing unemployed workers to be ready to labour in order to receive benefits. Further, the traditions of the welfare state, dating back to the Elizabethan Poor Laws and before, have maintained the principle that income from either the state or public charity should not 'undermine' provision by hard work and thrift. Each subsequent reform of social security has made sure that this principle remains intact. Traditional divisions between 'deserving' and 'undeserving' poor have been used to differentiate between those who should work for income – the ablebodied – and those who cannot – the sick and aged. Similar principles guide policy today with means-testing and work-testing of benefits, and making certain that private provision and thrift is not discouraged. Wage labour is considered the 'legitimate' form of self-provision while reliance on the state is discouraged except in particular circumstances in which the level of benefits is kept to a minimum.

Pensions historically have been tied to a worker's contribution record based on wages. This record determines whether or not a worker is eligible for a retirement pension, and how much this pension will be. The worker is forced to labour in order to become eligible for benefits. The traditional argument in defending this position is that benefits once established through contributions cannot be removed from the worker. Contributions thus establish benefits as a right. Why then is it only social security benefits that operate this way? Children are eligible for schooling, and all can receive health services regardless of tax paid or any means test. However, to receive a pension or unemployment benefits an adequate contribution record is required. Work or selling of labour power is central for pensions. This will be referred to throughout this book as 'work-testing'. For the origins of these contributions, a discussion of the struggles around the 1911 National Insurance Act is required and will not be pursued here.[10] More important, is that eligibility for pension and unemployment benefits is tied to wage labour and thus forms part of the domination of wage labour. As will be discussed, and demonstrated, there is no clear monetary link between the specific contribution made by a worker and future pension or unemployment benefits. Pension benefits and other work-tested benefits, rather than being only money paid out by the state to workers, are a form of relations defined by wage labour. The 'enhancing' aspect of the welfare state, then, is completely intertwined with capitalist class relations, and historically, in social security, work-testing has dominated in so-called insurance and pension programs in Britain.

Central to all aspects of the welfare state is the way that the state defines conditions under which programs are carried out. Relations of sexual domination or patriarchy are a central aspect of the welfare state. Women are defined in terms of motherhood and as housewives, regardless of their position as workers.[11] There are several ways in which the domination of women is expressed in the welfare state, in defining a woman's place through health, education, and in social security programs, particularly in the cohabitation rule. Patriarchy in pension benefits is subtle but none the less evident. The way that pensions are structured assumes the dominant family structure with the woman economically dependent on her husband as the major earner. The benefits received by the husband are to provide for his spouse in retirement. This is reflected in contributions. Until the 1975 Castle plan was implemented, differing structures of contributions existed for women based on the assumption of dependency. Further, and more important, unwaged housework has never been recognized as a basis of entitlement for pension benefits. Thus, although this form of labour — unwaged housework — is essential for capitalist reproduction, it does not allow entitlement to pensions in later years, assuming dependency

7

on a spouse's pension and therefore continuing the dependent position of women. Even with reforms creating formal equality of pension contributions and benefits for women, the inequality in the labour market producing low wages and unstable jobs for many women implies low level pension benefits in later years. The consequences of the forms of patriarchy implicit in state pensions are the poverty experienced by elderly women, the high number of these women dependent on Supplementary Benefits, and the poverty among widows. Again, a form of domination, in this case the domination of women, is interrelated and reflected in what might appear to be a benign pension policy. Further, in so far as more and more women are selling their labour power they are subjected in pension benefits to the domination of class.

In capitalist society, relations with the state are expressed in terms of individuals, and citizenship and not in class terms. A worker encounters the state not as a member of his/her class, but as a citizen with individual rights, liberties, and benefits.[12] This relationship of individualizing class relations developed historically out of property rights, and for workers it meant that the selling of their labour power to the capitalist, and more recently to the state, had an appearance of free exchange between equal individuals meeting in the market place. The implication of this form of relations is profound in welfare state provision. The state individualizes what are essentially class-based relations. The principle of pension and unemployment benefits contributions discussed earlier is a good example. Benefit decisions are based on individual participation in wage labour; that is, the fundamentals of class relations become translated through the state as a relation between the individual worker and the state. Pension benefits take the appearance of an individual 'saving' for his/her own retirement, and individual responsibility for retirement is perpetuated in this way, when in reality the conditions of the labour market determine this process. Individualizing of class and sex relations occurs in education, health, and a whole range of welfare state programs.

The process of individualization has important consequences for class struggle. As opposed to the workplace in which workers are brought together in the labour process, the worker experiences the welfare state as an individual, as a pensioner, a council tenant, or a student. In the workplace one of the major contradictions faced by capitalists is that labour is a collective process, and thus the struggle of workers grows out of it. Mobilization against the welfare state is more difficult because of the individualized nature of the state, and the class nature of the welfare state is obscured by the way the state fragments and divides the working class. In facing the state as individuals, the working class becomes divided, and this acts against the solidarity of workers.

One of the most profound forms of domination of the welfare state is the increasing control and penetration of the state into the daily lives of all people. The state, in providing more and more, removes control from people in the process, and increases powerlessness. The combination of technocratic rules and regulations, and increasing of the role of bureaucratic professionals takes more and more control out of the hands of the working class over daily affairs. Examples are wide-ranging; two ways in which this applies to pensions are as follows: first, the calculation of pension benefits and contributions have become so complicated that it is beyond the scope of most individuals to even come close to figuring out entitlement. Complicated formulae, that will be elaborated later, have made the calculations of pensions a limited expertise of those managing computers. Similar arguments can be made in education, health-care, and the personal social services, where the technology and organization of services allows workers to approach a maze of bureaucracy and technocracy such that it is almost impossible to do anything except receive services completely defined and packaged in advance.

Second, historically, particularly for retirement and sickness benefits, the state apparatus has superseded institutions organized and controlled by the working class. In this case the transition began around the 1911 National Insurance Act when the state began to usurp control of working-class forms of self-organization.[13] Friendly societies were organized by the more stable and skilled sections of the working class and provided benefits for sickness and unemployment. Although there were limits to their programs, and the growth of demand for benefits was creating financial problems, these were autonomous organizations of the working class, controlled by them. The state-organized system, in the name of greater access and universality, and through a series of reforms superseded these organizations. The point is not to glorify past achievements of the working class, but to understand that state provision is a historical form, one that should not be understood as permanent or as the only form. Historical precedents demonstrate the possibility of working-class institutions of provision autonomous of both the market and the state. This process has continued, and, through the technocratic transformation of the state, has removed the control of all social services from those it supposedly serves. The relation of domination through the daily experience of powerlessness is central in understanding the fundamental relations of the welfare state. At times these relationships have been resisted, and groups of women, neighbourhood groups and workers have mobilized against this form of domination, organizing popular committees; however, in response the state has tried to co-opt these groups into state planning bodies. The principle of self-managed community services is the direction of these struggles, but has not succeeded. This theme will be raised later.

In summary, any conception of the welfare state must include not only what the welfare state does, but, more importantly, the relations of domination expressed in it. These relations exist in tension and change with the continuing struggles of the working-class men and women against the state. The welfare state transforms and deforms struggles and defines the terms in which the struggles take place. The forms of domination expressed in the welfare state include class, patriarchical, individualization and technocratic forms of domination. These render the working class and individual workers powerless in relation to the state and fragment class solidarity. In understanding and analysing the welfare state it is insufficient to discuss it in terms of its good and bad features. By its very nature, the so-called good and bad, enhancing and repressive tendencies are woven together. Interaction with the state is a form of relations. The welfare state is a relation of power and domination; it defines conditions under which benefits are received. In addition to the growing technocratic and bureaucratic forms of relations experienced daily by all who interact with the state, relations based in class and patriarchical forms are characteristic of the welfare state in capitalist society. As a conception of the welfare state it is impossible to isolate the forms of relations of domination inherent in the welfare state from the benefits and services provided by it. Thus although the welfare state provides goods and services necessary for many workers, these are provided within a class, patriarchical, technocratic state that individualizes contradictions produced by broader relations of domination. The 'enhancing' and 'repressive' tendencies discussed earlier are an artificial division, that do not reflect the daily experience and practice of the welfare state.

The functions of the welfare state

Many writers on the left have discussed the state, and the welfare state, and in particular its development in terms of the functions it performs in relation to the totality of capitalist reproduction.[14] In class terms, this position argues that the welfare state, although providing certain benefits to the working class, is necessary for the capitalist class in so far as it plays a role in providing a pool of labour to exploit and manages some of the negative social consequences of capitalist production. Gough discusses two basic functions of the welfare state. Through its benefits and programs it is involved in the reproduction of labour power, and in the support and maintenance of the non-working population.[15] Much of the reproduction of labour power occurs through the market and unwaged household labour. Workers buy goods with their wages and family members, usually wives, perform such necessary services as shopping, cooking, and provide emotional support. Together, these activities allow a worker to labour. For women workers, there is a double task of performing both unwaged and waged labour. Along with these the state influences the quality of labour power by providing resources that influence household labour, such as children's allowances, or the labour power of workers through training programs, medical programs and education. Also, state programs are related to intergenerational reproduction through schooling and child-care programs. The second function of the welfare state is the maintenance of those who are unable to work. The state transfers money to those who for various reasons cannot work. Although these functions are conceptually separate, this distinction becomes more complex in practice because the reserve army of labour falls into both categories.[16]

With this general conceptualization, what functions do state retirement pensions perform? State pensions are involved in supporting those outside the reserve army of labour–retired workers. The question that arises in relating this function to capitalist development is what is the function of retirement. Some brief, speculative comments here might help to make connections between the needs of capitalist reproduction and retirement pensions. Forced retirement and now 'early retirement' from work is a relatively recent phenomenon. The consequence is to maintain a younger workforce with less conflict and obstruction in labour turnover. During recessions, early retirement reduces the pressure for redundancy and unemployment in both the state and private sector. Younger workers in manual work are supposedly more productive and adaptable to change in productive techniques. Also, with increased hierarchy and bureaucracy in work, job mobility plays a role in maintaining and stimulating competition between workers, in the game of job improvement. Orderly retirement of older workers helps in these functions. Pensions are the major way of insuring a planned and orderly retirement. Both occupational and state pensions perform this function. Thus pensions are important in terms of managing labour turnover. This is particularly functional during times of recession when large numbers of redundancies and unemployment occur.

Turning now to the relation of pensions to the reproduction of labour power, two related points can be made. First, traditional support for retired workers came from a mixture of family supports, communal agencies and perhaps limited savings, and sickness benefits through friendly societies. One change in advanced capitalist societies has been the gradual erosion of the extended family and a network of locally run communal supports. With this has been a steady growth of retired people dependent upon the state to meet many of their basic needs.

State provision has reduced the necessity of retired workers being supported by their families. This is a gradual historical process. Further, the possibility of labour mobility has increased, and is of particular importance in recent years with the increased mobility of capital. Thus, pensions have developed in a functional relation to the needs of capital. The state has freed the worker to some degree in supporting his/her parents and greater mobility is possible. Second, pensions can be understood in terms of wages. Traditionally workers had to save for their own retirement out of wages through savings. With the growth of state and employer pensions, this responsibility has shifted from the worker and at times his/her employer to the state. This has had the effect of reducing the cost to capital in at least a small way in the costs of reproduction of workers. The significance economically is minimal, but the link between the reproduction of workers and retirement is a connection that has been reduced by state pensions. These functions of pensions illustrate the relations between the needs of capital and how pensions function in relation to these needs.

There are several weaknesses and limits to this argument. First, although the functional interrelations of the welfare state to the needs of capital are important to point out, they are not an adequate explanation for the development of the welfare state.[17] As will be discussed later, the forces that led to welfare state reform are complex. An assumption that there exists a long-term design by the state is not warranted. Neither can capital perceive itself as a totality because of the dynamics of competition, nor can the state 'know' what is in the total or long-term interests of capital to foresee how the large number and fragmented pieces of welfare state legislation can play a functional role. The state more correctly reacts to the changing conditions of accumulation as a general form of class struggle.[18] These reactions are by definition limited and constrained, not always efficient, and cannot form the total pattern of reproduction implied in the left functionalist explanation. State pensions provide a good example of how the fact of pension provision does help capital in the reproduction of labour power, but the historical development of state pension policies is a response to other changing conditions. Then changes in the conditions of accumulation and class relations will explain the changes in pensions much more than any function they perform for capital.

Second, to imply that the state performs a certain function precludes the question of how else could a given function be performed. Social needs historically have been provided in four ways: by the state, through market relations, by charitable organizations, and by self-managed working-class organizations. In the present period, there is a tension between market and state forms. This tension exists in the major areas of social policies, for example, state and private education, state health-care and private insurance. Perhaps the most developed of the private sector forms is occupational pensions. Further, much of the pension debate in the post-war period has been around how state and private sector pensions should co-exist and what the balance, interrelations and conditions of operation of each should be. The point is, then, that the arguments derived from a left functionalist perspective tend to ignore the balance between state, market and other forms of provision. The question, then, is more historical and involves an analysis of the changing forms of capitalist reproduction. The post-war years in many cases involved a shift from reproduction of labour power from wage labour almost exclusively to a complex combination of wage labour, taxation and the state. With the present crises, perhaps there will be a return to increased provision through market forms. Because the state performs a specific function, it cannot be assumed then that this will continue indefinitely. The private and state forms of provision of retirement pensions have had important consequences. Workers have developed different interests in pensions. At times, workers in alliance with private pension interests have fought to protect those pensions against increased state involvement. The market-state relationship therefore needs to be specified and its consequences analysed. Third, because certain functions are attributed to the welfare state does not imply that they are carried out without contradictions. These will be explored in the next section, but it is inappropriate to assume that the welfare state performs those functions necessary for capitalist reproduction without contradictions, tensions and limits.

To summarize, a discussion of the functions of the welfare state is useful in locating the connections or links between the welfare state and the totality of capitalist reproduction. Further, this discussion implicitly debates the Fabian position about the content of welfare state provision. The welfare state, then, is to be understood not only as providing benefits for workers. At the same time as these may be useful to the worker, they also play an important function for the capitalist. To understand the welfare state, a left functional approach discussing the fact that the welfare state is in the interest of capitalists is limited but useful.

Limits and tensions of the welfare state

In recent times the welfare state in many capitalist nations has been subject to both cutbacks in and restructuring of benefits and services. This section will present the interconnections between capitalist production relations and the welfare state. The main argument used by Marxists in exploring the limits on welfare and state expenditures is that these constitute a drain on total surplus value. Thus surplus value produced by workers becomes siphoned off and is not available for profit and/or reinvestment by capitalists.[19] This argument links state expenditures to capitalist production. In this form the argument is limited and oversimplified, although the basic concept is correct. One criticism is that state expenditures, even those directed to the welfare state, are necessary for capitalist reproduction, and are indirectly productive because of their relationship to the reproduction of labour power.[20] Thus even though state expenditures are a deduction from total surplus value and divert value from expansion of accumulation, they are necessary for the process as it is defined in advanced capitalism. However, the problem with this argument is that it looks at the economy as a relation between objects and does not discuss production and the process of accumulation as a form of class relations. The following circuit of reproduction is one way of avoiding this error, and allows a more dynamic perspective on the forces in capitalism that put limits on welfare state development.

In this model,[21] the relationship between production, taxation, bureaucratization and individualization will be explored. For the purposes of this discussion the relation of production and taxation will be emphasized, not only as an economic relation, but as well as a relationship between classes. The discussion starts with the production of surplus value. Production, however, is a relation of struggle, particularly over the conditions of wage labour and the distribution of surplus value. How much of it will go through the circuit of production and be reinvested, how much will be taken off by the state in the form of taxation and how much will workers be able to increase their standard of living? For the moment, the question of crisis and restructuring will be omitted. With accumulation understood as a relation of struggle, the question of taxation can be introduced.

Taxation is the form in which surplus labour or value is transferred from production to the state.[22] Taxation is based on labour, but taxpayers appear not as members of their class but owners as a revenue source.[23] Thus the process of taxation is based on the labour of workers in production, and individualizes workers. But, if taxation is from surplus value production, who bears the cost of taxation? That is to say, is the capitalist or the worker less well off after taxation? Is it the living standard of the worker that suffers or is it the process of accumulation and profitability that becomes diminished? Ginsburg's work is helpful on this question. He points out:

> according to value analysis, the wage or price of labour power is the *net* wage after such 'stoppages' [taxation]. The worker has no control over that part of the gross wage which he/she never sees, and

it cannot be considered part of the exchange between capital and labour – the exchange of the commodity labour power for a wage. The ultimate cost of state expenditure falls therefore solely on capital.[24]

As he elaborates, the immediate increases in taxation tend to be a reduction in wages, and thus tend to bring about increases in the class struggle. Thus although in the long run there is a tendency to shift the burden back to capital, it is not always guaranteed and taxation represents, at least in the short term, an attack on the value of labour power. The argument that capital bears the cost of the welfare state is too simplistic and tends to be ahistorical. So long as workers can defend their post-tax and post-inflation standard of living, which has generally been the tendency since the war, then the burden of taxation falls on capital. But, as will be discussed in later chapters, a fall in the net income of workers can be worsened by increases in taxation. The ability of the state to raise funds is closely linked to the form of domination and struggle involved in surplus value production. Increases in taxation will intensify workers' struggles over their living standards, posing problems for capitalists as taxation increases have the potential of taxing some surplus value out of circulation, as well as increasing the intensity of class struggle. The limits of welfare state expansion, while appearing to be economic, are also broader and must be linked to the totality of class relations. As will be discussed later, in periods of intensified class struggle, or crises, the relationship between accumulation, taxation, and welfare state expenditures is highlighted. The other two aspects of this model – bureaucratization and individualization – were discussed earlier and will not be repeated, except to note the link between these aspects of the welfare state and capitalist production.

One other factor limiting welfare state expansion is its relation to the market. In many cases, in constructing new forms of domination, the welfare state does limit the full functioning of market relations and profitable outlets. Particularly when the unemployed receive state benefits, the *full* pressures of the reserve army of labour are buffered. In other areas the state constrains market forms of provision. These limits are flexible and will be modified according to broader changes in accumulation and other general conditions of class and other struggles. Historically, besides its being based on surplus value production, the welfare state is limited because it interferes with the full functioning of the market in labour, and in other areas. As conditions change, the balance between state and market forms of provision can change.

The implications for state pensions begin with the large expense that state pensions pose. Further, as the proportion of elderly increases in relation to the working population, and as people live longer then this expense will increase. A traditional question raised by the ruling class concerns the affordability of pensions and the consequences that the growth of state pensions have for profits and growth of the economy. Clearly, the fundamental dynamic linking welfare state expenditures, taxation, and surplus value production is embodied in state pensions. The specific aspects of this relation will be discussed in each of the chapters that follow. In each period, specific links will be made between accumulation, as a relation of class struggle, and the development of state pensions. Both the failure, and the limits of pension reform are linked to the basic form of class relations in|capitalism — surplus value production. Further, as private occupational pensions grew, these began to act as a limit on state pensions. State policy had always been to encourage to varying degrees these pensions, but their growth began to limit and form state pension policy, particularly because of the role of private pensions as investment capital. As mentioned earlier, the contribution by workers is a way of linking state pensions to wage labour. The strategy of increasing contributions and linking increased benefits paid out to retired workers with these contributions has been used as a way around the limits posed by accumulation. However, far from solving these problems, these increased contributions are another tax and the dynamics of increasing taxation on the working class discussed earlier|apply. Increasing contributions are understood as an attack on wages, and workers will struggle to maintain their standard of living. If they succeed then the burden will be passed on to capital, but there are no guarantees and only the balance of class forces can decide. The problem then is historical, and in periods of increased strength of the working class pension increases become a problem to capitalists, and act as a drain on surplus value.

In summary, the expansion of the welfare state is limited by the form of class relations implicit in capital accumulation. If workers are able to protect their take-home pay, which has been the case in most years in post-war Britain, then the burden of welfare state expenditures falls on capitalists and acts as a drain on surplus value and therefore on further accumulation. This then acts on the welfare state as a limit to its expansion. The relation of state and market forms also shapes and limits expansion of state provision. This is particularly important in the discussion of pensions that follows. The specifics of these relations require historical discussions which will be pursued in the chapters that follow.

The development of the welfare state

In this section, a general perspective will be outlined as the basis for historical discussion. It will explore the forces that lead to welfare reform and shape the welfare state. Writers on the left[25] examine the development of the welfare state through a combination of the functions the welfare state performs for capital and the struggles and demands of the working class for welfare state reform. This position is important in that it corrects errors of those who see the development of the welfare state either as a result of solely the needs of the capitalist class or the demands of workers. There are two problems associated with this position. First, the criticisms of left functionalism raised earlier apply here. Second, it is questionable whether the demands for the welfare state have been the demands of the working class.[26] Although, as will be discussed, trade union leaders have played a role in shaping the welfare state, it is not the masses of the working class that have mobilized for the welfare state. Although there are elements of the above perspective that are helpful a more comprehensive understanding is required. Specific welfare state reforms need to be situated in the context of broadly defined class and other struggles and the orientation and strategies of the state as a reflection of class rule at any particular time.

If the task is to situate welfare reform in a broader social context what aspects of society are important to analyse and how do these affect or interact with welfare state reform? In the broadest sense the welfare state needs to be understood as part of the changing form of capitalist social relations. The state reacts to changes in accumulation, and class struggle, and attempts to find strategies to establish conditions and social relations for growth and profitable accumulation. Capitalist production generates periods of crisis and intensified class struggle. This study will not present a theory of crisis,[27] but will emphasize the response of the state to crises and in particular the changing strategies and reactions through which the state tries to establish new conditions for accumulation. Welfare state reforms are one aspect of the way in which the state can respond to periods of intensified class conflict, but these reforms are part of larger changes in the conditions of capitalist social and class relations.

Historical analysis is the most important tool in this task. Changing social and class relations, and the reactions of the state through various social and economic policies need to be specified. This study covers the development and changes in state pensions in the post-war period. These changes will be discussed in the context of changing conditions of accumulation, understood as the changing forms of class and social relations. Three periods will be presented. The first includes the war years and the period of Labour government that followed. In it, a new form of class relations based on the policies of Keynes and Beveridge developed. These shaped social policy generally, and the conditions of

17

class and sexual domination for most of the post-war period. The second period corresponds to the long post-war boom, and discusses the pension debate in the context of the consolidation of the policies formed in wartime generally to be referred to as the Keynesian/ Beveridge mode of domination. Although by the end of the years of Conservative government the boom was slowing down and some policy shifts were beginning to emerge, those years will be considered the dividing point. The third section will discuss the crisis of British capitalism. Here more clearly than in either of the two previous sections, the links of the welfare state to the process and relations of capital accumulation becomes evident. The relations of domination begin to change with the crisis and intensified class struggle. Shifts away from the policies of Keynes and Beveridge became evident and prepared the way for Thatcher's orientation towards the state. Pension reform will be discussed in relation to the above shifts and changes in the state as a form of capitalist social relations.

Class and related struggles and the changing forms of capitalist domination are central to understanding the development of the welfare state. There are two ways to analyse this relation. First, periods of general increases in working-class strength and/or militancy are responded to by the state with welfare reform. These reforms may not be demanded by workers but are a response by the state to increased militancy from below. This is *not* the only possible response. The state can respond with force or cutbacks as a way to discipline the working class. Social policy reform, however, has been one of the main ways in which the state has responded to a general increase in working-class strength and militancy. At times of instability and crisis, welfare reform is used in an attempt to re-establish a stability in capitalist domination. These reforms may be a concession to the working class, improve materially their conditions, but they are a response to more generalized struggles, and changes in the balance of class forces. In this context, the debates and plans of intellectuals and social reformers can be located. Beveridge provides a good example. His proposals emerge in the context of a growth of working-class strength and the particular circumstances of the war. The option was either social reform or intensified class conflict. This general orientation will be followed in later chapters. Pension reform will be linked to shifts in the general struggle of the working class in its different expressions, and the general strategies or forms of relations used by the state to re-establish and change the conditions of relations of domination.

Second, the organizations of the working class play a role in the shaping of welfare state legislation. In terms of the development of the welfare state this role is secondary compared to the more generalized class struggle. The trade union movement, particularly as will be discussed in pensions, has accepted the boundaries of debate of welfare state legislation. They have pushed for improved benefits, and pressured Parliament, through media campaigns, and demonstrations. They have fallen short, however, of using strikes and other socially disruptive tactics to achieve their demands. They have accepted the forms of organization of pensions described earlier, and worked to improve private pensions for their members. In the context of intensified class conflict or the wartime changes in class relations, reforms supported by and in some respects initiated by the trade union movement have succeeded. These reforms were defined within the limits of the relations and conditions of the welfare state. The post-war welfare state, and pensions in particular, became an arena of negotiation between the trade union movement and the state analogous to industrial negotiations except with much less militancy. The trade unions negotiated general conditions of exploitation and domination, accepting the dominant forms of relations. This theme will be explored in more detail with each pension reform. The aim is to try to understand the relation of class to struggles over the welfare state, and to untangle two sets of relations — first generalized class and social antagonisms and its implications for social reform and second, the moderation and the ways in which the trade unions have accepted the relations of the welfare state and pushed for improvements within those definitions.

To summarize, this study will situate state pension reform in the context of the ongoing changes in class and social relations. The pressures of struggles from the working class, and the restructuring of these relations through the state, often in the context of crises of accumulation will form this context. The state will be presented as reacting to these changes and pursuing various strategies oriented toward profitable accumulation, growth, and social stability. Pressures from the trade union movement defined in a relatively narrow, and dominant framework will be explored as one aspect of this process. The chapters that follow will discuss the connections between the broader class struggles and relations and pension reform, and show that the welfare state, and particularly pensions, are limited by both capitalist social relations and its resultant economy, and that the welfare state has become part of the relations of domination in capitalism.

Summary

This chapter has defined the welfare state as a form of relations of domination. It sees it as playing a role in the totality of capitalist reproduction. The limits of the welfare state with its links to surplus value production have been explored. To understand the development of the post-war welfare state in general and state retirement pensions in particular, connections will be made between these developments and broader conditions of class struggle, and accumulation and the related changing state strategies. The chapters that follow will do this. Finally, some comments have been made on a libertarian socialist perspective and struggles around the welfare state.

2

Beveridge and the post-war Labour government

Introduction

The war, and the post-war period, brought with it a new form of class relations. The intense class conflict of the inter-war period was replaced by a strategy designed to accommodate the working class through improved material conditions based on a stable, profitable, and expanding capitalism. It was in the context of this shift in the form of class relations, or a change in the strategy of class domination that the post-war welfare state and reform of pensions was implemented. The war ended with the basic relations of capitalism intact, but with new conditions of exploitation. These included an active, interventionist state, full employment, accommodation of trade unions through increased involvement in state policy formation, wage improvements, and universal welfare state provision. These changes in the conditions of class relations have been referred to as the post-war settlement[1] and the Keynesian mode of domination.[2] The second of the concepts will be used in this book, as it more accurately describes the post-war conditions. The term Keynesian mode of domination is too narrow, and should be referred to as the Keynesian/Beveridge mode, reflecting the importance of Beveridge in developing this strategy of class rule. This mode of domination, however, is not only about changes in the specific policies mentioned earlier, but, more importantly, refers to a total reorganization of class relations.[3] This form of class relations paved the way for the period of stability and growth that characterized the immediate post-war period. However, as will be discussed in Chapter 4, the new strategies produced their own conflicts

and contradictions. This chapter and the next will discuss the development of the post-war policies as the context in which pension reform
can be discussed. There was agreement on this strategy of class rule
between representatives of both classes and the Labour and Conservative parties. Further, although the change in the mode of domination
was implemented by a Labour government, it will be argued that the
foundations of these policies were laid during the war in the coalition
government. The chapter will begin with a discussion of the coalition
government, focusing on the development of the policies that became
part of the Keynesian mode of domination. The next section will
discuss the Beveridge Report, its policies, and the response to it. The
emphasis here will be on the broad consensus that developed in favour
of the post-war social conditions. The Labour government's policies
in general and the pension reforms specifically will then be discussed.
An evaluation of those changes brought about will be presented. It is
important to situate the pension reforms in a broader social context,
particularly the changing forms of class domination brought about
during the war years. This will be the major objective of this chapter.

The war years

The years at war temporarily calmed the conflict between the classes,
increased the integration of both the trade union leadership and the
Labour party into running affairs of the state and resulted in promises
of a better future for the working class. The parliamentary Labour
party gave up its role in opposition and joined the Churchill coalition
government in 1941. In addition, Churchill brought Ernest Bevin, a
powerful spokesman for the trade unions, into his cabinet as Minister
of Labour. The urgency of the war required this participation; however,
the integration of the working-class leadership through its organizations
had been growing since the defeat of the General Strike of 1926. After
the intense conflict of the 1920s, the 1930s saw a gradual increase in
trade unions taking part in state activities.[4] With the appointment of
Bevin, relations between capital, workers, and the state improved
significantly.[5] By the end of the war many trade unionists felt that an
era of intense class conflict had ended. As Sir Walter Citrine, then
General Secretary of the TUC stated: 'We have passed from an era of
propaganda to one of responsibility.'[6]

   Although the trade unions were represented in the state apparatus,
and subsequently in the Labour government, their bargaining position
grew during the war in other ways. First, and most important, from
1941 onwards conditions of full employment existed. This was in
dramatic contrast to the inter-war years in which unemployment levels

averaged around 10 per cent. The war effort mobilized most of those able
to work. Further, the hours of work increased from an average of 48 to
approximately 54 per week.[7] Women were brought into the labour force
in large numbers in all sections of production and state employment.[8]

The growth of employment was reflected both in trade union membership[9] and wage rates.[10] However, by 1944 cracks were beginning to
appear in the industrial treaty. Wage rates had slowed down, especially
in the coal mines, and the number of unofficial strikes began once again
to increase. Bevin suspected Trotskyist agitation in the coal mines and
made it an indictable offence to instigate or to incite a stoppage of
work.[11] Also, the number of strike days increased steadily through
1942, 1943, and 1944, dropping slightly in 1945, but double what they
had been in 1939.[12] The implication of the increase in the standard of
living of the working class and its increased organizational strength was
that a return to the conditions of high unemployment, and attacks from
the ruling class as experienced in the inter-war years was impossible
without intense class conflict. Even though the leadership of the trade
union movement was actively participating in the implementation of
policies designed to reduce class conflict, this does not imply that the
working class would automatically follow. Capitalist labour relations
are based on exploitation and therefore antagonism is usual. Because
the trade union leadership had entered the chambers of state power,
and had increasingly become the full-time, professional managers of exploitation, does not imply that workers will comply with their orders.
The war years provided concrete gains for some and death and great
personal suffering for others in the working class. In both cases, a return
to the conditions of pre-war Britain was not possible. Popular attitudes,
and state intervention during the war years manifested themselves in
social policy outcomes both during the war and in the post-war welfare
state.[13] Miliband points out that the fight against Germany and Japan
was not only against fascism but also for democratic values and a cel-
ebration of the 'common man' which entailed condemnation of the
manner in which Tory governments had treated the working class in the
inter-war years. Large scale intervention was required by the war in
order to achieve victory. People assumed that state intervention would
continue when peace came, and would guarantee employment, welfare,
social security and educational opportunity. The vision for the end of
the war was not socialist or revolutionary, but based on bitter memories,
positive hopes and notions of social justice. There was a popular shift to
the left. This was reflected in support for the Soviet Union after its
entry into the war.[14] A survey by the Postal Censor in January 1941
reflects the attitudes of the working class:

They are looking forward confidently to a post-war levelling of class distinction and a redistribution of wealth. . . . They anticipate a post-war government which is either 'national' (with a strong socialist complexion) . . . or Labour.[15]

The Home Intelligence Office documented what they described as a 'home grown socialism',[16] implying less support for socialist forms of production but for increased state intervention, and social welfare provision. Both classes accepted these conditions as the promise for the post-war period.

A representative of the Federation of British Industry said of the Blitz: 'it has already linked London's east and west in a new sense of civic unity and responsibility'.[17] Seebohm Rowntree, at the end of 1940, wrote of 'a growing sense of friendliness between class and class'[18] The famous editorial from *The Times* on 1 July 1940 best summarized the popular attitude:

> If we speak of democracy, we do not mean democracy which maintains the right to vote but forgets the right to work and the right to live. If we speak of freedom, we do not mean a rugged individualism which excludes social organization and economic planning. If we speak of equality, we do not mean a political equality, nullified by social and economic privilege. If we speak of economic reconstruction, we think less of maximum production (though this too will be required) than of equitable distribution.[19]

The character of the war effort provided the most important propaganda of all for those on the left. Addison states:

> Taking the war years as a whole, however, the Right was politically quiescent while the Left kept up a barrage of activity and propaganda. . . . The roots of class remained untouched, but above ground there was much levelling and trimming.[20]

The general popularity of the ideals of equality was facilitated by and reflected in an increase of state action in a variety of social areas.

The growth of the power of the central state and its intervention into a variety of social areas was necessary because of the conditions of total war. Throughout the 1930s the Treasury had been the power behind Conservative policies, but with total war it became essential to plan resources first and finances second.[21] Before the war, social services had been developed to assist the socially underprivileged, but with the war, the government had to take responsibility for the welfare of all. The ideological consensus and the importance of maintaining the co-operation of the working class was reflected in a flurry of White Papers promising improved conditions in the post-war period, and improvements in welfare state policy during the war itself.

These papers and policy initiatives are important because they demonstrate the shift in policy and the wide range of state activity. Also many of the post-war Labour reforms had their origins in the social policies of the coalition government. Policy papers and reforms came about in the fields of education, health, urban planning and housing. In social security, supplementary pensions were introduced, and the dreaded family means test abolished.[22] The Beveridge Report, which will be discussed in the next section, was perhaps the most significant of the proposals and brought together many of the themes and visions for the post-war welfare state. It cannot, however, be analysed in isolation from these other policy initiatives.

In addition to these programmes, the coalition government committed itself to full employment. The White Paper on 'Employment Policy' accepted 'as one of their primary aims and responsibilities the maintenance of a high and stable level of employment'.[23] In order to accomplish this, the government would act to influence the location of new enterprise and diversify industrial composition of areas particularly vulnerable to high unemployment, to maintain stable wages and prices, to increase public investment when private investment declined, and to maintain a steady measure of consumption expenditure.[24] The policies of full employment had roots not only in the Labour party but also in the coalition government. Further, budgetary techniques were introduced to facilitate these policy objectives. Keynesian formulations for economic policy were brought in with the reforming of the 1941 budget. Keynes utilized figures on national income and expenditure as opposed to traditional figures of government revenue and outgoings. The budget was transformed into a market regulator. Forecasting and utilizing the control of aggregate demand became an instrument to regulate demand to a level, to maintain full employment or to prevent mass unemployment.[25] The importance of this innovation was that it became widely accepted and at least theoretically provided technical tools necessary for full employment.[26] A Keynesian orientation was a product of the depression and war mobilization and became adopted by both parties.[27] The war proved to be the testing ground for Keynesian principles and large-scale state intervention in the economy.

The Labour party, continuing its pattern of compromise and acceptance of capitalist social relations, reflected the popular support of the welfare state and full employment. Its participation in the coalition government gave it respectability. However, because it was both within the government as a partner in the coalition, and outside of it as a political party with its own ideology and programme, conflicts did exist.[28] Within the coalition, Labour ministers played an important role in the development of social policies. Often, as will be seen with the Beveridge recommendations, Labour ministers came into conflict with both backbenchers and their party. Labour policy proposals put forward during the war were neither particularly radical nor, with the exception of economic nationalization, that different from many of the policies of the Conservative Party. Labour's position can be summarized in their 1942 statement on reconstruction of 'The Old World and New Society'. In it the party endorsed the following four principles: a commitment to full employment; a rebuilding of Britain to standards worthy of men and women who have preserved it; a call to organize the social services at a level which secures adequate health, nutrition and care in old age for all citizens; and the provision of educational opportunities for all which guarantee that the cultural heritage would be denied to none.[29] The experience in government and the positions taken by the party formed the basis for the post-war welfare state and full employment. As Miliband points out, there was much agreement with the Tories on the social conditions for post-war reconstruction. The Tories agreed that post-war reconstruction would include a high level of employment and extended provision of welfare and social security, along with the need for economic controls. The major difference between the parties was that the Conservatives wanted a speedy return to private enterprise in which state intervention would play a marginal and mainly indirect role. Labour, however, with the memory of the post-First World War social disaster, saw the control of the economy as essential to post-war reconstruction and full employment.[30] Even with these differences, the central commitment to full employment and expansion of the welfare state with basic social security provision, a conciliatory attitude to trade unions and active state intervention emerged as policy from the major parties participating in the coalition. With this background, it is little wonder that Beveridge's report received such wide acclaim and popularity. Before turning to it, the main points of this general section will be summarized. Wartime and the coalition government brought about the following conditions. These form the general background for what has been described as the Keynesian/Beveridge mode of domination. The Labour party and the organized trade union movement were integrated further into the business of state and government. An increased strength of the working class because of the conditions of full employment manifested itself in a growth of trade union membership and increases in wages. General popular attitudes of reconstruction, social justice, with an acceptance of increased state intervention brought about expectations of better social conditions at the end of the war. These expectations in many ways were partially implemented and reinforced by a series of government White Papers and social welfare legislation. Keynesian economic techniques were adopted and contributed to post-war full employment and economic growth.

Both parties accepted the policies of full employment and an expanded welfare state.[31] Beveridge and his Report became part of these general conditions.

Beveridge and his Report

Within this climate of debate on social policies and reconstruction the Beveridge Report was produced. It played a vital role in the discussion and optimism for post-war improvements. People do not make history through personality and ideas, but rather it is the point in time at which these ideas emerge that is significant. Beveridge was ideally situated. His Report used the political, economic and social environment and helped encourage its direction. There were several other factors in addition to the general conditions that led to Beveridge. Addison summarizes them: first, the evacuation of Dunkirk coincided with an extensive Nazi campaign extolling the benefits and virtues of National Socialism for the 'common man'. The Ministry of Information in 1941 was concerned about the effect of this propaganda and commissioned various papers to guide their response. Keynes's paper named social security as the first priority both nationally and internationally for the post-war years. In May 1941, Anthony Eden repeated the pledge that social security for all must be the first object after the war. This principle, as a result of Labour ministers' pressuring Churchill, became embodied in the Atlantic Charter.[32] The promise of social security then was already held out to workers even before Beveridge, as a means of encouraging co-operation in the war effort.

Pressures on the cabinet from other sources at least partly led to the establishment of the Beveridge Committee. A committee was established in 1938 to investigate trade union complaints about the system of workman's compensation. Employers, as the war began, could not supply the necessary information; yet the Home Office was reluctant to abandon the inquiry. Thus, pressure existed for an investigation into one area of social security. An inquiry held into the practices of industrial assurance schemes in 1937 had criticized them for extravagant administrative costs — 40 per cent on management expenses — and a high incidence of 'lapsing'. Another provider of security had been under attack. Finally, and most directly, in 1940 the General Council of the TUC, after referring to the inadequacies of the National Health Service, came to the conclusion that a complete review of all social services was necessary. They sent a delegation to the Minister of Health (Conservative, Ernest Brown) in February 1941 and stressed the

27

need for a co-ordinated scheme to be implemented after the war. In May the government announced a survey of the entire social services would be conducted under the auspices of the Minister of Reconstruction, Greenwood, chaired by Beveridge.[33] This is not to argue that single events of this kind make history, but that the time was right, and the labour movement had the leverage to push for this kind of investigation because of its strength, the popular mood, the need to counter Nazi propaganda, and finally because of the recent history of investigation into the social services. These specific pressures were within a larger realignment of class forces and shifts in strategies for class rule described above. The specifics of the Beveridge Report will now be discussed.

The Beveridge Report

The discussion of the Beveridge Report will be divided as follows: at the general level, the assumptions and principles of the scheme will be elaborated. This will lead to a discussion of what Beveridge proposed and its under-pinnings. The general reception of Beveridge, and the positions taken both in the process of the preparation of Beveridge's report and the attitude towards it following its publication will be discussed next. The specifics of the pension proposals will be examined later in the context of the 1946 Labour government's legislation.

The assumptions and the principles of the Beveridge Report represent neither a radical departure from much of social policy discussed in the trade unions, the Labour party, and the coalition government, nor a break with social security tradition that emerged from the National Insurance Act of 1911 and continued through the 1925 Widows', Orphans' and Old Age Pension Act. The three principles of Beveridge were based on a combination of state intervention and concepts of justice. The first principle is that although the social security system should be developed from the full experience of the past, the new scheme should not be determined by it. 'A revolutionary moment in the World's history is a time for revolutions, not for patching.'[34] With this call to major reform, Beveridge turned around and adopted the basic principles of social security that had been entrenched in Britain since 1911. The second principle related social security to broader concepts of social improvement. Social insurance was viewed not only in terms of providing benefits, but as part of the struggle against Want. The report states: 'But Want is one only of five giants on the road of reconstruction and in some ways is easiest to attack. The others are Disease, Ignorance, Squalor and Idleness.'[35] Again, the rhetoric and promise was far greater than the proposed reforms.

Beveridge related the attack on want to the provision of subsistence level benefits. To some extent, this was an improvement to what existed at the time, but certainly is not the kind of assistance that would end 'Want'. The third principle was perhaps the most interesting, and in many ways its implications are the most important. It is as follows:

> Social security must be achieved by co-operation between the State and the individual. The State should offer security for service and contribution. The State in organizing security should not stifle incentive, opportunity, responsibility; in establishing a national minimum it should leave room and encouragement for voluntary action by each individual to provide more than the minimum for himself and his family.[36]

More than any other principle, this summarizes both the essence of the Beveridge recommendations and the principle underlying much of the history of the British welfare state and social security provision. It demonstrates the limits and the forms of social relation implicit in this plan. The implicit exchange between the state offering security for 'service and contribution' was and continued to be the basis of social security policy. Social security through insurance at a minimum subsistence level was not a right, but was contingent upon selling one's labour for a wage. Workers are required to establish eligibility through the labour market; this link between social provision and selling one's labour is the central condition of social security provision. This process of benefits being determined through contributions will be referred to as work-testing of benefits. This form of testing for eligibility contrasts with means-testing. In most cases, work-testing guarantees benefits but not the amount of the benefits, while means-tested benefits tend to be more arbitrarily administered. It is important to emphasize the centrality of work-testing in Beveridge's plan.

The principle raises the question of how much the state should provide and how much provision should occur through the private market. If there is any principle that has historically divided discussion between the Labour and Conservative parties it is the question of models of provision. In theory, as will be seen in their orientation to pensions, the Labour party has favoured the state's providing of benefits on a universal basis. On the other hand, the Conservatives have to a large degree, although not exclusively, favoured social provision to be through the market with state aid directed toward those on the bottom, who cannot 'buy' whatever benefits might be required. These are theoretical models and of course in practice have been modified. The point is, however, that Beveridge's principle combined elements of both of these models. He mixed universal benefits with market provision in such a way as to protect or to encourage the development of the market while at the same time the state would provide a limited level of benefit to all depending on contributions. It is this principle around which much of the debate on pension reform has been focused since Beveridge. In a sense, this principle has, to a large extent, remained unchanged, and coupled with the principle of subsistence, helped it pave the way for the growth of the private market in retirement pensions. The basic argument presented here is that based on the principles of Beveridge; once the rhetoric, vision and promise is stripped aside, what is implied is a rather traditional and modest orientation to social security. Along with these three principles, Beveridge produced three assumptions that were to complement his programme of social security reform. The first was a programme of children's allowances for all children up to the age of fifteen and sixteen if attending a full-time educational programme. Second, he advocated a comprehensive health and rehabilitation system available to all. Third, was the assumption of maintaining full employment, that is, avoiding massive unemployment.[37] Each of these three assumptions was to come to fruition either during the war or after it. The Report, with these assumptions, helped increase and maintain popular pressures for full employment and health services. The policies of a national health service and state commitment to full employment coupled with improvements in social security were the major concessions to the working class, and formed part of the conditions of post-war exploitation. The fact of their achievement is partly because of the popular pressures for Beveridge's assumptions. Again, none of these three assumptions are that remarkable in the context of the social policies of the coalition government. Each of these three assumptions was part of the Labour party programme. More specifically, on questions of social policy, the 1942 Labour Party Conference adopted the following position coincidentally anticipating and paving the way for acceptance of the Beveridge Report. The principles were:

1 one comprehensive scheme of social security;
2 adequate cash payments to provide security whatever the contingency;
3 the provision of cash payments from national funds for all children through a scheme of family allowances; and
4 a right to all forms of medical attention and treatment through a national health service.[38]

For social security, Beveridge saw three methods of provision, again reflecting the policy tradition already established. They were national assistance for special cases, voluntary insurance for additions to the basic provision and, of course, contributory social security benefits.[39] These three methods continued to develop after Beveridge. With his proposals six principles of social insurance were articulated. They were as follows:

(i) flat rate of subsistence benefit
(ii) flat rate of contribution
(iii) unification of administrative responsibility
(iv) adequacy of benefit
(v) comprehensiveness of coverage, and
(vi) for categories of provision and contribution differences in employ-
    ment position.[40]

These principles will be discussed generally here and returned to later in their application to pensions. The first two principles, flat rate contributions and benefits remained basic until 1959. Setting aside the rhetoric of equality, the principle reflected the commitment to the private market as a means of provision, the state as not competing with it, and providing a floor on which private pensions can be built. With flat rate benefits, the principle of subsistence is again put forward. The government, in Beveridge's view, would provide the minimum regardless of the standing of an individual. The notion of equality before the state, as opposed to inequality experienced in the selling of wage labour is reinforced here. The third principle of unified administrative responsibility applies in terms of how contributions were to be collected, how benefits were to be paid out, and a general centralization of social security organization in one department, in the central state. This recommendation, partly implemented by the coalition government, ended whatever local control remained over social security programmes. This local tradition dated back to the Elizabethan Poor Laws.

The fourth principle – adequacy – is perhaps the most important. The subsistence principle is embodied here: Adequacy is considered in terms of length of time during which a benefit will be received. On the question of time, Beveridge favoured an indefinite period without means tests as long as the need existed. This principle was struck down with Labour party legislation for unemployment benefits because the potential of long-term unemployed lingering on non-means-tested benefits was unacceptable to them and the Tories. The fifth principle – comprehensiveness – refers to both persons covered and their range of needs. This principle of universality provided a significant reform. However, the extensions necessary to reach the comprehensiveness prescribed by Beveridge were to the better paid workers and the self-employed. The comprehensiveness of coverage of a wide range of contingencies brought together and reorganized a wide range of existing programmes, rather than establishing anything new.

The final principle of classification recognizes the differences of 'ways of life of different sectors of the community' and sets out to provide correspondingly different contribution conditions and eligibility requirements. The six categories that Beveridge developed provided an administrative tool for the organization of state benefits. These categories were:

  (i)   employees
 (ii) others gainfully employed
(iii) housewives
(iv) others of working age
 (v) those below the working age, and
(vi) those retired above the working age.

The category that is of special importance is that of housewives. The reason for this importance is that it both reflects and reinforces the inequality of women, and institutional sexism in state pensions. Two orientations on housewives emerge with the Beveridge Report. First, women are defined as dependants, and in their role as housewives are considered to be entitled to benefits based on their husbands' contributions. The image of women as housewives and the sanctity of the nuclear family first and foremost is presented by Beveridge irrespective of the large increase in women in the labour force during the war. Also, unwaged domestic labour did not provide entitlement for pensions. This disregard of domestic labour is the basis of the poverty of many elderly women in the post-war period. Direct discrimination against women emerged if married women chose to remain in the labour market. Here, they were to make a choice. They could continue their contributions, but their benefits would not accrue based on those contributions, because of the assumed dependency on their husbands.[41] Further, married women who are working can decide not to contribute at all, and although the employer must contribute, these women are assumed to benefit from their husband's benefits. The question of the possibility of a woman being a primary breadwinner, or equality of roles is ignored by Beveridge.[42]

Finally, the question of financing the Beveridge proposals will be presented. This part of the proposal was to raise some difficulties, especially with Churchill and the Treasury. In preparation of the Report Beveridge worked closely with Keynes. The aim of this collaboration was to minimize cost to the Treasury. One policy that resulted was the phasing in of pension rates over a twenty-year period.[43] The transition period for receipt of full pensions in twenty years was arbitrary in the sense that it was estimated that twenty years of contributions would provide funds needed so that pensions could pay for themselves with a reduced contribution from the exchequer. Beveridge saw three sources of financing his scheme: the exchequer, the prospective recipient of payment, and his/her employer. He was most concerned about protecting the exchequer from large contributions.[44] Beveridge's policies placed an increasing burden of finance directly on the insured and employers. A practice of regressive taxation emerged. Workers, regardless of income, were required to contribute in order to become eligible for pensions. Direct taxation is, relatively speaking, more progressive. Beveridge's vision of a self-financing scheme based on actuarial soundness was never realized, but his proposal followed the traditions built in 1911. Social security was tied to wage labour and at the same time tried to get the working class to pay for their own social security. The question is more complicated than this. As discussed in the previous chapter, taxation may or may not be a drain on surplus value. As long as the working class can defend or improve its standard of living, taxes such as contributions to social security will be deducted from surplus value available to capital. In the context of the post-war period, as will be shown in the next chapter, with increasing standards of living of the working class, these contributions would tend to be borne by capital, thus acting as an impediment to accumulation.

In total, the Beveridge proposals promised improved conditions for workers in two ways. First, they ended the means-testing of many benefits, particularly unemployment benefits, and substituted work-testing. Second, the principle of subsistence, miserly in theory as well as in practice, did allow some minor gains for some people receiving benefits. On the other hand, the Beveridge Report, in its recommendations for social security, was conventional by all standards and built on traditions already established. Further, it allowed the continuation of and furthered the conditions within social security for the growth of a multi-billion-pound enterprise of private pensions. Beveridge set up the state as guarantor against starvation. The harsh realities of life at the bottom of the capitalist heap were buffered slightly. Reorganization, centralized planning and administration plus fiscal conservatism, work-testing and other conventional methods of social security delivery are the central aspects of Beveridge.

If this is so, then why (as will be developed) did Beveridge win so much popular acclaim and support, particularly from the left? There are several reasons. Perhaps the most important is the context of Beveridge. In a sense, he was a man in the right place at the right time. The general political environment was ready for the Report. Beveridge used the Report not only to introduce relatively modest social security reorganization, but also to support policies of full employment and national health services.

The rhetoric used by Beveridge conveyed social progress, and held out promise for the reconstruction of Britain based on principles of social justice after the war. This quotation demonstrates his position:

> they [the proposals] are concerned not with increasing the wealth of
> the British people, but with so distributing whatever wealth is avail-
> able to them in total, as to deal first with first things, essential
> physical needs. They are a sign of the belief that the object of
> government in peace and war is not the glory of the rulers or of
> races, but in the happiness of the common man.[45]

In ending his Report, Beveridge called for national unity.

> Freedom from want cannot be forced on a democracy or given to a
> democracy. It must be won by them. Winning it needs courage and
> faith and sense of national unity: courage to face facts and difficul-
> ties and overcome them, faith in our future and in the ideals of
> fair-play and freedom . . . a sense of national unity overriding the
> interests of any class or section.[46]

The promise of a better tomorrow in contrast to both the daily difficulties of war and the memories of the bitter class struggles, hunger and
unemployment at the end of the First World War were key elements of
the Beveridge Report and certainly account for much of its popularity.
Beveridge used the claim of national interest, more apparent in wartime, to smooth over the class nature of the society. Social policy was
national in scope and provided for all through the state which was
identified with the interests of 'the nation'. In this sense the Beveridge
Report blurred the class nature of capitalism by promising a reformed
capitalism based on a national consensus aimed at a just social vision.

Responses to Beveridge

This section will review some of the responses of the major groupings in
society as well as general indicators of popular attitudes to Beveridge.
In general, there was popular acclaim both reinforcing and pushing
forward the 'public' support for a vision of social justice after the war.
Interestingly, there was little criticism of Beveridge from left intellectuals or left-wing organizations. This is of tremendous importance when
one analyses the emergence of the welfare state and its development in
the post-1945 years. The failure of welfare reform seriously to attack
the fundamental inequalities and contradictions of capitalist society is
hardly surprising given the nature of the class system. But equally
surprising is the inability of the established left, particularly within the
Labour party, to push forward a serious alternative to the Beveridge

proposals. The only major exception to this was the Political and Economic Planning group. In their submission to Beveridge, they recommended a system of non-contributory pensions based on direct taxation. As well, they recommended the implementation of a minimum wage to maintain adequate incomes.[47] Perhaps part of this problem lies in the formal working-class organizations' acceptance of the premises, assumptions and directions of Beveridge. The Labour party, as mentioned earlier, generally accepted the principles of Beveridge as they put forward at their party conference of 1942. The demand of the party, pushed for by its parliamentary backbenchers, was the implementation of the social security legislation before the end of the war. Related to the legislation was Labour's pledge to nationalize private insurance while maintaining a place in the social security system for *bona fide* friendly societies.[48] The following quotation from a left-wing Labour Member of Parliament sums up the party position. Sydney Silverman stated at the Labour Party Conference of 1943: 'It [Beveridge] expresses the basic principle of this Party, the only thing which entitled us at the beginning and entitles us now to regard ourselves as fundamentally different from all other Parties',[49] or as Sir Walter Citrine, Secretary of the TUC, stated on Beveridge: 'It is evidence of the public conscience recognizing at long last that which the Labour Party has stood for.'[50] In addition, for the working class as a whole, the harshness of unemployment and means-tested benefits made the promise of Beveridge a major step forward by contrast. Although the support from the Labour party was generalized, there was criticism. Some members thought the proposed benefits were too low while others thought that there should be a time limit on all benefits (except, of course, retirement) in order to preserve the insurance principle. Further, there was a minority position within the party lead by Ernest Bevin that opposed family allowance as he feared extensive state provision would undermine the bargaining position of the trade union movement.[51] The support for a contributory system of benefits can be understood with the background of the dreaded means test of the 1920s and 1930s; yet support for a principle of non-contributory benefits as a right did remain as one strand in the Labour Party. This position was stated in 1944 by Aneurin Bevan:

> It is only with difficulty that Socialists could persuade themselves to back the Beveridge Plan in the first place. There is nothing particularly new or adventurous in it for them. The idea of an all-in social insurance scheme has formed part of their political propaganda for more than a quarter of a century.[52]

In the end, the support of the Labour Party went behind Beveridge. According to Marwick, so did that of the Communist Party.[53]

The organized trade union movement generally endorsed Beveridge's report; Bevin's criticisms were the exception. The TUC, in its submission to Beveridge, agreed with him in all aspects except on Workmen's Compensation.[54] The list of concrete proposals presented by the TUC closely follows the final recommendations of Beveridge.[55] Two points in their presentation are of interest in the light of events that emerged in the years after the war. First, they opposed private enterprise playing a role in social security provision. Second, they advocated, for those outside the insurance scheme, that a personal means test be maintained but improved and centralized.[56] On the whole, the general position of the two major institutions of the working class, the trade unions and the Labour party was a warm welcome for the Beveridge Report and its proposals.

The position that emerged from capital and the Conservative party was less clear-cut. In general, as mentioned earlier, there was support for welfare and social security provision as well as high levels of employment. In their submissions to the Beveridge Committee, the main representative of industry, the British Employers' Confederation, maintained general support for reorganized social security, but strongly qualified its support along two lines. First, and less important, was the timing of the reforms. It thought that it should wait until the end of the war. Second, and more important, were fears of the long-term costs of extended state expenditure on social services. The Confederation stated in 1942:

> It is imperative that the expenditure on these Services and the other Social Services, must be directly related to the industrial performance of the country on which they ultimately depend for their continuance, and that the benefits they provide should not be such as to weaken the incentive of the population to play their full part in maintaining the productivity and exporting ability of the country at its highest level.[57]

Other responses of capital to the report showed a similar mixture of support and reservation. Groups such as the Shipbuilders' Employers' Federation and the Mining Federation wanted delays. In November 1942, 120 industrialists prepared a position paper called 'A National Policy for Industry' which endorsed improved industrial relations and welfare provision, based on a form of corporate paternalism. They envisioned employers being responsible for the proper housing of employees, supplementing state pensions, and providing subsidies to prevent unemployment. They also endorsed state family allowances, and the raising of the school leaving age. There were attacks on Beveridge from the representatives of the insurance industry. In many instances the

Beveridge proposals did arouse hostility from sectors of capital. *British Industry* made no official comment except to release an article extolling the virtues of private enterprise, and a publication of the Conservative party presented a bland mixture of praise and criticism.[58] The division within the Tories and their position will be discussed a little later in examining parliamentary response to the report.

The support of both parties for Beveridge was influenced by its vast popular appeal. The Report itself was published at the victory of the Allied troops in North Africa at El Alamein. This was a turnabout in the war and the Report built on this sense of optimism and hope. The press with the exception of the *Daily Telegraph* were favourable to Beveridge.[59] More important, however, it was the public that showed the greatest enthusiasm. The Report was an immediate best-seller. Within two weeks of its publication, a poll taken found 95 per cent of those interviewed had heard of it; 88 per cent approved of its ideas of health care; and 53 per cent believed that the government would put the plan into operation while only 18 per cent doubted it. Another poll showed that 86 per cent believed that the Report should be adopted.[60] Beveridge and G. D. H. Cole, noted socialist intellectual, founded the Social Security League as a vehicle to canvass for immediate adoption of the social security scheme.[61] Even with its popular appeal, the Report and its recommendations had to come face to face with Churchill, the strength of the Tories, and the caution of the coalition.

With Churchill leading the way, the coalition government delayed any significant action on the Beveridge proposals. Churchill objected because he did not want to detract energy and attention from the war effort; and following the arguments of capital, he was cautious, and concerned about the costs of social security, and what large-scale commitment would mean in terms of post-war reconstruction. The Chancellor of the Exchequer, Kinsley Wood, cautioned Churchill in a memorandum of November 1942 that Beveridge's proposals involved an 'impractical financial commitment'. Cherwell wrote to Churchill that acceptance of the proposals might endanger the prospects of getting Lend-Lease arrangements from the United States at the end of the war, as the Americans may not want to finance welfare provisions far in advance of their own. Further, if the Beveridge Report were adopted, reconstruction plans for housing, agriculture, and education, as well as higher wages in general, might be less feasible.[62] Yet, Churchill was caught in a political squeeze. His own Ministry of Information had used the Report to build morale, and counter Nazi propaganda, and the Report had been widely read and supported. He was aware of the disaster of Lloyd George's pledges for reconstruction. Above all else, the war effort and subsequent reconstruction required the co-operation of the working class. The Tories were the party of the ruling class, and

Churchill in the pre-war years had not been a popular figure amongst the working class. He had to do something. Churchill appointed a secret committee of Conservative members of parliament to report the party's view. They recommended the acceptance of children's allowances, and the principle of universal contribution to old age pensions. They emphasized, however, that unemployment insurance should be kept substantially lower than wages, not be paid at a subsistence level, and limited to a duration of six months unless the unemployed person was willing to put his services at the disposal of the state. They recommended a compulsory health insurance limited to those with low incomes in order to preserve private medicine.[63] The strategy that emerged from the cabinet, however, was an acceptance of Beveridge in principle, but with no commitments to be made. Churchill proposed that only a renewed mandate from the electorate could commit the nation to such large expenditures. Dalton and Attlee feared losing ground with an election and subsequently supported Churchill's strategy of delay.[64] Churchill spoke to the nation on 4 March 1943, within a climate of parliamentary and public resentment about the delay on social reform commitment. He proposed a four-year plan for compulsory insurance and implementation of welfare measures. Although he avoided all direct mention of Beveridge, he did commit himself to a policy of 'national compulsory insurance for all classes and for all purposes from the cradle to the grave'. He also stated that there should be state intervention to support high levels of employment.[65]

The coalition faced a rebellion of backbenchers against the government delay. Labour backbenchers, as well as Liberals, and a group of Conservatives led by Quintin Hogg and Lord Hinchingbrooke called for immediate implementation of the Beveridge proposals. This marks a formal grouping within the Tory ranks in favour of a full commitment to welfare state provision.[66]

A compromise finally emerged in 1944 with a White Paper, *Social Insurance*.[67] The White Paper closely followed Beveridge's recommendation without the rhetoric, principles, and assumptions. Included in it are recommendations for a national, unified, social security scheme for all adults, based on flat rate contributions and benefits. The basic difference was that the paper did not support either subsistence level benefits, or indefinite periods of payments of benefits except on retirement. Also, the Report maintained the separation of means-tested from insurance benefits.[68] On the level of benefits, the paper proposed:

The right objective is a rate of benefit which provides a reasonable insurance against want and at the same time takes account of the maximum contribution which the great body of contributors can properly be asked to bear.[69]

38

In general terms, the paper linked social security provision to national recovery and prosperity.[70] It was more cautious than Beveridge's scheme, and toned down post-war expectations with its moderation, but it demonstrated the coalition's commitment to a comprehensive scheme of social security after the war. The achievements, and policy pronouncements of the coalition government paved the way for the social legislation that followed under the Labour government in 1945. Rather than departing from the traditions of the previous adminis-tration, the legislation of the Labour government followed it quite closely: as well, it embodied the forms and traditions of previous welfare state legislation in both form and content.

1945 – Labour in power – its welfare state

The 1945 election campaigns fought by both the Tories and Labour brought about pledges to expand the welfare state and commitments to high levels of employment. The Conservatives, in their election mani-festo, committed themselves to the implementation of the policies published in the 1944 White Paper.[71] Labour, in reminding workers of their 'shabby treatment' under Conservative governments, pledged themselves to rapid expansion of social insurance.[72] They linked these provisions to an efficient and prosperous economy and stated: 'There is no reason why Britain should not afford such programmes, but she will need full employment and the highest possible industrial efficiency in order to do so.'[73] In this context, no mention is given to what the government would do if this economic efficiency was not achieved. Under conditions of full employment and economic growth the question of unemployment benefits is relatively less pressing. The irony of Labour's position was that it did not address the problem of what they might do if economic difficulties produced high levels of unemploy-ment after the war.

With their victory Labour inherited a legacy of state intervention and policies from the war years. These included the commitment to the welfare state, Keynesian tools and approaches to economic manage-ment, limited nationalization and an ideology of increased state involve-ment with the state acting as guarantor of minimal levels of social provision. The coalition experience had brought the leadership of the parliamentary Labour party into close contact with the bureaucratic functioning and practices of the civil service. The government inherited a civil service who, according to Miliband, 'by social provenance, education and disposition were bound to conceive it as one of their prime tasks to warn their ministers against too radical a departure'.[74] The Labour party, by this time, had established political and economic

39

moderation, as well as a firm commitment to the assumptions of a modified private enterprise system. They eagerly took on the techniques, the orientation towards the working class and the state practices from the war that formed the Keynesian/Beveridge mode of domination described earlier. This is reflected in the moderate, non-radical nature of the Labour party's social security reforms. The principles of these reforms can be found in Liberal and Conservative administrations dating back to 1912 and followed through Beveridge and the coalition government. Marwick characterizes the incoming Labour government as embodying 'middle class radicalism and official trade unionism [rather than] left wing socialism'.[75] Within this, the Labour government faced a working class which had gained strength during the war and which held high expectations for reform on the one hand, and the economic conditions of a war-devastated economy, on the other. The government's commitment beyond all else was to the rebuilding of a 'just capitalism'; for this, the co-operation of the working class was necessary.

The Labour party's winning the election, as well as conditions of full employment and increased trade union membership, led to an increased strength of the working class to bargain for improved wages, yet, as Miliband points out, the government made it its business 'to moderate and discipline both their claims and their expectations'. Further, he explains, Labour's coming to office did not change the consultation received by trade unions during the war in economic and social matters. The unions could count on a sympathetic hearing, but in return the government expected and received a measure of co-operation in the maintenance of industrial discipline.[76] In order to establish working-class discipline, the social relations necessary for capital accumulation, reforms were necessary, both because of the combination of pledges of both parties, experience and hopes built on the war experience, and the strength of the working class. As well, these reforms were linked to the new mode of domination, and became part of the conditions of post-war exploitation.

The economic conditions were anything but conducive to reform that might involve high levels and future commitment of state expenditure. The following are indicators of the economic problems faced by the Labour government. The man/woman power demanded by war production and services drastically shifted deployment from production for consumer goods to armaments and state employment.[77] International trade and overseas investment, on which Britain depended, was almost entirely destroyed by the war. To finance the war effort, overseas investment, the return on which had for three-quarters of a century helped to bridge the gap between Britain's imports and exports, had been sold for approximately £1,000 million. As well, two-thirds of the gold reserve of 1939 was used up, while external debts were up by

£3,000 million.[78] Internal production was run down by the war effort. Domestic destruction and damage to property was estimated at £1,500 million, depreciation and obsolescence of stock was approximately £900 million, and the running down of personal consumer goods stood at £885 million. The debt service both in absolute figures and as a percentage of GNP increased drastically with the war. The total indebtedness at the end of the war was approximately £3,000 million.[79] Labour faced this economic situation with a mixture of Keynesian techniques and selective nationalization. Moreover, the road to reconstruction was to be paved with profitability, and continued exploitation of the working class, under improved conditions for workers.

The first step in economic reconstruction was to increase the money supply by borrowing heavily from the Americans. Keynes was dispatched to Washington to arrange loans. By the end of the war, Britain was in a weak negotiating position with the USA. The USA saw Britain as a trading rival. The agreement reached by Keynes with the US government further diminished the role of Britain in terms of world trade. Britain was to receive a loan of $3,750 million at 2 per cent interest. Repayments were to start in 1951, spread over a fifty-year period. Within a year of the loan, sterling was to be made freely convertible for purposes of current trading, imperial preferences were to be abandoned, and Britain was to settle with her sterling creditors before 1951 which would enable them to buy the US dollar. The agreement was signed in December 1945.[80]

There are two implications of this process. First, it demonstrates the economic devastation of Britain, and the tremendously weak economic position in which Britain had to attempt reconstruction. Second, the war consolidated and increased the position of the US as the hegemonic capitalist nation and further diminished Britain's role in world trade; yet, in relation to potential competitors in Europe Britain's productive capacity was intact. This factor put Britain in a strong economic position *vis à vis* Europe for at least a few years.

By 1947, there was a rapid dwindling of the American loan. Economic conditions were going from bad to worse. The conditions of trade continued to worsen.[81] Within these conditions, the government nationalized parts of the economy including the Bank of England, Cable and Wireless, railways, and the coal industry, paying compensation of £164,600,000 to private capital for the coal industry which was at the time a run-down and unprofitable enterprise.[82] The budgetary priority in these years was to keep a supply of cheap money available for expansion. The government tried and failed to expand capital investment, yet it was able to maintain full employment (unemployment at less than or around 2 per cent).[83] By the end of 1947, the Labour government had reached a watershed. It had passed most of its legislation, yet the economy seemed to be collapsing. By 1947 the deficit to the USA had risen to £655 million.

The Marshall Plan, signed in 1948, provided Britain with another $1,263 million to help bail out the economic problems. Without Marshall aid, Britain would have suffered severe unemployment and a reduced standard of living. By 1948, a partial recovery had begun, partly as a result of import restrictions, and an export drive. Output was up by 36 per cent in 1947 over the pre-war figures and by 50 per cent in 1948. By 1950, exports had reached a 75 per cent increase over the 1938 level. In summary, the recovery had been based on outside aid as well as a disciplining of working-class demands.

Wage increases were thought to be acting as a bottleneck in pro-duction and recovery. A wage freeze was proposed and accepted by both the Labour party and the TUC in 1948. Union restraint was maintained until 1950. Wage rates rose 5 per cent while prices increased by 8 per cent; between 1945 and 1951 weekly wages rose by 6 per cent in real terms. By 1950 the policy of wage restraint was finally rejected by the TUC against the advice of its General Council.[84] The final aspect of Labour policy in this period was the devaluation of sterling from $4.03 to the pound to $2.80 to the pound. The devaluation was accom-panied by measures to cut home demand in capital expenditures on fuel and power industries and as well on the expansion of education and housing expenditures. The cuts totalled £140 million, and were to become effective in the second half of the next year. The savings were to be over £100 million for the financial year 1950–1.[85] In the context of these economic conditions, the Labour government was committed to the development of the welfare state and full employment; also they faced a strong working class with expectations for state initiative and action on their behalf. The reforms that followed the 1945 election reflected a great deal of legislative ambition and, at the same time, a strong commitment to the continuation of a system based on capitalist social relations and domination.

The welfare state reforms brought in by the Labour government followed closely the proposals and policies of the coalition government. The most important principle that emerged with Labour's welfare state was its belief in universality of coverage and benefits. This principle was a major departure from pre-war policy. The previous principle of welfare state legislation was to provide services and coverage for those least able to help themselves through the market. The introduction of universal health benefits and services were supposed to reduce the stigma of the poor and the working class when they had to claim state benefits. The major innovation of the Labour government, following the wartime coalition, was the inclusion of the 'middle class' and the ruling class into the coverage of the welfare state. The most innovative reform brought in during this period was the establishment of the national health service.

In the first three years of their administration, the Labour government passed legislation in the following fields. Family allowances commenced on 6 August 1946. The level of allowance was 5s. per child after the first with free school meals and milk. Beveridge had recommended 8s. but the Labour goverment's policy was that free school milk and food compensated for the difference. The Industrial Injuries Bill was passed on 10 October 1945. Benefits were to be paid at a higher level than sickness benefits. This policy rejected Beveridge's position that higher level of benefits should start only after thirteen weeks of incapacity. Instead, the legislation provided a higher rate of benefit from the beginning of disability followed by a pension if the disability was prolonged.[86] The National Assistance Board was established in 1948. It brought means-tested benefits under the central state, and shifted the burden of finance from rates to general taxation. The means test and the traditional stigma that went with it were therefore continued. After extensive negotiation, and controversy, the national health service with a network of state hospitals and services passed into law in 1948. Although no separate Ministry of Housing was established, there were subsidies for conversion; increase in council housing generally for other than the working class, and 157,000 'prefab' units were constructed. Rent control legislation acted to protect the rights of sitting tenants by retaining rent tribunals and rent control. State intervention in urban planning was increased in the New Towns Act of 1946 and the Town and County Act of 1947. In education, the Labour party implemented the Education Act of 1944 passed by the coalition government.[87] The legislation was not particularly innovative and, with the exception of the establishment of the national health service, not particularly controversial. The working class did make limited gains, but these were linked to the post-war strategy discussed earlier. The form of class rule changed through the welfare state. Exploitation was muted by the promise of cradle to grave state provision.

Post-war pensions – 1946

National Insurance Act

This section will examine more closely the pension reforms that were the product of Beveridge and the post-war Labour government. Before beginning that discussion, it is interesting to note the support received by the National Insurance Act from the Tories. This support is a reflection of the growing consensus on social policy questions that began during the war. The type of question raised by the Tories was whether the financial commitment required to pay for the Act was too high.[88] There were attacks from Labour as well. Sydney Silverman led an attack on contribution conditions, arguing instead for a policy of work or maintenance as a fundamental right. His attempted amendment was easily defeated.[89] In all, the National Insurance Act of 1946 brought several changes, particularly in providing comprehensive coverage by increasing the number of beneficiaries and benefits such as marriage allowances and death grants, in extending periods of coverage, and, relatively speaking, it provided marginally higher levels of benefits. The goal of these reforms was not to reduce inequality but to provide a minimum subsistence level of provision in all circumstances.[90] The rest of this section will discuss the pension legislation. The presentation will be organized along Beveridge's principles of operation see p. 32. They were:

(i) flat rate subsistence, and through this principle a discussion of benefit rates will be pursued;

(ii) flat rate contributions, and through this principle a discussion on the financing of the scheme;

(iii) unification of the scheme will lead into a brief discussion of the basis for the continued separation of the national assistance or supplementary benefit scheme;

(iv) the principle of adequacy will be discussed under (i), (v) and (vi).

The comprehensiveness of coverage and system of classification will be discussed together in order to address the question of the real changes in coverage of the pension scheme. Through these points a critique of the legislation will be presented.

Flat rate subsistence

The principle of flat rate benefits was closely tied to Beveridge's and the Labour government's principle that pensions should provide a minimum level subsistence. At the time, Beveridge's view of subsistence was based on Rowntree's 1938 level plus 25 per cent, accounting for increases in prices; as well, this amount was to include the cost of rent, regardless of regional fluctuation.[91] Kincaid explains that this definition of subsistence was based on Rowntree's study of York in 1936. His study defined a minimum need for a family of five at 1938 prices at £2.90 per week. Beveridge used the figure of £2.65 dropping costs for 'personal sundries' such as travel and newspapers. This point is crucial because it has influenced benefit levels of social security since 1945.[92] Rowntree's notions, especially in his calculation of nutrition, were based on highly scientific work of nutritionists with sophisticated knowledge of purchases and food usage, far beyond what most people of all classes would know, and excluded cultural or social habits.

Further, for old-age pensioners Beveridge allowed only 75 per cent of this food value, then added 10 per cent extra for special food needs. He reduced even further the amount required for clothing and housing compared to a person of working age receiving national insurance benefits.[93] Labour added 31 per cent to the 1938 subsistence level, but by 1946 prices were already 45 per cent above that level. By 1948, benefits paid out to adults were only three-quarters of the level recommended by Beveridge. Even those original levels were not excessively generous and certainly left people in a precarious financial position. Further, in the 1946 Act, review of benefits was stipulated only every five years.[94] Certainly, these low levels of benefits coupled with the post-war increases in prices, did not put pensioners dependent upon 1946 state pensions in a very desirable position. The definition used by Beveridge and subsequently followed by the Labour government, and each government since then, is conservative in its estimation and provision of need. It is based on notions of prevention of starvation and life at a minimum standard of living. There are three important implications here. First, since the concept of subsistence can be argued to be inadequate in protection from poverty,[95] and even then, as the level of provision was below the definitions of subsistence, every increase that occurred over the years that followed maintained the inadequacy of benefits. Those people solely dependent on these benefits remained in poverty. Second, the very low level of benefits left a great deal of latitude for the operation of the private pension business. The post-war era saw the very rapid growth of private pension funds. This is to a large degree as a result of the very low level of benefits provided by the plan. Third, the low level of benefits was based on the perspective of 'financial soundness' encouraged by Beveridge and adopted as principle by both the Tories and the Labour policy-makers.[96] Even with the low levels of the 1946 Act, these represented an improvement. Table 2.1 compares benefit levels. It is evident from Table 2.1 that although the purchasing power of pensioners was improved by the 1946 Act, the low levels of benefits provided by the Act and the lack of any systematic review in relation to inflation pushed pensioners further into poverty. It was not until 1958 that purchasing power caught up to the level projected by the Beveridge Report.[97] In the early years after the war inflation and average wages rose much faster than pensions. Prices from 1946 increased on the average of 6¾ per cent compounded a year.[98] Thus by 1950 prices had increased close to 30 per cent. Yet if this is compared to the increase in pensions, retired workers did not do well at all. Based on Table 2.1, between 1946 and 1951 pensions increased by just under 20 per cent, falling well short of wages and inflation, on top of the meagre levels of subsistence established by Beveridge and then by the Labour government. In a comparison

TABLE 2.1
Benefit levels

Year	Single man or woman	1965 Equiv.	Married man and Woman	1965 equiv.
	£.s.d.	£.s.d.	£.s.d.	£.s.d.
Based on 1925 Act (1946)	10.0	1.13.6	1.0.0	3.7.0
Beveridge Report	1.4.0	3.0.0	2.0.0	5.0.0
1946 Act (1948)	1.6.0	2.11.0	2.2.0	4.2.6
1951	1.10.0	2.6.0	2.10.0	3.17.6
1952	1.12.6	2.7.0	2.14.0	3.18.0

(From G. D. Gilling-Smith, 1967, p. 21.)

between national assistance and national insurance benefits not much difference emerges. On national assistance, with the exception of those who were blind or suffered from tuberculosis, who received a higher level of benefit, a single person received £1.4s. while a married couple received £2 per week.[99] Thus the contribution conditions required in order to establish eligibility for national insurance benefits netted a retired couple £2 a week. Further, levels in national assistance benefits grew substantially faster than national insurance.[100] As well, national assistance benefits included a housing allowance making it relatively higher in relation to national insurance than it would otherwise appear. The promise of subsistence level benefits Beveridge put forward, even at minimum level was never realized. In effect, contributions in exchange for benefit rights brought nothing more than a marginal difference for those benefits provided by national insurance.

Contributions
The next principle put forward by Beveridge was that social security entitlement should be based on flat rate contributions in order to establish claims on the fund. This principle, besides having its roots in the 1911 National Insurance Act, was accepted as an alternative to means-tested benefits. Benefits became a right established by contribution and could not be withdrawn by arbitrary bureaucratic decisions. The memories of the harshness of both bureaucracy and the means test on unemployed workers during the inter-war years was certainly a reason for workers and their organizations to support this principle. However, the principle did two other things. First it reaffirmed and consolidated the policy of paying for much of social security benefits

out of a regressive tax on both capital and labour. The central concern of Beveridge, Tories and Labour was to limit and diminish contributions from the exchequer and therefore general taxation. Kincaid points out that the 1946 Act shifted more of the burden to labour. Capital's share of contributions in 1945 was 55 per cent, and after the new Act it was cut to 42 per cent.[101] Second, the principle of contribution can be analysed by the concept of 'state form' presented earlier. Pensions can be discussed not only by what they do, but in terms of the social relations implied by how they perform a specific function. The principle of contribution forms the important link between pensions and wage labour. Entitlement is not taken as a right in the same way as a citizen's right to vote, or free speech. It is a right contingent upon a worker selling his/her labour power for a defined length of time to an employer. The difference between these two forms of right is quite important and points to the connection between pensions and the social relations of production, the domination of the ruling class through the process of selling labour power for the production of surplus value. Of course, pensions are not the only way that this domination occurs, but the contingency of pensions upon the process of selling labour power and wage labour certainly strengthens the class domination and brings this form of class domination into other parts of the lives of the working class than does the direct relation of capital and labour at the factory gates.

The principle of contribution raises the question of funding of social security and pensions. As a background to the financing of pensions, a discussion of state expenditure is helpful. The years immediately after the war presented economic conditions that were not conducive to a large increase in state expenditure and the further expansion of welfare services. The fact that much of state financing was from loans from the USA made this even more difficult. From the earlier theoretical perspective, it was argued that although state social welfare expenditures are necessary for the conditions of accumulation, they play a contradictory role in that they act as a brake on capital accumulation and a shift of surplus value to the state. How then can the commitment to large expansions in the welfare state made by both major political parties be explained? First, given the conditions of social relations generally, and particularly the increased strength of the working class, the choice of *not* expanding welfare benefits implied intense class conflict that was not a realistic option with the major task at hand being that of expanding re-established 'normal' capitalist forms of exploitation with a compliant working class. Second, and perhaps more to the point, the end of the war marked a sharp reduction on central state spending as a percentage of GNP. During the war, state expenditures reached approximately 60 per cent of GNP; however, by 1947 these had dropped to about 22 per cent of GNP. In 1938 state

expenditures were 20 per cent of GNP.[102] The increase comparing 1938
and 1947 was not significant, given the level of state activity. The end
of the war brought with it a freeing of a substantial percentage of the
GNP to the private market. The expansion of the welfare state paralleled the re-establishment of more market-oriented production which
was disrupted by the war. Similarly, for the social services, the early
post-war years did not represent an extensive growth in relation to state
expenditures. In 1930, social services represented 42.3 per cent of state
expenditures. This climbed to 47.0 per cent in 1934, then fell to 37.6
per cent in 1938. By 1950 social services represented 46.1 per cent of
state expenditures, and then dropped to 42.9 per cent in 1951 and
finally grew to 44.6 per cent in 1955, still *relatively* below the 1934
level. Social insurance as a percentage of state expenditure did not
grow substantially either. In 1938 it represented 13.6 per cent, in 1949,
10.6 per cent, and in 1950 still only 11.3 per cent.[103] Again, it is
important to note that although both the war and the early years
after the war produced a great deal of social legislation, the relative
position of social service and social security expenditures in terms of
state expenditure did not change.

The major principle of financing of social security and retirement
pensions was that they should be self-financing through an agreed upon
level of contributions from the exchequer and contributions from employers and employees. As well, there was a reserve fund established,
left over from other state schemes. Beveridge envisioned the scheme to
be an insurance scheme with an expanding reserve fund, and actuarial
soundness. This was to be achieved by phasing in the scheme over a
twenty-year period, thus allowing the accumulation of the reserve fund.
This never came to pass as the 1946 Act allowed the claiming of full
benefits right from the beginning of the scheme. Pensions and all the
social security schemes became based on the principle of 'pay-as-you-
go' in which those working supported those collecting benefits. The
role of the reserve fund became less and less important as a proportion
of total social security expenditures. In the early years after the war,
the contributions from the exchequer as a percentage of total receipts
began to diminish. In 1950, exchequer contributions represented
approximately 24 per cent, by 1952 it represented 18 per cent, and in
1953, 12 per cent.[104] The total excess of receipts over payments grew
between 1949 and 1951 and then began to decline. The fastest drop was
between 1952 and 1953, when the excess dropped from £97,378,000
to £23,151,000. The difference is attributable to a 16 per cent increase
in demand for service, and a drop in block grants to the scheme by
approximately £39,200,000.[105] Compared with the absence of increases
in benefits in the early years of the scheme, workers' contributions
grew rapidly. The changes are illustrated by Table 2.2.

TABLE 2.2
Contributions to national insurance

| | Changes in contribution rates 1938 = 100 | | | |
	1938	*1944*	*1946*	*1950*
Employee's contribution	100	118	345	364
Index of average weekly earnings	100	170	177	239
Cost of living index	100	146	150	184

(Adapted from Peacock, 1952, p. 17.)

What emerges in the early years of the pension scheme and follows subsequently is the policy of minimizing the contribution of the exchequer and to as large a degree as possible maintaining a surplus of receipts over expenditure. Contributions can be seen as nothing more or less than a direct tax on the working class, and particularly with flat rate contribution, a regressive taxation. Capital too paid contributions, but these were, of course, deductible as a cost against profit, and in terms of competition between capitals, these contributions were standard nationally, and similar internationally. The two main reasons for the relatively large surplus of funds that accumulated besides the taxation policies were, first, the low level of post-war unemployment. Post-war projections for unemployment were $8\frac{1}{2}$ per cent, but the reality was less than 2 per cent during those years. Second, as in most new programmes, the number of retirement pensioners claiming in the first few years was relatively small.[106]

The importance of this form of funding pensions, consolidated by these reforms, is that priority had been given to maintaining a surplus in the national insurance fund. The means of doing this was to limit exchequer contributions, and increase worker/employer contributions. A part of wages was removed in the name of saving for retirement. All that could occur was that workers would struggle to protect their take-home pay. Further, welfare state provision would be closely linked to wage labour not only through establishing eligibility but also through a direct tax on wages.

Administration
The next principle of operation of the Beveridge scheme was unity of administration. This principle was formally enacted by the coalition government with the establishment of a Ministry of National Insurance. The 1946 Act carried through this principle by bringing into this

49

ministry the total range of social security programmes through one system of contributions and benefits. In reality, two state systems of social security continued to develop at the end of the war. The first, national insurance, is based on the principles of contribution and benefit rights; the second, national assistance, is based on a means test and does not entail a formal legal entitlement. Beveridge, in his Report, foresaw that as the national insurance programmes grew over the years, and as people established their contribution rights, the dependency on means-tested national assistance would diminish. This has not been the case. From the beginning of the 1946 Act, and continuing since then, more and more people have been forced to turn to these benefits as their sole or primary means of support particularly because of the miserly national insurance benefit levels. In the years immediately after the war, as expected with a new scheme, there were many claiming national assistance, but, instead of diminishing in the years after the war, the number claiming national assistance increased.[107] The major category of recipients particularly in the years following the war were retired workers and their dependants. The inadequacy of the level of benefits is reflected in the large number of retired workers claiming national assistance benefits who were also receiving national insurance funds. In December 1949 just over 62 per cent of those claiming national assistance were retired workers, of whom 48.2 per cent were receiving national insurance benefits. The number of retired workers and their families dependent on national assistance continued to grow in the post-war years. The proportion of all those receiving national insurance retirement benefits who also received national assistance benefits remained about the same between 1951 and 1965 at 23 per cent.[108] The low level of benefits prescribed by Beveridge and the miserly reforms brought in by Labour are reflected in this tendency. Further, as stated earlier, the fact that national assistance provided housing allowances and other discretionary benefits increased the difference in the level of these two benefits. Also among retired workers themselves several divisions were emerging, reflected in the form of retirement benefit to which they were entitled. These divisions became more clear with the rapid development of private pensions in the late 1950s. The fact remains that right from the beginning the levels of benefits provided by the 1946 Act resulted in a two-tier state system with contributory national insurance benefits and large numbers of retired workers forced into means-tested national assistance.

Coverage
The final principle of Beveridge was comprehensiveness of coverage in relation to the population. This will be discussed, particularly in terms of who became covered for retirement pensions. In order to understand,

the limited accomplishments of 1946 reforms, particularly the 1925 Act and subsequent developments, will be reviewed. Briefly, the 1925 Old Age Widows' Pensions Act introduced contributory pensions for retired workers covering them from age 65 to 70. Those over 70 were covered by the 1908 non-contributory scheme. Contributions were administratively linked to contributory schemes for health insurance established in 1912. One of the major shifts in 1925, in terms of pension legislation, was to establish the principle of contribution, and this policy reduced demands on the Treasury, under a great deal of pressure at that time. The pensions themselves did not begin until 1928 in order that the Treasury could accumulate some contributions before payment. The level of benefits, even according to Chamberlain, was inadequate but he thought that it was in line with what the nation could afford and provided the basis for personal savings and industrial pensions. In addition, the cost to the Treasury at the time was not large.[109] It is important in understanding Beveridge and the Labour reforms to note that even with its inadequacy and its low cost, low benefits approach, the 1925 Act brought much of the working class into a programme of contributory pensions. It was the Conservative party that brought in these pensions, and this, to some extent, explains their support for the principles behind Beveridge, which were largely, except for the principle of universality, the same principles that they used in the 1925 reform. In 1929, the Labour government added half a million people to the pension scheme by giving pensions to widows of insurable men at age 55.

Orphans' and Old Age Contributory Pensions extended rights to independent workers with incomes between £250 and £400 per year, and allowed workers to subscribe at age 55 for a 10 shilling pension between ages 65 and 70. In 1940, the maximum age for joining the scheme was dropped to 40, and the pensionable age for women was dropped to 60 for insured women or wives of insured workers. As well, supplementary pensions with increases for the cost of living were administered by the Unemployment Assistance Board.

The net impact of these policies was to establish, albeit in a haphazard way, contributory pensions that covered most of the population. The history of pension development is such that small groups became covered for pensions with each reform. The Labour/Beveridge reforms completed the process and provided universal coverage for all workers. Not untypically, because of the centrality of wage labour, unwaged domestic labour, that is, women in the family, remained excluded, leaving large gaps and severe poverty in old age for widows and many elderly couples. Thus the post-war pension reforms added a relatively small number to the scheme and established a universal scheme for all excepting unwaged domestic labourers — women in the home.

In total, it has been argued, in this section, that the 1946 National Insurance Act, especially in terms of pension reform, brought very small gains to the working class. The social security reforms, particularly in the early years after 1948, did not bring any increase in state expenditures in relation to the GNP beyond the highest level of the 1930s. On the specifics of pensions, the only gain under the 1946 Act for the working class was a slight increase in benefits on retirement. However, these benefits in no way reached a level of subsistence defined by Beveridge, even at that low level. The 1946 Act consolidated the principle of contributions established by the 1911 National Insurance Act. The consequence of this principle was that a regressive form of taxation was maintained and subsequently developed, as the basis of pension financing. Further, contributions became the basis for conditions of entitlement, and thus linked pensions to the process of the selling of labour power and thus the pension form was a reflection of class domination. The pension reforms laid the foundation for a three-tier system of benefits that developed in the years after the war. The three are private occupational pensions and individually purchased pensions, state contributory national insurance pensions, and means-tested national assistance benefits. The first, private occupational pensions, emerged through a deliberate social policy in Beveridge and before of leaving the state sector with a minimal role in terms of the subsistence principle of provision, consequently encouraging the growth of the private sector. The state insurance sector, although universal in coverage, provided benefits at a level so as not to compete with the growing private sector. The growth of means-tested benefits was also a direct result of the low level of benefits provided by national insurance and the inability of many workers to reach the contribution conditions necessary to be eligible for benefits. Both of these problems point to basic failures of the 1946 Act in the terms defined in the Beveridge Report and the goals of the Act itself. Finally, the 1946 Act furthered the coverage of the 1925 and subsequent legislation to only a relatively small number to bring about universal coverage for pensions. In total, then, the gains of the 1946 National Insurance Act in terms of pensions can be described as quite limited, and built on well-established traditions.

Summary

This chapter has situated the 1946 National Insurance Act in the context of a changing form of class relations. The new form of relations that emerged was referred to as the Keynesian/Beveridge mode of domination. It developed out of wartime class collaboration, and the coalition government. A new strategy of class relations was required because of the increased bargaining strength of the working class, that developed as a result of relatively full employment and the need for co-operation of the working class in order to defend against and to defeat fascism. The new mode of domination was accepted by the trade union and Labour party leadership, as well as the Conservative party and to a large extent other representatives of the capitalist class. There was popular support for a more just and humane capitalism after the war. The components of the post-war reforms included the state's actively intervening to maintain a growing, prospering, and stable capitalism. This intervention was supposed to accommodate the demands of workers and capitalists. Workers would be protected through high levels of employment and welfare state coverage from the cradle to the grave. Capitalists would enjoy a stable environment, and more systematic state intervention to guarantee a profitable and tranquil capitalism. The Keynesian/Beveridge mode of domination defined new parameters and conditions of class relations for the post-war period.

The Labour government followed closely on the path paved by the coalition with the exception of limited nationalization of industry. It faced difficult economic circumstances but brought in welfare state reforms anticipated in the coalition, and followed a policy of restraining the demands and limiting the militancy of the working class. It was in these circumstances that the 1946 Act brought about pension reform.

As discussed, the reforms closely paralleled the Beveridge Report. They embodied the traditional forms of social relations of the welfare state expressed through the work-testing of benefits and contributions. The benefits provided were miserly, creating a legacy of poverty for the aged, especially for elderly women and widows. Also, the low level of benefits created some of the conditions that enabled private pension development in the years that followed. The low level of benefits is partly a reflection of the fiscal caution of Beveridge, the coalition government, and the Labour government. Providing a long-term commitment to high levels of pensions was difficult to accept, given the unstable nature of post-war capital accumulation. Pension provision was linked to the assumption of a growing and profitable capitalism. In total, the pension reforms did not deviate from a tradition well established in British social policies, and reflected a limited commitment to social reform and the general moderation of the Labour party. Social policy was not to interfere with or to impede directly the post-war attempts to reconstruct a prosperous capitalism based on a new form of class rule and limited social reform.

The next chapter will follow these themes, particularly, how the post-war boom continued to accommodate the Keynesian/Beveridge mode of domination. The debate on pensions and pension reform will be situated in the context of the post-war boom and its implication for class strategies and struggles.

3

Pensions in prosperity

Introduction

This chapter will discuss the development of state retirement pensions during the years of Conservative government from 1951 to 1963. The major reform was the introduction of earnings-related or graduated pensions in 1959. Although the period was one of Tory party rule, far more important was the context. It was characterized by the long, post-war economic boom. The combination of relative prosperity and a decrease in class conflict seemed to herald in a new kind of capitalism. By the end of the period, however, the economic prosperity was drawing to a close. More important, the Keynesian/Beveridge mode of domination was consolidated. Shifts in orientation of both major political parties resulted in a convergence of strategies. The period of prosperity brought with it full employment, a consolidation of the welfare state with some reform, and state policy designed to manage a growing, prosperous capitalism. These conditions formed the context for the strategy of class rule, and the debate and reform of pensions.

This section will discuss the emergence of graduated pensions and situate their development. In order to do this the economic boom and its relationship to the working class will be discussed in section 1. Section 2 will discuss developments in the two major political parties, in the context of the boom and how each party perceived the welfare state. Section 3 will explore the debate on state pensions, and the major reform in this period, the 1959 National Insurance Act.

1 Capital accumulation and the boom years

The years of Conservative government from 1951 to 1963 took place
during a period of extensive economic growth, and prosperity. However,
towards the end of this period the crisis of British capitalism, so evident
in the late 1970s, was becoming apparent. In this section, an overview
of the period from 1951 to 1963 will be presented. It will cover the
characteristics of the period starting with the general conditions of
accumulation followed by some specific considerations such as the
economic difficulties that went along with this period of prosperity,
state policies that emerged, and the position of the working class.

On the whole, the years between the early 1950s and the early
1960s can be described as a period of slow but sustained growth, of
rising incomes, and consumer spending. Unemployment virtually
disappeared; profits, with the exceptions of 1952, 1957 and the early
1960s, rose steadily, doubling between 1946 and 1955, and increasing
by one-third again by 1960.[1] Under the Conservatives, [the sun] shone
brightly on private enterprise and private consumer expenditure.[2]

The prosperity of the post-war years was not without its fluctuations; however, in comparison to the patterns in the period before the
war, these were mild.[3] In contrast, the years considered here were ones
of remarkable stability, especially in contrast to the pre-war experience.[4]

Although this period was one of exceptional growth and prosperity
for Britain, it is much less favourable if viewed in an international
context. In comparing Britain's average annual GDP with other OECD
nations, its rate of growth was lowest.[5] The rate of growth, which was
rapid in relation to other periods in British history, was not as good as
its competitors. Further, in profitability, the UK performed poorly by
international comparisons.[6] Not only were the levels of profits and
growth rates lower than other countries, but so was Britain's rate of
investment.[7]

Lower investment, relatively slower growth and lower profitability
were present in the context of the boom. The importance of these
patterns is that the period of the boom in Britain was weak by international comparisons. The tendency for crises to emerge in all capitalist
economies was certainly increased in Britain by these weaknesses.

Two other difficulties that were defined as major during this period
were the balance of payments, and related to that the difference of
interests pursued by finance and industrial capital. The problem of
maintaining a balance of payments surplus was one of the major deter-
minants of government economic policy in these years. Britain was
losing in the international scene, reflected in her falling behind in competition in industrial production, in her dependence on imports of food
and natural resources, and increased competition for export markets.[8]

56

The separation and competition between finance and industrial capital weakened accumulation in general. Glyn and Sutcliffe[9] argue that the split in these interests has origins early in the history of British capitalism. Traditionally, and continuing in the post-war period, finance has favoured high interest rates to attract foreign funds and maintain reserves while industry wanted cheaper money to finance investments. Further, finance capital tended to oppose high levels of government spending when industry might have benefited from increased demand. One important consequence of the position of finance capital was uneven industrial growth and investment. Finance capital defined itself in relation to world-wide investment, and the investment needs of British industrial capital suffered because of it.[10]

To summarize, the years from the early 1950s until almost the end of the Conservative government in 1963 was an era of sustained growth and prosperity. High profits, stability, low unemployment and general economic optimism were in sharp contrast to the pre-war years of the 1920s and 1930s. However, although Britain's economy did well in relation to its past performance, it did not in any way keep up with the level of the boom in other advanced capitalist countries. Further, several major economic problems — weak balance of payments and trade, interests that were defined differently by finance and industrial capitalists and lack of capital investment — further weakened Britain's position. One of the important characteristics of this period and related to these problems was the state's attempt to manage economic development.

State economic policy

This section will briefly summarize some themes in the development of the economy and the response of the government to these changes. In general terms, the shift from Labour to Conservative ministers was not very dramatic. Both faced similar problems and responded with similar policies. The term 'Butskellism' was coined by *The Economist* to describe the similarity of policies.[11] Three important themes can be identified during this period. First, was a shift from direct control techniques to budgetary techniques. Second was the famous 'stop-go' policies of the Conservatives, and third were attempts to regulate wage levels of labour. Each of these will now be discussed.

The one major change brought in by the Conservative government was the abandonment of planning controls that were instituted during the war and continued during the Labour administration.[12] In general, the price system was left to operate virtually free of rationing, licensing and direct controls.[13] With this shift, the budgetary policies described as 'stop-go', which were strongly identified with the years of Tory rule, were implemented in an attempt to regulate inflation and growth.

By the time these measures had been introduced, demand had already slowed down and industrial investment was needlessly reduced. The 'go' was presented in the 1953 budget which reduced income tax and the excess profit levy restored initial allowances and liberalized building licences.[14] There were no balance of payment problems between 1952 and 1955. Further restrictions were removed, and a drop in the bank rate took place. By the end of 1954, problems in balance of payments seemed likely as consumption and imports were growing faster than production and exports.[15] Butler delayed the next stop until after the 1955 election. This stop included sharp increases in taxation; the bank rate was raised to 5½ per cent, and restrictions imposed on hire purchase agreements with sharp cuts in the investment plans of nationalized industries.[16] It is not necessary here to review each of the subsequent budgets. This general pattern was followed with a fair degree of variation throughout the Tory years in power, reflecting an attempt at state management of the economy. The government tried a strategy of encouraging investment through the establishment of the National Economic Development Council (NEDC) in 1961. It set targets of 4 per cent for annual growth of investment but it failed to reach these goals as Britain's investment in industry fell behind its European competitors.[17] The Conservatives continued to play an active role in the economy partly because of the traditions established by Labour, partly because of the continual mild crises of one kind or another, and partly because of the policies of full employment and government responsibility for economic growth that had become part of Conservative policy.[18]

The other important aspect of state policy was the periodic attempts to regulate wage increases. The major determination of wages during this period was through direct bargaining with little state intervention. It was during periods of crises that policies to regulate wage claims developed.[19] The working class were not to concede their gains. The policies tried to integrate the trade union leadership into the process of wage restraint, and formalize their role as managers of exploitation. The strength of the working class in the context of full employment presented a situation in which the restraint of wages could not easily work. In total, even with the active role of the state, the problems and contradictions of British capitalism could not be contained, and the strength of the working class would not allow wage cuts.

The working class and economic growth

As discussed at the end of the last chapter, the conditions of the capital–labour relations that emerged at the end of the war and in the period of the Labour government were based on commitments to full employment and the welfare state on a universal basis. Although these conditions were challenged in a very general way by Churchill in his election campaign of 1951,[20] once in office neither of these basic policies were substantially altered. Certainly in comparison to any other period, conditions of full employment were maintained and the welfare state was consolidated. The conditions of sustained economic growth and profitability provided the basis for full employment and the welfare state, and, at the same time, the conditions of full employment increased the strength of the working class to protect their material gains within this form of class rule.

The previous section described the economic conditions of accumulation. It is, however, a one-sided description. Accumulation is based on class struggle, and it cannot be separated from it. The contradiction that emerged during the boom was that although material gains were made by the working class, there was not tremendous overt trade union militancy. Thus, although there may have been relative calm in terms of the class struggle, it cannot be understood as a period of working-class weakness, or a period that was to herald the end of class conflict. The boom provided the material condition to allow, at least in the short term, a period of class calm. The position of the working class will now be discussed in more detail.

In general terms, the conditions of prosperity brought with it greater consumption by the working class, and appeared to reduce class distinction between the working and the so-called middle class.[21] Mass consumption and spending became a central feature of this period with the image of the 'affluent worker'. The symbols of affluence included ownership of homes, televisions, and automobiles, with a large increase in consumer spending.[22] Macmillan's famous quotation, 'You never had it so good', in some ways indicates popular perception.[23] The period was one of optimism for the working class, particularly after the harsh years before and during the war. The Conservatives promoted the idea of a 'property-owning democracy' and 'partnership in industry'.[24] These increases in working-class consumption reflect an increase in wages and an improvement for many in conditions of employment.

Employment

If there was one single factor that helped to strengthen the position of the working class in Britain, this was the long period of full employment. In these circumstances workers can push forward their wage demands and the combination of economic expansion and strong worker positions in the labour market tends to benefit workers. The main reason for the strength of the working class was the absence of the reserve army of labour, nationally reflected in low levels of unemployment.[25]

Wages

The wage gains made by workers in this period were significant. Not only did wages rise, but they rose faster than prices and productivity; as well, wages gained as a share of the GNP as compared to profits.[26] The wage gains in this period were important and reflect the combined effects of prosperity, growth and relatively full employment. It was clear, however, that by the end of this period the state was becoming more concerned with these gains, and beginning to develop strategies to curtail wage increases, foreshadowing the conflicts between workers and the state that followed.

Trade unions and class struggle – whose consensus?

The combination of growth and general prosperity produced conditions in which wage claims were more easily achieved, particularly in the 1950s.[27] Particularly in the early years, the co-operation between capital and labour based on full employment, consumption, and wage increases was historically exceptional. By the end of the period, it was rapidly beginning to break down.

Beginning with the election of the Conservatives, co-operation was assured by the TUC, as they stated in 1951:

> We expect of this government that they will maintain to the full this practice of consultation. On our part we shall continue to examine every question solely in the light of the industrial and economic implications.[28]

As discussed earlier, in the period after the election, wage negotiations tended to be free from government intervention. This was in the context of the rapid decontrolling of the economy after 1951.[29] Up to the 1955 election there remained a low level of strikes and days lost. Following, but not related to, the election, stoppages began to rise. In the years 1955–8, the annual number of stoppages due to strikes and lockouts continued to increase. During this period there were several major strikes, for example, London bus drivers, and railway workers.[30]

In addition, an unofficial system of bargaining emerged at the plant and shop-floor level through shop stewards. Conflicts, perhaps, were not great at a national level, but did continue at the local level through shop stewards' movements.[31] This grassroots movement perhaps was the key to workers' defence and strength, in effect acting against the trend of routinization, greater centralization and co-operation between trade unions and capital. By the end of the 1950s trade union conflict was on the increase. The hard line taken by the government through the Council on Prices, Productivity and Incomes in the strike of the London bus drivers and conductors led to the intervention of the TUC. The strike was not successful in making any substantial gains for the workers.[32] This general trend in government policy to limit wage increases was formalized in 1962. The earlier pay pause was to end in March 1962, and a $2\frac{1}{2}$ per cent guideline on wage increases, as well as an invitation to the TUC to join NEDC was issued. The TUC refused to regulate wage claims, but reluctantly joined NEDC. The final pitch of the Conservatives, just prior to their defeat in 1964, was a cabinet house cleaning bringing in Maudling, who attempted to engineer a brief pre-election period of expansion through budgetary measures. Along with this, Macmillan established a weak and short-lived National Incomes Commission. This Commission was to investigate wage claims, particularly their impact in terms of the 'national interest'. The TUC refused to join this Commission.[33] The period ended with a foreshadowing of a major change. The state was to attempt to play an active role in regulating wage claims, and, further, to incorporate representatives of the trade union movement. These two strategies were to form the areas of bitter class conflict in the years of crisis that followed.

Although the number of work stoppages showed a gradual rise during this period, with the exception of 1957, 1959 and 1962, the aggregate duration in working days of stoppages was not increasing substantially, remaining at approximately the same level as the closing years of the Second World War.[34] Further, although the trade union movement was growing, it was not growing rapidly, only increasing its membership by approximately 635,000 on a total membership of just over 10,000,000.[35] By the end of this period it was clear that class conflict was intensifying. This was expressed in terms of increasing strikes and militancy especially through shop stewards, and conflict with government-imposed wage policy. Also, the façade of 'the end of ideology' prevalent in the era was beginning to break down. The nuclear disarmament movement, and the emergence of the 'new left' were signs of new forms of conflict that, coupled with increasing trade union militancy, were to challenge the relative calm of the era.

Summary and implications

The following are the major themes of the era. The period was one of rapid economic growth, stability, and relative profitability. Within it, however, there were some economic difficulties. The prosperity encompassed economic fluctuations, reflected in slumps that by any other historical standard were minor. Further, in relation to other advanced capitalist nations, Britain's boom was weak. Growth was slower, and profit rates were lower. The state played an active role in attempting to regulate the economy. The prevailing policy was expressed as 'stop-go', with policies encouraging expansion alternating with policies designed to slow growth. The latter were policies of economic restraint and here connections were made to slow down the growth of public sector expenditures. The period was one of full employment. The working class gained with increased wages and consumption. Although class struggle, expressed in terms of strikes or mass protests, was reduced, this does not necessarily express a weakness on the part of the working class, but rather reflects the conditions of prosperity. By the end of the period, greater economic difficulties were becoming apparent. One response by the state was to attempt wage regulation, and to involve trade unions directly in this process. These themes became a central part of the crisis that followed. In general, the period suggested that the era of a capitalism producing severe contradictions and class hostility had ended. The basic assumption upon which this notion was based was that growth would continue. As long as growth continued, and prosperity seemed indefinite, then increased wages and profitability seemed compatible.

The implication of importance here is that the Keynesian/Beveridge mode of domination that grew out of the war years continued and was consolidated in this period. The conditions of full employment, stability and relative class harmony implied the success of these strategies of class relations. As long as the conditions continued, improved conditions for the working class seemed compatible with the needs of private enterprise. The state appeared to be able to balance class interests and maintain general economic growth. As well, the conditions of full employment and increased occupational stability meant that an attack on these policies by the government would have brought about increased and intense class conflict with a working class in a strong bargaining position. A strategy of class accommodation through the Keynesian/Beveridge mode of domination seemed a preferable option as long as the period of growth continued.

The general conditions of economic success and class relations provided the basis for the increased acceptance of the state as economic regulator, provider, and the institution of capitalist society that would be able to solve social and economic problems. In other words, action by the state was, as will be discussed in the next section, accepted as a strategy. The contradictions of increased state expenditures and functions did not seem to be extensively questioned. As long as economic growth continued, the state could perform its various functions, and when economic growth faltered it would be the state that, if correctly used, could help stimulate growth. Capitalist stability through the state was a basic assumption and implicit in both the Conservative government's and Labour's oppositional positions throughout the period. The contradictions of these policies did not emerge until later. Further, one can argue that the reformism and relative political conservatism of the period was one consequence of these conditions. Yet, crises are the other side of capitalist prosperity, and with the crises the 'solution' of state intervention, economic management by the state and welfare reforms were to be challenged by capital. It is because capital accepts the welfare state on the assumption of economic growth that when crises appear the expansion of welfare state activities is challenged. More generally, any growth of capitalism is based on class domination. Therefore, the continuing challenge to capital is to reproduce these relations that are based on conflict, and instability. The Beveridge/Keynesian form of domination, with its welfare state and state commitment to full employment, worked as long as economic growth and prosperity held up. As the crisis began to appear at the end of this period the terms of class domination would become more shaky and would undergo periods of conflict. The next section will discuss the positions of the Conservative and the Labour parties and how at a basic level the policies of state intervention and the Keynesian/Beveridge solution were maintained.

2 Consolidation of the Beveridge/Keynesian mode of domination

This section will review the orientation of the Labour and Conservative parties, including the major political debates and positions on the welfare state. The significant feature of this period is the general acceptance of the Keynesian/Beveridge mode of domination. This section will describe the emergence and the leadership of the Conservative party by what Andrew Gamble calls 'Right Progressives'.[36] Similarly, after their defeat in 1951, the Labour party underwent a shift to the right. With these shifts, both parties shared a fundamental policy commitment to full employment, and the welfare state, and active state economic intervention. This section will set the background context for state pension policy and debates.

The Conservatives

After the defeat of the Conservatives in 1945, the party faced two possible options. The first was to accept the new conditions of social relations that developed in the coalition and were rapidly implemented by Labour after the war; second, they could return to the politics of class confrontation, and high unemployment that characterized the pre-war period.[37] With the exception of Churchill's anti-socialist attacks and the 1950 party manifesto, the first option prevailed. This contrast can be seen in the party manifestos of 1950 and 1951.[38] This shift reflects the policies that had been developing in the party since the 1945 defeat. These reflected the strength of the Tory reform group who gained influence within the party and with the leadership.[39] The leadership of this wing of the party in government was Macmillan and Butler. Their position is reflected in the writing of Macmillan. It is based on an enlightened self-interest of the ruling class, and ideas of social progress, expressed for example in Macmillan's *The Middle Way*. Here, he links concepts of economic efficiency and growth with the improvement of social conditions.[40] It is not only out of goodwill that social progress is necessary, but also out of the fear of revolution.[41] The state was seen as the vehicle for social stabilization and industrial growth. This theme became strongly expressed in the Industrial Charter in 1947. It contained a commitment to full employment, to improve social services, and for the government to play an active role in controlling and regulating the economy.[42] This position reflected a shift from *laissez-faire* capitalism to a form of capitalism in which the state plays an active role in managing and regulating the economy. Another significant point is the stress put on the concept of national interest. The orientation was supposed to benefit all classes. As Macmillan argued:

> Any action we can propose, therefore, which would have the effect of maintaining business activity and employment at a high and stable level would serve the interests of every class in society.[43]

It was, of course, not only the ideas of the 'right progressives' that were important, but the conditions in which their ideas dominated. The approach worked because capitalism was in a period of unprecedented growth. As long as it was increasing, these policies were not seriously challenged and in general terms had the pragmatic quality of attempting to respond to the mild fluctuations in the economy. The Conservatives, when elected, had an ideal opportunity to apply this approach. Their domestic policy was based on two main assumptions — that the state sector was to be administered and not dismantled, and that the unions were to be appeased. With the years of affluence, the Conservatives could make the claim that they could run a system of welfare capitalism. Further, the combination of the new Conservatism, and the vigour of capitalist growth made the defensive positions of the 1930s seem obsolete.[44]

The Conservatives and the welfare state

Within the general context of the economic boom and the orientation described above, it is not surprising that the Conservatives did not dismantle the welfare state. In general, this was a period of consolidation of services and some relatively minor changes. The first theme that the Conservatives developed during this period was the linking of welfare state provision to both economic growth and the limits of taxation. This is not to argue that Labour did not make these connections, but with the Tories, the limits of state-financed welfare schemes were made explicit, and constituted a major party position,[45] pointing towards the assumption that the welfare state could expand only within the context of general economic growth. These connections to economic growth were consistently expressed.[46] In 1951 this connection was made very clear:

> The Conservative aim is to increase our natural output. Here is the surest way to keep our people fully employed, to halt the rising cost of living and to preserve our social services' hard work, good management, thrift — all must receive their due incentives and reward.[47]

In this context and in contrast to the position of many in the Labour party, the Conservatives saw the welfare state in limited terms:

> All must be secure in the possession of a basic standard of life; and all must be free to rise above it so far as their industry and talents take them. . . . We denounce the Labour Party's desire to use social services . . . as an instrument for levelling down. We regard social security not as a substitute for family thrift, but as a necessary basis or supplement to it.[48]

Thus, not only did the Tories see the welfare state as limited by economic growth and taxation, but also, social services were not a tool for remedying of social inequalities. Related to this was the Tory policy to encourage, as much as possible, the use of the market as the primary means of social reproduction.

If there is one major difference of emphasis between Labour and Conservative parties in this period, it is the degree to which the market was understood as central to welfare provision. The Conservatives were clear in their position. The welfare state as a form of provision must neither compete with market provision not undermine it. The consequence of this position was to limit state provision both in quantity and in allocation. The state was not to provide services to *all* people, but it was to act as the guarantor that service would be provided. This position in practice pertained mainly to housing and pension provision. Expressions of these themes can be seen in Conservative party manifestos. In 1950 the position was put forward in terms of social security and housing.[49] This theme of a 'property-owning democracy' was returned to many times during their years in power.[50] To this end, in 1955 the manifesto emphasized expansion of home-building through the private sector, an increase in schools but protecting grammar schools, and new hospital-building but including private practice, and pay beds.[51] The message was clear: the state was not to interfere with the institution of private property, but to encourage it. Further, the welfare state must be maintained but it should not undermine the values of individualism, self-reliance and thrift. The welfare state was linked to traditional values of private property and capitalist social relations as the desired social relations. In contrast, as will be described later, although the welfare state under the Labour party followed these general policy orientations, it was perceived quite differently.

The Conservatives followed along the same direction as Labour and the coalition government. They consolidated the post-war reforms and brought in other improvements. For example, in health provisions, the government reviewed the costs of health care and discovered a shortage of capital funds being spent on the NHS. A plan to build new hospitals and renovate old ones was introduced.[52] In education, the government brought out the Robbins Report on Higher Education in 1963, recommending a rapid expansion of higher education. This expansion was to be implemented by the Labour government after 1964.[53] Increases in both the private and public housing stock was one of the major accomplishments of the government. The large increase involved a shift from local authority council housing to private housing.[54] In order to do this the government attempted to create conditions favourable to private home ownership such as tax concessions to those paying off mortgages.[55] The government tried to decontrol rental housing with resulting controversy, particularly in London, giving an important issue to Labour and its leader, Harold Wilson.[56] With the moderate recession of 1957–8, the government tried to stimulate the location of industry in areas of high unemployment, particularly Merseyside and Scotland, through the use of grants and loans provided in the 1960 Employment Act.[57] In the years between 1955 and 1965 expenditure on social services increased as a percentage of GNP from 16.3 per cent to 20.6

per cent, and total public expenditure rose from 36.4 per cent to 40.8 per cent of GNP.[58] Growth was slow, but steady.

In total the period of Tory government policies did not produce the dismantling of the welfare state envisioned by Labour. The 'right progressives' were in the leadership of the party, and government policies in this period reflected their orientation. Their policies did not exist in a vacuum. The conditions of class domination inherited by the Tories were working, and this policy orientation during this period of economic growth and prosperity made sense. One of the limits imposed by the Tories was that the growth of the welfare state should be kept in line with economic growth, and that the direct costs to the exchequer would be controlled. In practice, there was not that much difference between what the Tories did and what Labour did in the years after the initial reforms. It was the moderation of the Labour party itself that made these similarities more apparent. The policies of the Conservatives in general faced a moderate Labour party without clear alternatives to Tory policies.

The Labour party

During the years of Labour in opposition there was a distinct shift to the right. The policies and general orientation of the 'right progressives' in the Conservative party and the centre and right of the Labour party were virtually indistinguishable except for rhetoric and Labour's very weak commitment to nationalization and a vague goal of redistribution through welfare state reforms. In opposition, Labour's defending of existing reforms and consensus with the Tories on most issues of foreign policy made it impossible for them vigorously to oppose government policy.[59] The Labour election campaigns of 1950 and 1951 were fought in terms of defending the reforms of the years 1946-8 rather than by pushing forward new proposals. In 1950 they asked 'Can these Conservatives be trusted to safeguard the welfare of the sick, the poor and the old?'[60] This was not to be the case. The central policies of Labour — full employment and the welfare state — were maintained by the Tories, and Labour had little room to manoeuvre.[61]

After the defeat in 1951, the shift in Labour's position was gradual. The main issue in home affairs was the debate on nationalization; in foreign affairs, the question of rearmament and nuclear arms was the major focus of debate. Two important groups emerged at this time. The trade unions with their block votes tended to be a voice of moderation.[62] The left rallied around the leadership of Bevan, but even with a strong position on the national executive of the party, failed to articulate clear alternatives.[63] Towards the end of the 1950s these left-right distinctions were breaking down with unions defending nationalization, and in 1959 supporting unilateral disarmament, breaking ranks with the leadership.[64] Further, Bevan himself seemed to shift towards the centre of the party, particularly in foreign affairs, when, in solidarity with the rest of the party executive, he did not dissent in supporting German rearmament in 1954.[65] The position of the Labour left was significant in that with the exception of their position on nationalization, it was not that far left of the centre of the party.

The general shift in ideology can be seen in the party manifestos of 1955 and 1959. In 1955, after four years of opposition, and the Tories *not* having produced an economic disaster nor dismantled most of Labour's policy, the party did not produce any clear-cut socialist option, and subsequently lost the election.[66] The debate in the party that followed was strongly influenced by the work of Crosland. His position was accepted by the new leader, Hugh Gaitskell, whose election accentuated the rightward shift and gave it 'sharper ideological and political orientation'.[67] In his book *The Future of Socialism*,[68] Crosland argued a position which in many ways was similar to the position of Macmillan and the 'right progressives' in the Conservatives. He posited that post-war changes in Britain no longer made it a capitalist society. The question of who owned the means of production was of less and less importance; and class struggle had become more moderated along with the weakening power of the 'business class'. The major focus of political discussion should be in terms of equality.

Further, and this is the major point of convergence with the 'right progressives', the state was understood to be able to regulate and stabilize economic activity in order to prevent the crises of previous eras. The state had removed strategic decisions from the market and was the regulator of society, with the ability to correct the market and solve basic social and economic problems.[69] This faith in the state's ability to resolve the contradictions of capitalism and produce an equal and just society is the main feature of this position.

Crosland's position reflected the specific period of the boom, particularly his belief that the state could achieve these kinds of goals. The position gained credibility in the context of that particular period of rapid growth, increasing wages and a general rise in the standard of living. The growth of these ideas has to be situated as well in an international context. Richard Fletcher[70] points out that Crosland had been involved in a number of international seminars sponsored by the Congress for Cultural Freedom (CCF). In this group were a number of prominent American social scientists such as Daniel Bell and Irving Kristol. There is evidence to show that the CCF was at least subsidized by the American CIA. Its activities were strongly anti-Communist and a number of progressive, but anti-Communist journals, such as *Encounter*,

New Leader, and *Socialist Commentary*, were affiliated with it. Ideas influenced by this view found their way into the Labour party document of 1957, *Industry and Society*, which diminished the importance of nationalization in the party programme and emphasized the 'mixed economy'.[71] A formal commitment to nationalization was retained in the defence by the left against Gaitskell's attack on Clause 4.[72] In total, even with a formal commitment to nationalization, the Labour party became ideologically a party of the centre with the state playing the role of manager of a more just capitalism.

The Labour party and the welfare state

The major focus of the Labour party was defending the reforms brought in early in their administration. They did propose certain reforms in opposition, but these were not particularly bold. The major difference between their position, and that of the Tories, was that the Labour party emphasized the necessity of the state providing for all on an equal basis, without the market, or the market playing a secondary role, and the welfare state, to some degree, redistributing income to the poorer members of the society. The 1951 manifesto emphasized the theme of equality: 'Labour will press forward towards greater social equality and the establishment of equal opportunities for all.'[73]

The Labour manifesto of 1955 can be used to contrast Labour and Tory social policy. Housing was viewed as a social service. Labour's position was to subsidize local authority house-building and to ask local authorities to submit schemes for the gradual takeover and modernization of rent-controlled private property, subject to 'fair compensation', and secondarily to help those who wish to buy their own homes.[74] The NHS was to drop all charges, and need for treatment not private beds would determine policy priorities. In education, Labour's policy was 'a radical reform of our educational service'. This included increasing the number of teachers, improving education in rural areas, removing primary school eleven-plus exams, encouraging comprehensive secondary schooling, and providing scholarships for university based on need.[75] Labour saw the ability to expand the welfare state as being closely linked to expanding production in the private and nationalized sector. They concluded the manifesto of that year with the following: 'The signposts along our road are work for all, abolition of want, fair distribution of income and property, better education.'[76] As will be discussed later, retirement pension reform was the centrepiece of the 1959 manifesto. Besides that, their position on the welfare state remained much as it did in 1955. The financing of the welfare state was linked to economic growth and tightening up in the existing tax system;

additional revenue was available by closing tax loopholes and catching up with tax dodgers.[77] The shifts in the party were reflected in this manifesto with its emphasis on social justice, fair shares and the welfare state, as opposed to socialism and nationalization.

On the whole, the period was one of the coming together of the main political parties. The shift to the centre by the Labour party and the capture of Conservative party leadership by the 'right progressives' were indicative of this process. The major differences that separated them at this time was Labour's commitment to a very watered down programme of limited nationalization, and its emphasis on the welfare state as an important mechanism for reducing inequalities. The Conservatives maintained a commitment to full employment and the welfare state. It can be argued that both the positive economic conditions and the strength of the trade unions were equally responsible for these positions. The similarity between the parties was based on a philosophy of political pragmatism rather than idealism, and a managerial approach which saw the state as a regulator, and planner that could control the basic contradictions of capitalism.

3 Pensions: debate and reform 1953–63

The context

Before beginning the discussion of the debate on pensions and their subsequent reforms, related factors can be discussed. First, the growth and changes in financing state pensions will be presented. This factor was of central importance to the government in determining their policies on pensions. Second, the impact of the Beveridge/Labour reforms will be reviewed in order to understand the level of income provided to retired workers. Third, the growth of private occupational pensions, particularly as they affected the working class will be summarized. Each of these factors influenced in a substantial way the development of the 1959 reforms, and the debate around these reforms.

Pensions: fiscal developments

During this period, state retirement pensions grew consistently, not only in absolute terms, but also in terms of percentage of GNP, and total state expenditures. Table 3.1 summarizes these changes. Although pensions showed this consistent pattern of growth, it was the changes in pension payments in relation to the national insurance fund that was

70

TABLE 3.1

Year	Total expenditures on retirement pensions (£ millions)	Retirement pensions as % of GNP	Retirement pensions as % of state expenditure
1951–2	279	2.0	4.8
1952–3	321	2.2	5.3
1953–4	339	2.1	5.6
1954–5	353	2.1	5.7
1955–6	439	2.4	6.7
1956–7	455	2.3	6.5
1957–8	489	2.4	6.7
1958–9	629	2.9	8.2
1959–60	670	2.9	8.1
1960–1	690	2.8	7.5
1961–2	800	3.1	8.2
1962–3	824	3.0	7.9

(Analysis of Public Expenditures – Central Statistical Office.)

of importance. From 1952 to 1958 there was a drop in the excess of receipts over payments in the national insurance fund. Further, there were deficits in the fund from 1959 to 1961.[78] The major policy principle guiding government thinking was that national insurance should be financed by employee/employer and exchequer contributions. Beveridge's principle of financing pensions was beginning to break down. The national insurance fund was beginning to work in deficit. Further, the total exchequer contribution, even though it was formally reduced in 1951, as a proportion of total receipts from 1953 to 1958 was beginning to rise.[79] As well, the exchequer made additional contributions of £39, £46, £43.4 million in the years 1959, 1960 and 1961 respectively.[80] These facts, as will be elaborated later, became central issues in slightly different ways for Labour in opposition and Conservatives in government as they both attempted to retain actuarial respectability for the national insurance fund.

Pensions, poverty and older people

Under this heading I will review the financial conditions of old people in this period, and the level of benefits they received. What is striking is that even with the supposed gains made through the Beveridge reforms, those retired and dependent on the state remained in poverty, and poverty among the elderly reflected the failure of the Beveridge reforms.[81]

State retirement pension increases were subject to review every five years during the Labour government. Subsequently under the Tories the reviews and increases in pensions were most frequent and tended to be haphazard, that is, not based on any established policy. Pension increases were not formally linked either to changes in prices or to the level of earnings of workers; however, they did grow faster than the rate of inflation during these years, and made some small gains in relation to wages.[82] As pointed out in the last chapter, these gains are relative to miserly levels to begin with and did little to improve the conditions of the elderly. Further, as Table 3.2 shows, pension increases fell behind wages until 1958, and only really caught up to them in 1963.

TABLE 3.2

Date of increase	Weekly pension rate for single person	Weekly pension rate for married couple	Weekly pension as % of average weekly earnings
1948	26/-	42/-	18.9
1951	30/-	46/-	18.1
1952	32/6	54/-	18.2
1955	40/-	65/-	17.9
1958	50/-	80/-	19.5
1961	57/6	92/6	18.2
1963	67/6	109/-	20.1

(Michael Pilch and Victor|Woods, 1964, *New Trends in Pensions,* London, Hutchinson, p. 120.)

Further, means-tested national assistance increased faster than national insurance.[83] Also, national assistance benefits included a separate grant for rent and rates and, in addition, other special allowances. In effect, what workers were paying for through enforced contributions was not as adequate as what a means-tested benefit would provide. Beveridge's principle, of national assistance playing a residual role, was turned on its head, and if a worker was willing to go through a means test then he/she would do equally well in terms of retirement benefits.

The very failure of national insurance to do anything to solve the problems of poverty and low level of benefits in retirement pushed many old people into claiming national assistance benefits. In December 1949, 62.1 per cent of all those receiving weekly assistance through national assistance were over the pension age. In December 1965 this had increased to 68.9 per cent.[84] It is a reflection of the failure of contributory pensions that this number should increase both relatively and absolutely sixteen years after the introduction of the Beveridge reforms. The main reasons for this were two initial decisions. The first was the principle of subsistence which as was discussed earlier was never implemented even in Beveridge's terms; second was the fact that rent was supposed to be averaged into the total benefit.[85] A big proportion of a retired worker's expenses was not adequately covered by definition, particularly for those who lived in urban areas with higher than average rents. In total, then, the retirement benefits continued to be inadequate in terms of the original definition and in subsequent measures of poverty.

Occupational pensions

Another important factor that shaped pension policy in this period was the growth of private occupational pensions, particularly among those in the traditional industrial working class. This growth is important because it seemed to imply that pensions could be provided through the private market to large sections of the working class.

The growth of private pension plans in the 1950s and early 1960s was very rapid, particularly in the years after 1955. In the private sector, 60 per cent of the schemes began after 1955, and 16 per cent between 1950 and 1954.[86] The total coverage of pensions grew as a proportion of the total labour force. This is illustrated in Table 3.3. The total labour force at the time of the 1963 survey was approximately 25,000,000.[87]

TABLE 3.3
Estimated total numbers of persons employed by firms having pension schemes and estimated total numbers of pensionable employees (millions)

	Private sector		Public sector		Total	
	1956	*1963*	*1956*	*1963*	*1956*	*1963*
(A) Total employees						
Men	7.1	10.1		4.0		14.4
Women	3.0	3.8		1.6		5.4
Total	10.1	13.9		5.6	10.1	19.8
(B) Pensionable employees						
Men	3.5	6.4		3.0		9.4
Women	0.8	0.8		0.9		1.7
Total	4.3	7.2		3.9	4.3	11.1

(*Occupational Pension Schemes: A New Survey by the Government Actuary*, 1966, p. 7, Table Two with addition of 1956 data, and *Occupational Pension Schemes: A Survey by the Government Actuary*, 1958, pp. 4–5.)

Both the number of firms and the proportion of all workers in those firms covered by occupational pensions grew rapidly. Almost 80 per cent of all workers were in a firm with some kind of occupational pension plan. This proportion is high especially when it is pointed out that the 25,000,000 above includes both self-employed and unemployed workers. The actual number of pension schemes grew from 37,500 in 1956 to 60,000 in 1963.[88]

In this period, the number and proportion of manual workers enrolled in occupational pension schemes increased significantly along with the general growth. The focus here is on the private sector, as the state sector provides proportionately more coverage for manual workers. The structure of the schemes themselves differentiates between manual and non-manual workers. Thus in the 1963 government survey, 50 per cent of the schemes covered both manual and non-manual workers while 40 per cent were for non-manual only and 10 per cent for manual only.[89] Pilch and Wood found that of the companies with pensions responding to their study, 28 per cent had no scheme for manual workers, 40 per cent had a separate scheme, and in 32 per cent of the schemes both manual and non-manual workers were enrolled.[90] They argued that in many companies in which manual workers were in the same scheme as white-collar workers, more stringent age and service qualifications were required of the manual workers for pension plan enrolment. Further, the majority of schemes defined as being for manual workers only offered little more than the bare amount necessary in order to satisfy conditions of contracting out from the state scheme.[91] The structure of the schemes discriminated against women workers. In terms of general qualification for participation in private sector white-collar schemes, women had to be older to begin, 25 as opposed to 21 for males, and received their pension at age 60 as opposed to 65 for males.[92] If all other conditions were equal, then women could not possibly qualify for pensions at the same level as their male co-workers, given approximately 9 years less contributions. During the period 1956 to 1963, manual workers in the private sector made the most gains. With the exception of those in state employment, women did not fare well, and women in the manual worker category lost ground.

It is difficult with the available data and the relative newness of many of the pension schemes to speculate about the consequences of these pensions in terms of retirement income. By 1963 there were approximately 1.8 million pensioners or widows drawing benefits from the schemes of which 1.1 million were from the public sector.[93] The private sector schemes had not begun to return benefits to retired workers in large numbers. The benefits themselves were not very high. It is clear that 50 per cent of those receiving benefits were receiving less than £2 per week.[94] If it is assumed that manual and women workers would tend to be at the bottom of this scale, then it can be argued that at this point these benefits did little for manual and women workers except perhaps make them ineligible for national assistance grants.

The growth of occupational pensions was important because it reached into the working class, and many workers were becoming members of these schemes. This growth was facilitated by several factors. First, the low level and flat rate benefits provided by national insurance increased the appeal of private plans. Second, taxation conditions benefited and encouraged these plans for both employers and workers.[95] Third, the conditions of full employment made the issue of labour shortages a problem. Occupational pensions were supposedly one way of decreasing labour mobility. Fourth, and finally, the growth of employment in the state sector and the long tradition of pension plans as conditions of employment led to many workers being part of pension plans. The increased participation of many workers in these plans seemed to indicate that the private market could provide for the retirement needs of many in the working class. The early indications were that the level of benefits provided did little better than either national insurance or national assistance. This fact did not raise any serious doubts, as will be evident in the pension positions that were debated.

To summarize, the following issues were central to the debate on pensions that took place in the years 1953–64: the cost of pensions was rising steadily, and as will be elaborated, expected to rise much faster; further, the financing of the scheme as defined by Beveridge and the 1946 National Insurance Act was beginning to break down, with decreasing surplus followed by deficits in the national insurance fund (by any objective standard, the pension plan failed to abolish poverty among the aged, and forced more and more old people on to National Assistance benefits); finally, there was a rapid growth in those covered in occupational plans. With these factors, the discussion will turn to the development of state pension policy, and related debates.

Government policy

Under this heading I will present and analyse the specific development of state pensions leading up to the 1959 National Insurance Act which introduced earnings-related retirement pensions. The major issues that arose during this period related to the expectation that the demand for retirement pensions would grow at a more rapid rate than those employed could pay for the pensions. Further, as prices increased so did pensions, yet how were these increases to be financed? Both of these problems posed serious threats to the 'actuarial basis' of state pensions. The assumptions underlying this question were that the living standards of the elderly could not be substantially eroded and that the so-called 'actuarial basis' must be maintained. That is, the financing of pensions must be by the workers and employers with a relatively small proportion coming from the exchequer. The Labour party shared this assumption, but in addition tried to develop a policy that was oriented towards the elimination of poverty in retirement, and *to a limited degree* the redistribution of income, and the reduction of inequalities. Because of the shared assumptions of the major protagonists on pensions finance, the central issue that will be examined in this section is the 'actuarial basis'. This will not only be examined in the context of financing of state pensions, but also in terms of the continuing development of the form of pensions, and the implications of this form to broader capitalist social relations.

I will begin with a review of government reports, and in particular the Phillips Commission. From there, the debates in the TUC and Labour party and their pension proposal will be discussed. Finally, the 1959 reform will be presented and analysed.

First Quinquennial Review

In the early years of the Conservative government there were two major reports on pensions and social security. The First Quinquennial Review of the 1946 National Insurance Act was prepared by the Government Actuary. The second was the Phillips Report. The Quinquennial Review presents a useful summary of changes in pension legislation from 1946 to 1954. Both the changes in benefits and the financial arrangements will be reviewed. Changes in benefits were not dramatic. The 1951 National Insurance Act raised retirement benefits for men over 70 and women over 65. This increase was extended as a transitional measure to women over 60 and men over 65. The 1952 Act increased benefit rates and restored the principle of a common basic weekly pension, 25 per cent above the level of the 1946 Act. These were accompanied by increases in contributions payable by insured persons, employers and exchequer.[96] Two important tendencies were maintained. First was the linking of benefit increases to contributions, and second was the continual concern about the level of exchequer contributions, and attempts to either reduce it or maintain it even with increased benefits.

The 'actuarial contribution' played an important role in these discussions. Because of its centrality, its definition, and its relation to contribution levels will be explored. The Quinquennial Report defined the actuarial contribution as follows:

the evaluation of future benefits to the individual in terms of the weekly contribution which an entrant at the initial age would have to pay throughout his contributory lifetime in order to provide, on average, for the cost of benefits to which he and his dependents will become entitled.[97]

Although this concept of an actuarial contribution was retained, its connection to workers' contribution was non-existent. The major deficiency emerged because many contributors entered the scheme after the age of sixteen and, more important, increased benefits were paid to all contributors regardless of whether they paid the corresponding increase in contributions.[98] This second reason was to become more important as inflation worsened. The Report pointed out that national insurance was not funded and no arrangements were made to liquidate additional liabilities, mainly increased benefits, by special deficiency payments or a liability fund.[99] Further, even with revenue in the national insurance fund at this time outstripping costs, total contributions were set at a higher rate than the defined actuarial contribution. Table 3.4 illustrates this point.

TABLE 3.4
Comparison of actuarial contribution and present (1954) weekly contribution for adults (p/week) for employed adults

	Man	*Woman*
1 Present national insurance contribution less NHS contribution		
(a) By insured person and employer	110	87.0
(b) Exchequer supplement	18.0	13.5
(c) Total	128.0	100.5
(d) Deduct 1951 increase	4.0	4.0
(e) Total excluding 1951 increase	124.0	96.5
2 Actuarial contribution	113.2	94.2
3 Margin (+) or deficit (−) in present contribution (including exchequer supplement but excluding 1951 increase) compared with actuarial contribution	+ 3.2	+ 7.2

(*Report by the Government Actuary on the First Quinquennial Review, National Insurance Act 1946, House of Commons Papers*, 30 November 1954, p. 15.)

The point here is that there was in fact *no* actuarial basis for the scheme. Although, within the framework of the 1946 Act, the term 'actuarial contribution' might have made some sense, there was no relationship between contributions and benefits. Further, there was no recommendation that the scheme return to an actuarial basis. The Report estimated that in the next 25 years, the insured population would remain roughly constant at between 23 and 24 millions. At the same time the number of retired workers would increase from $4\frac{1}{3}$ to over 7 millions. The ratio of retired to those working would decrease from one retired worker to five contributors in 1954 to one to three by 1979.[100] In terms of deficits, the Report argued:

> Annual deficits are not as a result of an unfavourable experience nor are they unexpected. They arise from the grant of full insurance rights when National Insurance was introduced and wherever pension and other benefit rates are increased to practically all existing contributors . . . although past contributions of adequate amount cannot have been paid. The cost of benefits of one generation is thus met partly from the contributions of the next generation of contributors and employers.[101]

The evidence was clear that there was, in fact, no real actuarial basis for pensions, yet the mythology was continued in the debates that followed.

Following the argument made in the last chapter, national insurance contributions can be understood as nothing more or less than another type of taxation, and a highly regressive one at that. Table 3.5 supports this point, and points out that these contributions were the fastest growing type of taxation. Not only did these contributions increase, but they could be used in a general way to raise state revenues, so long as the actuarial basis, and the mythology of benefits as tied to contributions was kept intact. Related to this was the fact that the number and frequency of contribution increases grew far more rapidly than did increases in benefits.[102] The link between increased benefits and contributions was rigidly adhered to. For example, around Christmas of 1962, Maudling, the Minister of the Exchequer, proposed that increases in pensions be paid out several months before increases in contributions were introduced. This would have provided a large, short stimulus to the economy at a time when it was needed, then the increase in contributions could counter the stimulus shortly thereafter. This proposal was defeated by the Ministry of Pensions at the time.[103] Brittan comments on this affair:

> Somewhere in the background . . . was the moralistic belief that if the link between contributions and benefits was broken, only for a few months, the whole myth of an insurance scheme would be shattered.[104]

TABLE 3.5
The structure of taxation 1938-59 (percentages of GNP)

	1938	1946	1951	1959
Taxes on Personal Income				
On incomes from Employment	1.1	5.6	4.8	5.1
On dividends, interest, rent and trading incomes	4.6	6.5	4.4	3.5
Taxes on Corporate Incomes	1.8	7.4	5.8	4.6
Taxes on Capital	1.5	1.6	1.5	1.0
Taxes on Expenditure	8.0	14.6	14.8	11.9
Total	16.9	35.8	31.4	26.1
National Insurance Contributions	2.1	1.9	3.5	4.3
Insured persons N.I. Contributions	1.1	0.9	1.9	2.3

(J.C.R. Dow, *The Management of the British Economy 1945-1960*, NIESR, Cambridge University Press, 1964, p. 188.)

Insurance contributions were used as a means of taxation, and as long as the myth of insurance was upheld then they were supposedly not viewed as an increase in taxation but as payment for future income. The mythology, however, remained, at least in the formation of government policy.

The Phillips Report
The Phillips Commission was appointed in July 1953. Its terms of reference were 'to review the economic and financial problems involved in providing for old age, having regard to the prospective increase in the numbers of aged'.[105] The major problem raised by the Report was the anticipated increase in demand for pensions. Several of the themes discussed earlier were documented in this Report. The large and growing number of retired people receiving national assistance benefits was presented. The rapid growth of occupational pensions, particularly for government employees, was noted. One important aspect of the Report, alluded to in the Quinquennial Report and elaborated, was the rapid growth of retired workers in relation to non-retired workers.[106] Having completed this review, the authors turned to the question of the financial difficulties posed by the situation. In unambiguous terms they anticipated a major problem in the financing of pensions. They stated: 'The current costs of national pensions falls far short of the pension rights that will ultimately have to be met.'[107] The following factors were expected to lead to increased demands for pensions: in 1958, there will be a large influx of people into the scheme who had to wait

ten years from 1948; in addition, and more important in the long run, there were the demographic shifts. The Report predicts an increase in the elderly population of 40 per cent between 1954 and 1979, and the number receiving pensions to increase by 80 per cent. The consequences of these shifts for state pensions by 1979 would be increasing pressures put on the exchequer.[108] This concern about an increased commitment from the exchequer and the consequences for capital accumulation formed the central theme of the Report.[109] This concern with the long-term growth of demands for pensions and the decreasing capacity of the working population to finance the scheme were reflected in the recommendations of this Report. They did not foresee major problems in the short run of the next twenty or thirty years based on the assumption of a steady growth in the national income, but pensions were not the only item| in the budget, and had to be viewed in the context of national priorities.[110] One of the most important recommendations related to contribution conditions and the financing of pensions. They noted that for all pensioners, the amount of contributions paid by and for them was 'on the average only about 1/20 of what it would have cost to purchase their pensions on ordinary commercial terms'.[111] Yet, the scheme was projected to run into a deficit. They accepted the basic financial arrangements of the scheme but emphasized the need to link closely contributions and benefits. In doing this, they made explicit a basic argument for maintaining links between contributions and benefits. The links are not only financial but more importantly emphasize the fundamental social relations and discipline implicit in pensions and social security. They argued that the virtue of contributions is that pensions are established as rights, and| payment of contributions is the precondition for receipt of benefits. The Report goes on:

> We think that contributions provide an important measure of social discipline since everyone is aware that higher rates of pension must at once be accompanied by higher contributions. The existence of an accepted actuarial basis is a useful safeguard when rates of benefits are under consideration; it imposes some check on reckless increases by reason of the need to have regard to the amount required to pay for them, and to some extent removes the difficult question of rates of contribution from the arena of political controversy.[112]

Along with this was the recommendation that exchequer contributions remain stable at 1/7 of total contributions, that a fund be maintained, and that each increase in pension should have a corresponding increase for entrant contribution and, as well, an additional sum not covered by age sixteen contribution to be paid by contributors.[113] The recommendations reflected the realities of the scheme. It was *not* a pension scheme in the traditional sense of the word, but a means of transferring funds from those working to those who had retired, and linking contributions to benefits in a *quid pro quo* fashion. The major focus was to maintain a very limited exchequer contribution that would not have to increase at a rapid rate. The scheme was to be continued as a taxation scheme, a regressive one, based on worker and employer contributions. More important are the clear links between work and benefits. Workers were *not* to get something for nothing, but must continually re-establish their rights to pensions by selling their labour power. The links between pension increases and pension rights was also firmly recommended, even though there was no financial basis for this argument. The social relations of daily life, based on labour power as a commodity, were then strongly reinforced by this Report.

The Phillips Report recommended further that the official age of retirement be raised from 65 to 68 for men, and from 60 to 63 for women. This recommendation reflected the existing conditions in which over one million men and women above the pension age remained at work. However, according to the Report, the savings involved from this proposal were small. This change was to be implemented gradually.[114] Turning to the level of retirement benefits, the report argued against a fixed formula for raising benefits.[115] The reasons it outlined were changes in the cost of living, the extent of an increase of pensioners turning to national assistance reflecting inadequate pension levels and the implications of increasing benefits for contribution rates and exchequer contributions.[116] The Report went on to state:

> A contributions' scheme cannot be expected to provide a rate of pension which would enable everybody, whatever his circumstances, to live without other means, such a pension rate would be an extravagant use of national resources.[117]

This position represents a further attack on the principle of subsistence. What Labour had done in practice, Phillips and the Tories would attempt to do through formal policies. This statement reflects as well the general support within the Phillips Report for occupational pensions and, in its view, the importance of pension funds for helping out the post-war shortage of capital.[118] On the whole the Phillips Report did not challenge the operating principles of the 1946 Act, but recommended limited exchequer financing, a large area for the development of occupational pensions, a tight link between benefits and contributions and an attack on the principle that pension rates should provide a subsistence minimum. Some comments on this Report will illustrate positions taken on pensions at that time.

The issues raised by the Phillips Committee were pursued in the press. The Report was published at about the same time as the 1954 National Insurance Act raised benefits and contributions. *The Times* questioned the long-term economic and financial implications of the pension scheme and advocated private superannuation as an alternative to the state scheme.[119] The Report was attacked by two of the major adversaries in the debate on the welfare state in this period, Enoch Powell and Richard Titmuss. Powell, writing in the *Daily Telegraph*,[120] was critical of the Phillips Report and the 1954 Act for their short-sightedness. As discussed earlier, one of the main assumptions made by the Report was that there would be a rise in the national income and productivity sufficient to cover pension increases for at least the next twenty to thirty years. Powell questioned this assumption along with that of continued full employment. The question he posed was how could pensions be funded, and the implications of the accepted arrangements for growth and accumulation. He saw the consequences of the Phillips Report and the 1954 Act as putting increasing pressures on the exchequer which in twenty-five years' time would be carrying three-quarters of the cost of retirement pensions. Powell's position can be understood in the context of his attacks on the principle of universality of pensions, particularly the negative economic consequences that were likely to result because of universality, and redistribution through general taxation.[121]

Countering this attack, Titmuss[122] argued a case for redistribution and challenged the above assumptions. The cost to the exchequer for pensions, he argued, is considerably less than it was anticipated in 1925, 1940, 1942, and 1946,[123] and therefore the concern of the Phillips Report and by implication that of Powell is at least highly exaggerated. His proposal was in the tradition of Fabian socialists. He stated:

> the obvious answer is that these costs – the long-term and foreseeable dependencies of old age – should be shouldered by progressive taxation just as the long-term dependencies of childhood are.[124]

He went on to argue against the inequalities and the regressive nature of the contribution system, and summarized his position as follows: 'The higher the contributions are pushed because of the real or supposed "burden of ageing" the more regressive in its effects will this poll-tax become.[125] Titmuss's position is important because it illustrates a growing awareness of the structure of pensions themselves, and provides an example of a position on the 'left' at that time. Further, he was involved in Labour party policy debates and proposals on pensions; therefore his thinking on these issues is important. Before turning to the Labour party's proposal on pensions, a brief summary of the Phillips Report will be presented. This Report was discussed here because it was the major government evaluation of pensions during this period. It argued that the method of financing was adequate in the short term as long as national productivity increased. It emphasized the actuarial basis of pensions and the 'social discipline' implied in contributions. Further, it saw private pensions as an important means of providing for retirement, and one that should be encouraged. As well, it challenged the subsistence principle. In a peculiar way, some of the concerns of the Phillips Committee were to find their way into the Labour party proposal, particularly the emphasis on the actuarial basis, worker contribution, and at least non-interference with the private pension schemes.

Labour's pension reform proposals

Getting there – positions of the Labour party and TUC

Here I will review the positions taken by the Labour party and the TUC in the years leading up to the 1957 Labour party pension proposals. The Labour manifesto provides a good beginning in looking at the development of pension policies. In the 1950 party manifesto, Labour was self-congratulatory in terms of the 'square deal' provided for pensioners. They promised that their policies would be continued, and that a review of national insurance would be carried out.[126] More important, the 1950 manifesto raised a direct challenge to the right of private ownership of some pension schemes. It stated:

> Those who supplement their standard of life in old age or protect themselves against any of the hazards of life by voluntary savings through the Industrial Assurance Offices should receive the best possible return for their money. The Labour Party, believing that the interests of policy-holders should be paramount, therefore proposes that the Proprietary Companies should be taken out of the realm of private profit and mutually owned by the policy holders themselves instead of by private shareholders.[127]

Although this statement was mild, it provided a challenge to private pensions. Subsequent modification, and backing down from this policy was its future.

Next, the TUC conference of 1954 made some important points on pensions policy, that reflected the position of the organized trade union movement and was to influence subsequent debates within the Labour party. The report of the Social Insurance and Industrial Welfare

Committee[128] credited the establishment of the Phillips Committee to pressures from the TUC over their demands to restore the buying power of pensions to the 1946 level. They argued that the reason why pensions had fallen was the policy of restricting exchequer contributions. The TUC policy can be summarized in the following points.[129] First, retirement pensions along with all other national insurance benefits should be restored immediately to their 1946 value. Second, full consideration would have to be given to the economic burden of retirement pensions in the light of the information resulting from the Phillips Committee. Third, the insurance basis of the national insurance scheme should be maintained, and in order to strengthen the insurance basis, consideration should be given to the possibility of funding the contributions of entrants to the scheme at age sixteen. Fourth, the exchequer is under an unavoidable obligation to meet the growing gap between income from insurance contributors and expenditures. Fifth, every effort must be made to retain reasonable stability in the cost of living in order to ensure the value of insurance benefits. Sixth, the exchequer supplement should be restored to its pre-1951 proportion. With this, it would be unreasonable to oppose some increase of contributions on an actuarial basis in order to secure higher benefits. Finally, the existing retirement condition of pensions conditional on retirement should be retained. Their position reflects the general acceptance by the trade union movement of the dominant orientation towards pensions and the assumptions within it. In relation to proposals that followed, the TUC took a relatively conservative position. It defined the level of subsistence at the 1946 level and, as was argued in the previous chapter, this level was inadequate from the beginning. It accepted without question the mythology of the actuarial basis for pensions, and although it wanted the exchequer contribution increased to the pre-1951 level, it was concerned that pensions should not be too much of a burden on the exchequer. The TUC position is summed up in the following quotation from committee chairman Alfred Roberts:

> The General Council has no intention whatsoever of being party to any proposals for dealing with the problem which would undermine the basic principles of the social security scheme. They are convinced that the scheme, as originally conceived, is sound and any such proposals from whatever quarter, will be resolutely resisted.[130]

The Labour party position on pensions in 1954 centred on its demand that pension benefits should be brought back to the equivalent of the 1946 level. In a resolution which was part of their statement 'Challenge to Britain', the Labour party affirmed:

As part of its policy of establishing an adequate minimum standard of living below which no member of the community will be allowed to fall the next Labour Government will immediately restore all National Insurance benefits to the purchasing power which these commanded when the National Insurance Scheme was introduced. There will be an annual review of the cost of living and in any year in which there has been an increase immediate steps will be taken to ensure that the real value of benefits, pensions and allowances needed to maintain that standard is restored.[131]

Once again, the theme of return to Beveridge and that level of subsistence is presented as policy. Two other themes were brought forward in this discussion. First, Sidney Silverman suggested that pensions should replicate superannuation on a national level. He said:

I should like to see for every citizen . . . some form of superannuation system which will relate his ultimate pension to his standard of living and to his surroundings exactly as is done in the case of town clerks, civil servants.[132]

Second, protests and concern were presented about the low standard of living and poverty faced by many elderly at that time.[133] Both of these themes, the poverty of retired workers and the idea of further superannuation, would become central in later conferences.

Next, the TUC conference of 1955 rejected the recommendations of the Phillips Committee and reaffirmed its commitment to the system as it stood. Regarding the 1954 National Insurance Act, the conference accepted the higher rates of contribution if the exchequer contribution was to be increased, and if that increase would cover new liabilities.[134] One interesting event that reflects the general attitude of the TUC at that time was the attempts by the National Union of Miners to push for an increase in the basic rate of pensions to 50s. per week. Their motion was defeated.[135] Even relatively minor attempts at reform, then, were thwarted.

The 1955 conference of the Labour party brought the beginnings of a lively debate on pensions, and reflected the division within the party with the left led by Bevan, and the more moderate position of the TUC, particularly on the issue of pensions. Again, there were statements calling for a review of levels of pensions in relation to increases in the cost of living.[136] However, the main debate on pensions emerged when Bevan moved the following resolution:

This Conference is of the opinion that the National Insurance Scheme requires reviewing and that

(a) the scheme should be removed from its present actuarial basis and should be financed wholly through the Exchequer and employers, and the principle of equal benefits should be strictly adhered to;

(b) the earnings rule regarding retirement pensions be abolished and all pensions should be related to the cost of living index.[137]

These proposals were directly in opposition to previous positions put forward by both the TUC and Labour party. Bevan went on to say that the term insurance was a misnomer and that it was a poll tax, further, that the same could be said for unemployment benefits, and workers should be entitled to unemployment benefits as rights beyond any formal contribution period.[138] The motion was opposed by Roberts who repeated the TUC position and argued the classic position of the Labour movement that the elimination of contributions can lead to more arbitrary cutting of benefits as they would be completely in the hands of the exchequer, and the Tories would use that opportunity to introduce a means test.[139] Crossman responded for the National Executive Committee (NEC) and moved that Bevan's motion be remitted to the NEC. In his speech he did not argue for the proposals but spoke forcefully on the need for reforms in pensions. He reminded the party of their position to nationalize superannuation schemes and stated:

> I would prefer myself to see a full-scale nationally owned scheme if it were ever possible. . . I myself as a Socialist do not see why we should be afraid of the principle of superannuation, that is, the principle of each person being allowed to contribute year by year while he is working to a scheme which assures him that he will be able to have . . . at least half pay.[140]

In his speech he noted that the Tories had stolen the Labour party's position on pensions and it was time that Labour put forward a clear option. This debate, and Crossman's speech, foreshadowed the Labour party's policies to follow, some of the disagreements about them, and the important role that pension policy was to have in the 1959 Labour manifesto. Before turning to that plan, the position on pensions presented by Labour will be reviewed.

The policies presented to the electorate in 1955 were predictable. Again, the promise was made to review both national insurance and national assistance benefit levels annually in relation to the cost of living, and to reorganize the administration of national insurance to remove 'the last trace of public assistance'.[141] More important for subsequent discussion, it reaffirmed in a most unambivalent way its commitment to private pensions. The manifesto stated:

Welcome the growth of superannuation schemes in industry and commerce as valuable additions to National Insurance pensions. We shall consult with the TUC and industry with a view to extending similar schemes on a voluntary basis to all kinds of employment, and will seek whenever possible to arrange for pensions to be made transferable.[142]

This position was a 'U turn' in policy from 1950, and represents the increased stake of the working class in private pension plans, and the moderation of the party itself. This policy was practised throughout the Labour period in government, and by the Tories as well.

Labour proposals
The Labour party proposals on superannuation and pension reform drafted by Titmuss, Abel-Smith, and Pete Townsend,[143] strongly pushed by Crossman, marked a clear shift from Beveridge's principle of flat rate benefits and contributions. The major emphasis of the plan was the provision of a state superannuation scheme to all workers in the long term and an improvement in the level of pensions in the short term. One objective of the plan was to improve the conditions of retired workers whose pensions had not kept up with the standard of living, and who were increasingly being forced on to national assistance. The proposals in any objective sense were certainly more beneficial to workers than those enacted by the Tories in 1959, and would have involved some redistribution between workers of high and low wages. In later discussion it will be argued that it was also very traditional in its approach to pensions. One of the most important features of this plan was that it was launched shortly before the 1959 election campaign. The pension reform was a central aspect of Labour's election manifesto, and in many ways, given the agreement between the two major parties on most issues, was an important point of departure between them. The manifesto proposed an immediate increase in social security benefits from £2.10s. to £3 per week, and proposed indexing them, on an annual basis, to increases in the cost of living.[144] Given the Phillips Report and the support it had received in many quarters, the decision to index pensions on an annual basis was an important advance. This promise was contrasted to the Conservative party's refusal to increase pensions substantially. The major selling point of Labour's scheme was that it made superannuation available to all employed and self-employed workers. With full implementation of the scheme, retired workers would receive half pay on retirement, and some low pay paid workers would receive up to two-thirds of their pay. The plan will now be presented in detail.

National superannuation can be discussed under three headings:

benefits, funding, and relations between state and private occupational pensions. Benefits[145] were divided into two parts. First, the flat rate benefits would continue, and increase to £3 per week except for those who were 70 and under and who had contributed to National Insurance for less than ten years. They would receive only a proportion of this increase according to the number of years of contribution. Second, superannuation benefits, modelled on private pension schemes, would be in proportion to wage levels. A complicated formula determined these benefits. For those employed between age 25 and 45 entitlement would be 1/240th per year of average earnings, and for those under 25 and between 45 and 65 entitlement would be 1/120th per year of average earnings. The total maximum pension was not to exceed 75 per cent of total earnings. The scheme brought with it some redistribution within the earnings-related scheme. For example, a worker who earned on average £4.10s. per week would receive a pension of £3.7s.6d. per week while a high paid worker who earned £24 per week would receive £11 per week. It is important to note that the build-up period before maximum benefits would be received was fifty years of contributions. Workers would receive proportionately less depending on the years of contribution and could benefit five years after the plan had begun. The major issue facing any pension plan is the protection of benefit levels in the face of growing prices. This plan had a clear safeguard on the flat rate and the earnings-related portion. Increases were to be based on a cost of living index specially related to the expenditure of the elderly. A complex formula was proposed whereby a special index would be established relating individual earnings to average national earnings. This figure would be used as the basis to preserve the real value of pensions for which contributions have been paid. In this way the value of the pension would be maintained in relation to the actual contributions|made.[146] Even with these proposed improvements, an actuarial basis was attempted in which a clear linking of contributions to benefits was maintained. In other words, the plan involved strict work-testing of benefits.

Contribution conditions[147] were similar in a general sense to what had already been established. For the flat rate part there were some shifts. The employer was to pay a slightly higher share at 5 per cent of each employee's earnings, and employees were to pay 3 per cent of the same. The exchequer was to contribute 24 per cent of the combined contributions of both employee and employer. This was substantially higher than the practice in 1957, and higher than the level Beveridge favoured and what was in the 1946 Act. This was one way in which some redistribution of income would take place in the scheme. Contributions for the earnings-related part of the scheme would be a flat rate of 3 per cent of earnings. The range here was wide and provided further redistribution of income based on wages. This is of particular interest given the relatively narrow wage bands that were to follow in subsequent schemes, and in particular the Tory scheme of 1959. Contributions were to be paid by those who earned roughly between £6 and £50 per week. The upper limit was approximately four times the average wage of that year. One of the most important aspects of the plan was that the earnings-related part was to accumulate a fund before benefits were to be paid out. This was an attempt to copy private insurance schemes, and make the scheme more 'responsible' in terms of the exchequer. In essence, as Kincaid[148] points out, welfare expenditure could be dramatically increased over the long run without requiring higher income groups to pay more taxation. The proposed fund, as will be discussed later, was attacked from both left and right.

Finally, the plan was to allow private occupational pensions to continue if they were approved based on the following criteria:[149] contributions and benefits must compare favourably with the state superannuation scheme; the private scheme must be funded or guaranteed by statute, with each member possessing an equal right to his/her pension; pension rights must be transferable, and membership of an approved scheme must not be a condition of employment. Along with this, those in approved schemes would only have to pay a modified flat rate contribution that would cover higher flat rate benefits. They would, therefore, be exempt from the wage-related contributions. One final improvement in the proposal was to grant formal equality to working women. By forcing private plans to be at the same level as the state plan, many of the occupational plans providing less benefits would have to have been abolished. The state plan was to set the conditions for private pensions. The consequence of the plan would have ended many plans that were not providing benefits comparable to that of the state scheme. The proposal was one in which the state was to compete with the private sector particularly for working-class|pensions. Ironically, the actuarial assumptions that prevailed in the private sector were to be shifted to state pensions.

Some critical remarks can be presented on this scheme, both within the general logic of the scheme and at a more general level. The proposal established pensions based on a fraction of earnings for a given number of years. It set up fractions of 1/120th of earnings for younger and older workers, and 1/240th for the middle aged. In this way the scheme discriminates against manual workers, particularly unskilled and semi-skilled. These workers would tend to earn relatively more in the years between 25 and 45 taking account of their skill and strength, and in particular their ability to work overtime and extra shifts. On the other hand, as they get older it is more likely that their earnings decrease. A pension plan designed to favour them should have reversed those fractions. This problem was acknowledged in the document, but it was left unresolved at that time.

It can be argued that the wide earnings band in the wage-related part of this scheme is progressive and redistributes wages from the upper to the lower levels. This is certainly true as it was described, but it ignores one major fact. The scheme also exempts those in approved occupational pensions schemes from contributing to the earnings-related or superannuation part of the pension scheme. If it can be assumed that those earning higher wages are part of approved schemes, then much of the redistribution within this part of the scheme can be challenged. As long as those earning higher wages can opt out of contributing, then the basic weight on contributions will fall on relatively lower wage earners.

In many ways the underlying assumption of the plan is the centrality of workers' contributions. This theme is expressed in other ways. The scheme attempted to duplicate private pension schemes, and adopted an actuarial approach. If this scheme is compared to those in the private sector, workers were far worse off. First, workers could not receive full pension rights until fifty years after they had started contributing to the scheme. Private superannuation schemes at that time required forty years of contributions for maximum benefits. As well, blue-collar workers received 1/80 of their wage per year and at times 1/60th, reaching half of their final salary at the end. White-collar workers did even better with 1/60 of their wage per year up to two-thirds of their final salary at the end.[150] Although it can be argued that the low paid would never get into these programmes, and they would do far better in a government superannuation scheme, it can be countered by arguing that low wage workers would do as well with a relatively more adequate flat rate scheme without the façade of superannuation. Further, when the fact that contributions to private schemes were generally tax deductible is added to this then the state superannuation scheme as proposed for many manual and most white-collar workers could not compete with private sector schemes. One further criticism is that given the Labour party's position on private superannuation proposed in 1950 and Crossman's speech it is strange that such a weak position is taken in relation to the private sector, particularly in terms of transferability of pension rights. This lack *cannot* be explained only by the fact that many trade unionists had a stake in occupational   not pensions, because even if they were not to be nationalized, trade unions would have a stake in strong legislation protecting acquired private rights, which was not proposed but reflects the increased moderation in the party.

This pension plan was the boldest and most redistributive put forward in Labour party history, and even then it is fundamentally constructed on assumptions of capitalist social relations such as linking retirement benefits to both work and earnings records, and making the working class itself bear the lion's share of payment for retirement. The assumptions and method on which the scheme is based is on bourgeois actuarial methods more oriented towards protecting the exchequer and the ruling class from high taxation, and showing that the Labour party could be responsible pension managers. Even with all of these precautions, the plan was attacked by capital, and initially divided the Labour movement.

The response of the TUC and its support for the plan represents a turnabout in their policy on pensions the year before. One reason for this shift might have been their failure to get the government to raise basic pension rates. The TUC's representatives had demanded that the government restore pension rates to the 1955 level and establish a committee to re-examine the concept of subsistence. The government rejected this, falling back on the Phillips Committee's position that the state should *not* provide a pension that would enable people to live without any other means. National insurance benefit rates were interpreted to rest with the discretion of the minister.[151] In the light of this response, the Social Insurance Committee put forward the following position on Labour's superannuation scheme: in recognizing the shift in their position, their argument was that uniform, flat rate benefits had become synonymous with inadequate benefits; further, Labour policies represented a long-term policy. What concerned them were the immediate hardships of retired workers in the short term; hence, they pressed for increased flat rate benefits. As well, they linked this demand for increases in other benefits such as unemployment benefits.[152] In discussing occupational pensions, they demanded an inquiry into the relation of private and state pensions and a safeguarding of private pension rights for workers in these plans.[153]

The Labour plan was acceptable for two main reasons, first it provided short-term gains for retired workers, and second, it safeguarded private pensions secured by parts of the working class. The committee argued against the abolition of the retirement rule pointing out that this policy would lead to a subsidization of wages of workers above the pension age who continued to work.[154] They pressed for the accumulated fund to be a source of capital investment. This would strengthen the national insurance fund, increase the nation's productive assets, and in the long run reduce the burden on the exchequer of providing higher pensions.[155] In presenting a resolution supporting the national superannuation scheme, the argument was based on a criticism of both the Labour and the Conservative parties' inability to maintain the subsistence principle.[156] The general tone of support was cautious, and reflected some conservatism and an acceptance of the dominant approach to pensions. They recommended acceptance in the following way:

> If we of the General Council want to proceed with caution it is not
> because we are unduly critical but because we want to be quite sure
> that it is financially and economically sound, workable and equit-
> able.[157]

One attack argued in favour of earnings-related contributions, and
against earnings-related benefits, arguing that as it stood the scheme
took from each according to ability and returned 'to each according to
snob social level'.[158] The strong Transport and General Workers' Union
criticized the use of pensions funds to buy equities, and described this
policy as a 'blood transfusion for private enterprise'.[159] In the end, the
motion supporting the plan was easily carried. Also, the motion reaffirmed the subsistence principle, and demanded immediate increases
in benefits in line with the cost of living.

The debate in the Labour party itself reflected some division on this
scheme with the left losing in the end to what was supposed to be the
left leadership of Crossman. Several resolutions were presented that
were critical of national superannuation. One resolution rejected wage-
related benefits as being unsocialistic.[160] Another argued that the
benefits should be financed directly from the exchequer.[161] Another
criticism argued that the pensions scheme would emphasize inequalities
within the working class. The speaker went on to argue:

> that the architects of national superannuation in their concern to
> keep the scheme on a sound financial basis, have approached the
> problem of caring for our old folk in much the same way as an
> orthodox insurance company would; and in doing so have lost sight
> of socialist belief.[162]

Another argued against the fund itself, and stated that its investment
policies 'will help perpetuate the capitalist system almost into in-
finity.'[163] But in the end the day belonged to Crossman. In what was
described as an outstanding speech and one which placed him as a rising
star in the Labour party, he argued that the plan contained a short-term
strategy to raise pensions immediately, a transitional one, and a long-
term proposal to eliminate destitution and poverty among the aged.[164]
Worker contributions were defended on the grounds of defending
pension rights against Tory Chancellors of the Exchequer.[165] Of course,
the same argument could be made of Labour exchequers between 1945
and 1951. He argued that the state scheme was to provide competition
for the private sector and concluded with the following appeal:

> One of the things we have to do is to take pensions out of party
> politics and see that the pensioner gets his right whatever party is in

power . . . poverty in old age is the great disgrace and challenge of
the 1950s. . . . Friends, you can transform the position of the aged
in this country, you can abolish poverty in old age once and for
all.[166]

The victory of this scheme ended principles of equal benefits for the
Labour party, and even though this proposal was the most redistributive
policy on pensions to be proposed, it reflects the limited vision of the
party, the abandonment of any socialist principles, and reflects its
attempts to compete with the Tories in terms of the politics of moderation, respectability and pragmatism.

Even with these restraints, the Labour proposals were attacked by
the Tories and the media. The major attack focused on the plan to
accumulate a fund that could be invested. This was interpreted within
the ruling class as a strategy of back-door nationalization. After publication of the plan, £2.4 million was wiped off the value of Prudential
Insurance Company shares on the London stock exchange in four
days.[167] The Life Officers' Association, representing the private pension
and insurance business, launched a major attack on the plan.[168] The
Labour party, predictably, spent their time denying that the fund
would be used for nationalization of any kind.[169] The Labour party was
trapped by their own concern for 'actuarial soundness'. They presented
a sophisticated plan that did not attack the rich, but attempted to
upgrade the standard of living of retired workers in the long term, and
at the same time seem responsible in fiscal terms. The 1959 Labour
manifesto and election campaign offered improved social services
without increased tax rates. This was based on the assumption of
increased growth in the GNP. This was attacked by the Conservatives,
and contributed to the downfall of the Labour's electoral campaign.[170]
As one commentator pointed out: 'Journalistic enterprise and Conservative eloquence consolidated the picture of Labour leaders bidding
for votes with a succession of wild fiscal promises.[171] The promises for
better pensions failed because of their complexity, and the Tory
proposals which, as will be argued later, on the surface were quite
similar to those of Labour. In an election campaign, and within the
working class, elections are not won and lost on the basis of sophisticated, technical pension proposals which promise no poverty for the
aged in forty or fifty years time. As Crossman acknowledged after the
election: 'Our scheme last time was too complicated to understand.'[172]
Although the Labour party at this time was committed to increasing
equality with redistribution through the welfare state, the major plans
for achieving this were bound up in such highly technocratic detail that
its political impact was lost. The Tory pension reforms were clearly an
inferior offering, but in the election bidding the Labour party lost out.

1959 National Insurance Act – the Conservatives' copy of 'superannuation'

As Labour tried to copy actuarial techniques for the provision of pensions, the Conservatives copied the appearance of Labour's plan, and passed their pension plan into legislation before the 1959 election. The plan was influenced by the Phillips Committee Report, and was concerned with the state's increased liability for the cost of retirement. The scheme had three aims: to place the national insurance scheme on a sound financial basis, to institute a graduated pension for those employed workers who were not members of one at work; and to preserve and to encourage the development of occupational pension schemes.[173] The aims were quite similar to those of Labour with the major differences in emphasis, particularly in the discussion of the financial aspects and the centrality of private pensions. The assumptions presented in the plan were typical of the Tory approach to the welfare state. Pension provision by the state was not to interfere with either individual provision or occupational pensions.[174] Financing of retirement pensions in such a way as not to overburden the exchequer was the dominant theme of this scheme, therefore the graduated part was not protected against inflation. Further, clear links were made between limiting the exchequer contribution, and making workers responsible for financing their own retirement. The problem with the financing of retirement pensions was presented in terms of the deficiency in the national insurance fund; the anticipated growth of this deficiency was attributed to benefit increases and demographic shifts in population age and, with these, anticipated large increases in the exchequer contribution.[175] The proposal for the reform emphasized the need to restructure pension financing:

> To leave the scheme dependent on rapidly growing subsidies from general taxation would amount to drawing a blank cheque on the future. It would also undermine protection given to the individual by the fact that the benefits he receives depend on the contributions he personally makes. The Government have no hesitation in rejecting a system of pension benefits predominantly financed from taxation . . . [it is] dangerous in itself, and likely to be unacceptable to the people as a whole.[176]

The solution was the introduction of earnings-related benefits, and contributions. The proposal stated:

> the increased contribution revenue made possible by graduated contributions could secure that the large emerging deficits . . . . would

94

be eliminated and the Exchequer's share of the cost would be properly defined.[177]

The government was determined to protect and to encourage private pensions schemes; therefore, it built in the option of contracting out of the state scheme for those whose occupational scheme obtained a prescribed minimal standard. These standards were similar to those in Labour's proposal, but because the general benefit levels proposed were lower, then the conditions of contracting out were easier. They were as follows: occupational pension benefit rights must be equivalent to the maximum equivalent pension rights under the state scheme; adequate provision had to be made for preservation of benefit rights at least up to the level of the maximum in the state scheme; and the occupational pension plan had to be sound financially. The employer would be responsible for deciding on whether or not to contract out of the state scheme.[178] Within this general orientation and framework, the specifics of the plan follow.

The structure of the scheme was similar to Labour's, with a flat rate, and wage-related component. The basic difference was that the benefits in the Conservative scheme were miserly. There was not a direct correspondence between contributions and benefits. Benefits were based on contribution units or 'bricks'. Each £1 contribution, matched by the employer, would constitute a unit, and fifteen of these units would provide a male contributor an additional pension of 1s. per week upon retirement at age 65.[179] This was in addition to the flat rate benefit. The low level of benefits reflects the policy of non-competition with the private sector. The policy was to encourage the development of the private pension sector and assumes that most workers would be enrolled in some sort of occupational pension. Benefits were to be paid contingent upon retirement. Further, the graduated pension was not to be protected against increases in prices, making it essentially a meaningless gesture in the longer term. The flat rate component was to be increased at the discretion of the exchequer and parliament, again not guaranteeing any protection against inflation.

The contribution conditions[180] of this plan were clearly structured for financial reasons and limited exchequer contributions. There was to be no fund accumulated in the way that Labour had envisioned it. The earnings-related contribution can be interpreted as nothing more than an additional tax on wages. Further, the Tories defined the earnings band from which contribution would be taken in very narrow terms, closely related to the average manual worker's wage. The band was defined as between £9 and £15 per week. The actual contribution was divided approximately in equal parts between employers and workers. The total contribution was $8\frac{1}{2}$ per cent of the earnings-related component. The exchequer did not contribute at all to this part. Further, in the proposal the exchequer contribution was to be stabilized at £170 million for an indefinite period, and would not fluctuate with employer and worker contributions. Thus the exchequer contribution would diminish in relation to worker/employer contributions. It was anticipated that this structure of funding the plan in the short term would not keep pace with the growth in the cost of flat rate retirement pensions, and would require periodic increases in contributions of workers and employers. Through these financial arrangements a contin- ual decrease in the deficit of the national insurance fund was antici- pated to begin in 1961 when the plan was implemented with a surplus showing beginning in 1971.[181] The Conservative plan was basically one of regressive taxation, designed in such a way, with contracting out, that those in the plan would shoulder the bulk of the financing of *all* retirement pensions. These workers would tend to be the lower paid, and even without contracting out higher paid workers would only contribute on a limited basis. In essence, those workers paying into the earnings-related part of the pensions would be subsidizing all workers receiving flat rate pensions. There can be little doubt that this plan was a way of increasing tax on the working class, providing little in return, keeping the exchequer as far as possible from increasing contributions, and finally making sure that the private occupational pension sector prospered. Even *The Economist* commented on the obvious objectives of the scheme:

> The main feature of the scheme, indeed in some ways its whole es- sence is that it is expected to save the Exchequer £99 million in its first year of operation, rising to no less than £428 million in 1981–1982.[182]

In contrast to the Labour scheme, in which women were to be treated with formal equality in pensions, the Conservative scheme maintained the ambiguous position on women present in Beveridge. It is important to note that even with the formal equality of women, their weak position in the labour market and greater periods of disturbance of work for child-rearing greatly diminish earnings-related and occu- pational benefits. This is, of course, a more structured sexism in which society reinforces roles because of a clear lack of options such as sufficient child-rearing facilities, and then penalizes women further by not crediting years spent child-rearing as equivalent to work for pur- poses of pension calculation. Women then become dependent on their husbands' contributions for their benefits in retirement or after their husbands' deaths. This study is *not* considering widows' benefits, but will point out some of the features of this Tory plan that discriminated further against women. First, it accepted the fact that women retired earlier than men, continued past pension traditions and codified this in policy, and then, because women therefore contribute for less time, and live longer, they would receive less benefits.[183] To be consistent, the policy should argue that because men (assuming the class bias in university education) spend longer in the education process then male university graduates, by the same logic should receive lower benefits (particularly those with PhDs!). Second, if a married woman was working she would continue to have the option of whether or not to contribute to flat rate contributions, but if she earned more than £9 per week then she was expected to contribute to the earnings-related part. For part of the scheme, then, she was assumed to be a dependent but when she earned enough for it to be taxed on an earnings-related scheme, the contributions would be handed over to the state. With only the earnings-related part, the pension would be miserly. In implementing the scheme, it was the system of units or blocks in which the discrimination was implemented. When it took a man £15 to gain a shilling a week pension, it took a woman £18.[184] Finally, even with the assumed dependency of women on their husbands' record of earnings and contribution, a full pension based on her husband's contribution record was not to be received. Thus a widow of a man receiving a graduated pension or having contributed to one would only receive half of this pension on his death.[185] It is little wonder, given this discrimination, on top of the more structural sex inequalities, that it was mainly women who had little choice except to queue for means-tested national assistance benefits.

The Labour response to the Conservative proposals can be seen in the House of Commons debates on the White Paper. H. A. Marquand was the primary Labour speaker. The main points he raised were on the meagre benefits provided by the scheme in the short run, and the failure of the scheme to provide an adequate plan to prevent poverty among retired workers in the long run.[186] More specifically, the plan was criticized because of its inadequate coverage particularly of low wage workers. The Tory plan would provide coverage potentially to 13 million (including those contracting out) which represented only 54 per cent of the 24 million insured under the national insurance scheme. Further, with the £9 minimum as the cut off, $7\frac{3}{4}$ million workers were excluded from the plan.[187] This group is the lowest paid workers, and would be completely without any form of superannuation, and dependent upon arbitrary decision for levels of flat rate benefits and ultimately upon means-tested national assistance. Labour acknowledged recent improvements in the flat rate benefits, but attacked their low level, and the continuing large numbers of retired workers on national assistance.[188] The debate was confined to a scope predefined by Labour's own superannuation scheme, and although many of the points they made were interesting, these were kept within a very limited parameter.

There were several minor changes from the original government proposals to the subsequent legislation.[189] First, the method of evaluating the exchequer contribution was modified. Instead of a fixed contribution of £170 million per annum, a formula was established whereby the exchequer contribution would total one-quarter of the combined contribution of the employer and the employee at the flat rate minimum. This was a return to the Beveridge formula. This formula would imply a drop in exchequer contributions to £150 million. Because of this, the £170 million was maintained until such time as contribution levels would surpass that level at which exchequer contributions could be raised above £170 million. Second, the financing structure in the Bill provided for a quinquennial review of contributions, beginning in 1965. Because there was no intention of building up a surplus in the scheme, it would be possible by order to reduce the level if the scheme was balanced. Third, for those workers who continued to work after the retirement age the number of contributions necessary to increase final earnings-related pensions was reduced from twenty to twelve contributions per unit. With these modifications, the Tory legislation was passed on January 27, 1959, and was implemented beginning in 1961. One further addition was brought in in 1961. The Conservatives extended the earnings band of the scheme from £15 to £18 per week, reflecting the increase in the wage of the average manual worker. More important, it was a way of raising more money for the exchequer with only negligible increases in pensions in the long term.[190] The shell of Labour's superannuation was maintained in a bill that was to be more of a fancy book-keeping device for the exchequer and a stimulus to private pension plans than a bill aimed at adequate provision for retired workers.

Summary

The period considered in this chapter is dominated by the relatively long post-war boom. However, even in the midst of this economic growth and prosperity, Britain's economy was weak in comparison with her competitors. In the context of the boom, the working class was able to make important gains in its standard of living, and protect these gains particularly because of strong shop-floor organization and full employment. The Beveridge/Keynesian mode of domination was consolidated. Full employment, a universal welfare state, particularly in health, education and to some extent in social security, and the state as manager of economic and class relations were all maintained and developed by the Conservative government. The working class was able to defend its gains against very limited attempts at wage control. The Conservatives shifted clearly to the centre as did Labour, sharing a common orientation. The trade unions, as well, accepted the new conditions, and became managers of exploitation, and active in policy debates. Although in general terms both parties shared similar approaches, Labour saw the welfare state as a vehicle for increasing social equality through redistribution, and emphasized the state as the major vehicle for social provision. The Conservatives in many instances saw the state as secondary to market provision. This was the major difference on pensions. The Labour party proposed a universal superannuation programme with limited market provision while the Conservatives brought in very limited earnings-related pensions, with more concern for maintaining fiscal responsibility than providing adequately for the elderly. They questioned the limits of pension reform and linked it to economic growth and development. The limits to welfare state expansion were clear to them. The working class made a very small and hardly significant gain in these reforms but seemed unprepared to mobilize from below for anything else. The state pension as a form of relation was maintained, and contributions as a form of work-testing seemed to be accepted by almost all concerned. As well, divisions in the working class began to appear. Many were enrolled in occupational pension plans, others were solely dependent on contributory national insurance, while increasingly those at the bottom, particularly women and low wage workers, were forced on to means-tested national assistance. For most, however, poverty became synonymous with old age regardless of these divisions. Even in the context of economic prosperity, to be old still meant to be poor. The next section will take up on the development of the crisis and how it affected the development of pensions.

4

Capitalism in crisis and pension reform

Introduction

This section will discuss and analyse the development of state pensions from 1963 to 1975. The major pension legislation occurred in 1975 so the focus will be on that reform. In addition, two other attempts were made at pension reform, one by the Conservative party and one by Labour. Neither of these was implemented. As in the previous two sections, before discussing the pension legislation, the context of the attempted and 1975 reforms will be developed.

In contrast to the thirteen years of Conservative rule, the years that followed were ones of controversy, intensified class conflict, and a visible decline in British capitalism. The strategy of class rule implied in the Keynesian/Beveridge approach began to produce its own contradictions, and policies established in the previous periods were attacked. By the end of the period, rather than being a solution to the contradictions of capitalism, the contradictions of increased state action and expenditures were becoming prominent. Shifts and changes in state strategy will be reviewed in more detail in subsequent sections, and form the general context for the discussion of pensions. Prior to that, a review of the economic background will help situate the discussion of these issues.

Economy in crisis

This section will outline the major economic changes in this period. It is clear from what follows that Britain experienced a period of economic deterioration. However, although economic aspects will be presented, the economy is a form of class relations and struggle. The crisis reflects the impact of the strength of the working class and the failure of the bourgeoisie and the state to find new strategies to extricate itself from the contradictions of capitalism.[1] More important, for this study, than the causes of the crisis are its implications, particularly for state policy. Specific attempts by the state to re-establish a profitable growing capitalism form the context of welfare state, increasing class conflict, and the general condition of wage labour.

Not only did capital accumulation falter and decline during this period in Britain, as it did in other developed capitalist countries, but Britain's decline was worse than other nations in every category.[2] The consequences of this decline are more important for this study as they establish the general context in which pension development and reform took place. It is inappropriate to reduce reform to narrow economic categories. Accumulation is a form of class struggle and involves changing strategies by both capital and the state to restructure production relations and to re-establish profitable accumulation. The standard of living of the working class becomes a central issue here. The state and capital in attempting to re-establish profitable accumulation attempted to weaken the strength of the working class and attacked its standard of living.

The working class and the crisis

The period that is being analysed was marked by a combination of high inflation and increased taxation. How did the standard of living of the working class change? The first and most important point is that the gains made by the working class expressed in terms of real take-home pay of the average manual worker were defended or improved but by 1974, workers were experiencing a decline in real wages.[3] The decline in take-home pay corresponded to the years of the 'Social Contract' between the TUC and the Labour party. This particular attack on the standard of living of the working class will be discussed in greater detail later. When a comparison is made between real disposable income per head and annual increases in prices for the years 1965–1977, there was a fairly close correspondence, until 1973 when prices leapt ahead. Disposable income per head did not catch up until 1977.[4] Thus, although workers did make small gains, it was against a background of high inflation and increased taxation.

Women became an important source of labour power in this period, and were part of the reserve army mobilized into low wage and unstable jobs.[5] Trade unions in this period grew, as did their militancy. Membership increased from 10,259,000 in 1966 to 12,707,000 in 1977. As a percentage of all employees, members of trade unions increased from 43 per cent in 1966 to 53 per cent in 1977.[6]

The major change between the previous period and this one was the growth of trade union militancy and its strength in challenging government policy, particularly policies that tried to limit trade union strength and incomes. Statistics for this period show an increase in aggregate duration in working days of stoppages in progress in a given year. The highest number of days lost in the years 1958–64 was 5.27 million. By contrast, in the years 1970, 1971, 1972, 1973 and 1974 aggregate loss was approximately 11, 14, 24, 7 and 15 million days respectively.[7] These were years of intense class conflict not only in Britain but throughout Europe.[8]

The state

The Keynesian/Beveridge mode of domination continued to form much of state policy in this period. However, as the crisis of British capitalism became apparent many specific policies associated with this approach were abandoned. Full employment slowly disappeared and successive governments introduced strategies to limit trade union power and attacked living standards of workers. By the end of the period, and particularly after 1976 cuts in welfare state expenditure and a reorganization of many programmes took place. The form of class and social relations that went along with a relatively stable period of accumulation became more of a burden and a barrier to profitable accumulation and the period of crisis produced a transition or restructuring of class relations. The main symptom of this was the increased conflict between the working class and the state. The state reacted to the crisis with successive strategies each attempting to increase economic growth, productivity, international competition and profitability. The governments of the period each had general approaches and strategies but in each case these attempted to restructure conditions of wage labour – of production and reproduction. Before looking at each of the strategies, a general overview of state expenditure will be presented.

State expenditures

Total public expenditures as a percentage of gross domestic product rose continually during the 1960s, peaking in 1975 and then dropping slightly. This is elaborated in Table 4.1.

TABLE 4.1
State expenditures as a percentage of GDP at factor cost

Year	%	Year	%	Year	%
1964	43.6	1968	51.0	1972	50.1
1965	45.3	1969	50.3	1973	51.1
1966	46.2	1970	50.6	1974	57.3
1967	50.1	1971	50.1	1975	59.3

(*Hansard*, 2 February 1976, Column 453, and 8 July 1976, Column 663, cited in *The Campaign Guide*, Conservative Party Research Department, March 1977, p. 56.)

With the IMF crisis of 1975, and the subsequent cuts in state expenditures, these dropped from 55.2 per cent of GNP in 1975 to 50.1 per cent of the GNP by 1977.[9] Table 4.2 summarizes the distribution of state expenditure by category. It shows the welfare state's relatively fast rate of growth.

TABLE 4.2
The growth of state expenditure by category as a percentage of GNP at factor cost

	1961	1971	1975
All social services	17.6	23.8	28.8
Infrastructure	4.8	6.3	6.8
Industry	4.9	6.5	6.3
Justice and law	0.8	1.8	1.5
Military	7.6	6.6	6.2
Debt interest and other	6.3	5.9	6.3

(Ian Gough, *The Political Economy of the Welfare State*, London, Macmillan, 1979, p. 77.)

The public sector borrowing requirement grew substantially. With this growth, extensive pressures increased on the government to cut expenditures and restrain growth. According to Gough, the borrowing requirement increased as a percentage of GNP at factor cost from 1.7 per cent in 1971 to 11.3 per cent in 1975.[10] Public sector debt interest payment in millions of pounds grew from £1,470 million in 1965–6 to £4,845 million in 1975–6, an increase of over 300 per cent.[11]

The financing of state activities continued along a pattern established after the war with taxation on individuals through income tax, taxes on expenditure, and national health and national insurance contributions forming the bulk of revenue sources.[12] Not only did sources of taxation falling on individuals increase, but taxation sources which tend to be more regressive such as taxes on expenditure, for example VAT and rates, and social security contributions tended to increase, thus in relative terms putting more of the burden on the working class. In addition, the tax threshold as a percentage of average earnings fell; that is, more and more people who earned less began to pay taxes on their income.[13] With both increased state expenditures and borrowing requirements, more and more of the revenue to meet these came from workers, and workers earning relatively less. There are two important implications for this study. First, as will be discussed later, social security contributions were to become an increasingly significant tax, and one which by definition tended to put relatively more of a burden on lower wage earners. Second, the trend to put taxation more on the shoulders of the working class could only intensify class conflict. Workers concern themselves with their take-home pay. Gross wages are eroded by both increases in taxation and rapid inflation. In order to protect take-home pay, high wage demands become necessary. These demands occurred in a period of slow growth and shrinking profits. The battle over surplus value can only be made intense with increasing taxation of workers. State expenditures in this period acted as one way that living standards of workers were attacked, as well, these expenditures presented an increasing burden to capital. Not only did they increase indirectly the wage demands of workers, but they acted as a drain on surplus value in the context of reduced productivity, slow growth, low levels of investment and low levels of profit. The state, although appearing to solve the contradictions of capitalism through Keynesian/Beveridge strategies, produced its own contradictions and intensified class conflict.

The next section will present an overview of the orientation of state social and economic policies. Each government of this period faced different manifestations of the crisis of British capitalism, and both Labour and Conservative governments shared the same basic goals of re-establishing profitable capital accumulation. The major differences between the parties was in emphasis and strategy.

The inability of any of the governments or the parties to overcome the crisis and re-establish a profitable growing capitalism speaks less\of a question of will than of the more fundamental contradictions of capitalism. Labour governments particularly dominated this period. If there had been any doubt about Labour's acceptance of capitalism and its abandonment of socialist transition during the first post-war government and the subsequent period in opposition, then the years in power from 1964–70 and 1974 onwards certainly confirmed Labour's commitment as a party whose aim was the restoration and development of British capitalism.

Wilson's years 1964-70

Before looking at the specific strategies and crises faced by the Wilson administration, a short review of the party ideology at this period will be presented. The revisionists still remained in control of both party ideology and the party apparatus.[14] During the long period of opposition, the strategy adopted by the party was that it must gain power at all costs, and to do this Labour's image became that of a 'responsible, socially-conscious rather than Socialist . . . that was less interested in ideology than practical social reform within a moderate framework'.[15] This was expressed in Labour's economic approach. In the 1964 election they sought to modernize the British economy through the use of science and technology. The goal was to get the economy moving with the state playing an active role through national planning within a 'mixed economy'.[16]

Wilson's belief that Britain's economy could be transformed by an infusion of technology was summarized in his speech in October 1963. He referred to: 'the conscious, planned, purposive use of scientific progress to provide undreamed of living standards and the possibility of leisure ultimately on an unbelievable scale.'[17] The orientation to economic growth and development proposed 'a renovated capitalism, freed from its aristocratic and gentlemanly accusations, dynamic, professional, entrepreneurial, numerate, and efficient'.[18]

Wilson's policy assumed Labour to be a classless party. As Miliband points out, Labour would not attempt to do much about the evils that they were ready to denounce because to do so would be to challenge capital at a fundamental level which they were not prepared to do. Also, Labour would do their best to demobilize their supporters, and turn against them when the occasion required.[19] In both cases this orientation was used as a way to pursue policies that became defined in 'the national interest'. The Labour party was moderate, with radical rhetoric, committed to national economic planning, technological growth, and a mixed economy. With these policies it faced the crises of the years 1964 to 1970. These policies of economic restructuring and containment of the working class went hand in hand, but were neither able to achieve great economic gains nor class harmony.

The period of Wilson's first premiership from 1964-70 moved from one crisis to another. These formed the context and set up the limits of social policy development in the period. The promises of even limited social reform were quickly forgotten as the Wilson government faced the crisis of the pound and balance of payments. The government chose to make itself respectable to the world and British financial and business communities and restrain working-class demands. The consequence was that this government, although claiming to be a party of economic

105

stimulation and growth, was one of deflation, stagnation, and unemployment.[20] Unemployment began to rise; the government attacked and attempted to limit trade union powers; and parts of the welfare state were cut while others were allowed to stagnate.

In the first period from October 1964 to March 1966,[21] the government had commitments to very limited and moderate social welfare reforms, such as pension increases and the abolition of prescription charges. It also wanted to establish itself as a responsible government in the context of world capitalism. Even with this moderation the first financial crisis began with a run on sterling. The government response was to strengthen sterling through overseas borrowing and to increase the bank rate. Shortly after, the government began its attempts at wage restraint by establishing the National Board for Prices and Income, that included representatives of capital and labour to monitor wage increases and prices. In March 1965, the government published a paper arguing that wages should be limited to a $3\frac{1}{2}$ per cent increase. This was ignored as wages increased by approximately 9 per cent. The government's strategy of wage restraint was not working.

With the government's passing of the Trades Disputes Act in 1965, it persuaded the TUC to accept the establishment of the Donovan Commission to look into the problems of industrial relations. Further, just before the election of 1966, the government put more pressure on the TUC to accept compulsory wage restraint. This was refused and, prior to the election, the cabinet contemplated regulation of wage increases through legislation.[22] This period set the tone for the Labour government. The limits of social policy and wages were set by outside constraints, such as protecting the value of the pound and showing itself to be a responsible government.

The economic and social strategy of the period 1966 to 1970 was centred on the devaluation of the pound, establishing a balance of payments surplus, and again regulating wage settlements. The government, in its throne speech, introduced programmes for steel nationalization, extension of public control of the docks, establishment of a Land Commission and an Industrial Reorganization Corporation. Social welfare measures included the development of comprehensive education and the establishment of a ministry of social security.[23] It was not these reforms, however, that preoccupied the government. The government was almost immediately confronted with a major strike and another sterling crisis. The National Union of Seamen went on strike from May until July. The strike had severe consequences for the economy and further weakened exports and precipitated a further run on sterling.[24] The government responded with deflationary measures and a statutory wage freeze which was to be followed by a period of 'severe restraint'. This strategy was used to prevent devaluation of the pound, at that time.[25] Again, the government attacked the standard of living of the working class in order to preserve a strong pound.

However, the government was forced finally to devalue the pound. With devaluation Britain received $3 billion credit including a loan of $14 million from the IMF.[26] After devaluation, the main goal of government was to establish a balance of payments surplus. The policies of deflation continued.[27] Part of the conditions of the IMF loan was that the government was to cut home expenditures by £750 million. Defence expenditures were cut, and there was the implementation of a charge for prescriptions with some exemptions, increased dental fees, withdrawal of free milk for secondary school children, reduction in housing programmes, and delays in raising of school leaving age were all announced.[28] In spite of these measures, the balance of payments continued to deteriorate. The combination of a high level of imports and the international gold crisis in 1968 led to further deflation; as well, steep increases in indirect taxation and cuts in public expenditures were introduced. Along with these measures, the government continued in its attempt to limit wages by setting targets for wage increases. These policies had the effect of increasing tension between the government and trade unions.[29] Further, they had little or no effect in restraining either wages or inflation.[30] However, this was not the only tactic the government had in curtailing the strength of trade unions.

The Donovan Report raised the issue of how much state interference there should be in the process of wage negotiation. It recognized the increased importance of the 'informal system' of wage settlement and the increase in unofficial strikes in industrial relations, but it thought the state could do little to remedy these problems. The solution should be worked out directly between trade unions and employers. This was not an adequate solution for Barbara Castle, the minister responsible, and Wilson, who supported the need for legislation of certain aspects of collective negotiation. *In Place of Strife* was published in January 1969. Although there were some concessions to trade unions such as the guaranteed right of every employee to join a trade union, the bulk of it proposed state regulation of trade unions. This elicited broad-based opposition from both the Labour party and the TUC. Not deterred, Castle and Wilson, in April 1969, presented parts of this policy in conjunction with termination of the compulsory powers under the Prices and Incomes Act. The Industrial Relations Bill incorporated the conciliation pause and gave the state powers to settle inter-union disputes. Again, large-scale resistance developed, even in the cabinet. Only the possibility of parliamentary defeat persuaded Wilson and Castle to back down and agree to a compromise proposal of the TUC that contained a 'solemn and binding undertaking' that they would regulate and intervene in unofficial strikes.[31]

The government had attempted and failed to use state powers to limit the powers of trade unions. This, along with incomes policies, were the strategies followed by the Wilson government, with deflationary budgets and devaluation to get British capital going. The programmes finally paid off in a very limited sense when, in the context of an expansion of world trade, monthly trade figures moved into a surplus by the end of 1969.[32] In total, Wilson's and Labour's vision of a capitalism growing with technological innovations and planning was shattered. The defence of the pound and the acceptance of Britain's place in the world capitalist order blocked even this limited vision of a reformed and restructured capitalism. The dominant concerns that limited both economic and social policies in the 1964–70 period were the defence of the pound and restoring a positive balance of payments. Part of doing this involved deflation of the economy, leading to higher unemployment and most important attacking the trade unions through both incomes policies and legislating 'solutions' for industrial relation problems. In the latter case, the policy did not succeed and only widened the conflict between unions and the state. The commitment to full employment and trade union autonomy to negotiate increases in standards of living were both attacked, yet the problems of British capitalism and the class struggle did not disappear. They were there for Heath and the Conservatives to deal with, although with initially different strategies.

Heath

On election, the Heath government was committed to policies that were a departure from both his Conservative and Labour predecessors. The policies represented a shift from the strategy of large-scale state involvement in the management of the economy and a departure from 'Beveridge' welfare policies. The Heath years brought with them intense class conflict and eventually the downfall of Heath and his policies. A shift in policy took place during the period of Conservative opposition from 1964–70.

In the 1964 election, the Conservatives campaigned on a platform of economic growth and modernization with active state involvement in this process. Heath initially was seen as a follower of the 'Right Progressive' orientation including a commitment to a politics of technique and pragmatism rather than hard line principles.[33] However, the right in the party began to mount an offensive and appealed to a wide range of Conservative party members and supporters. They gained in strength. Many of their following felt that a programme of economic modernization was inadequate, and a far more comprehensive programme was required to remedy the ills of British society.[34] New policies were required to arrest the growth and intervention of the state. These included strong measures to get the British economy going again, particularly curbing the power of trade unions and the restoration of law and order. Market forces would rule instead of the state, particularly in industrial relations and welfare state provision. The state itself was to be administered more efficiently.[35] The general orientation of their programme and their political and economic strategy broke with the traditions established by Macmillan and Butler and as well, for the first time since the war, promised a major shift from Labour party 'socialism' based on state management of the economy and extensive welfare state provision.

When Heath came to power he was faced with the problem of inflation. In 1970 wages had risen by 12 per cent, prices by 6 per cent, while productivity had fallen by 2 per cent.[36] His immediate tasks were to reform the tax system, to create incentives, to reduce public spending, to limit trade union income gains without resorting to an incomes policy, and to reform trade unions. In Spring 1971, he cut taxes by £546 million and introduced further tax reductions in July. Inflation was not brought under control. Strikes continued to grow. The main attack on trade unions was through the Industrial Relations Act. The Act was to bring extensive legal restrictions to trade union affairs, particularly to limit unofficial strikes. The National Industrial Relations Court was created to regulate much of the activities of trade unions. It had the authority to impose a conciliation pause or 'cooling off' period in industrial disputes, and it could require secret strike ballots in major disputes. It had the power to fine unions. The Act attacked the closed shop.[37] Massive resistance followed the introduction of the Bill. The trade union movement called a series of one-day strikes and large demonstrations, and was committed to defying the Act after it became law. The major point of opposition was against the registering of trade unions with the government. Several early decisions by the National Industrial Relations Court resulted in gains for workers, the most significant being the awarding of a 20 per cent wage increase to miners after militant strike action. The court defined miners as a case for special treatment. Heath had aimed at wages increases of 8 per cent. Unions continued to pursue large wage increases, and trade union militancy was paying off and leading to increases in wages. By 1972 wages were rising faster than the 7–8 per cent inflation rate, the GNP was increasing at approximately 1 per cent per year, unemployment reached 900,000, with a large balance of trade deficit. The government announced a further devaluation of the pound from $2.61 to $2.42. Heath and the cabinet, faced with these circumstances, tried to put a lid on rising wages through re-establishing an incomes policy. The policy began with a ninety-day wage freeze followed by three phases of wage restraint. Phase III provided a 7 per cent wage increase except in cases of unsocial hours and some cost of living flexibility. As this phase was being implemented, the Yom Kippur War broke out bringing a fuel crisis. Further, the miners' wage claim was ruled out as being too high. The miners imposed an overtime ban. The result was the three-day week and cuts in electricity. A miners' ballot for strike action resulted in a mandate to strike on 10 February. In a climate of intense class conflict, Heath called a general election and was subsequently defeated.[38]

Heath's brief period in power represents an attempt to restructure industry, the economy, the state, and class relations. The major economic goal, according to Guttman,[39] was to rationalize British industry using the market rather than the state. Large-scale rationalizations were planned for the public sector industries. The government abolished several programmes of direct state intervention into the private sector established by Labour, so that those industries unable to compete would go under. The market was to function, with reduced state interference, to restore British capitalism through the elimination of unhealthy capitals and the restructuring of others to make them more competitive in a world market. These strategies proved largely ineffective. Entry into the EEC increased imports, and the increased competition proved a greater threat to British industries. Deficits from nationalized industries increased and put increasing demands on credit supply. Attempts at 'reprivatization' of the public sector failed largely because there were hardly any profitable industries to be taken back. Finally, the government policy of allowing weak capitals to go bankrupt failed, and the government either bailed out private companies or nationalized them, such as Rolls Royce, Harland and Wolff, and the Liverpool Docks.

The attempt to use the market to restructure capital was not a success, but it was not only the restructuring of capital as an economic unit that failed but the attempt to restructure, as describd above, class relations which brought about the most intense class conflict in the post-war period and led to Heath's defeat. Heath's brief period represents an attempt to move away from the post-war Tory and Labour strategies, but in its failure, Heath returned to a statist strategy of large-scale economic management, but that too did not succeed in getting Britain out of its crisis. The working class had refused to bear the costs of the crisis under the conditions of Tory policies. The election was fought by the Tories on the issue of who is running Britain, and by Labour on how well they could manage class relations in order to get Britain going again.

Labour, crisis and the Social Contract

The major point to be discussed here will be Labour's strategy, especially the 'Social Contract' as a means of managing class relations. Further, the major crisis of 1975 with its implications for cutbacks in state expenditures and subsequent restructuring of the welfare state will be introduced, although not discussed in detail. The Wilson/Callaghan period can be divided into two parts. The first, around the two elections, was one of reform in the way that it was envisioned in the Social Contract. The second period was dominated by crises and resulted in major restructuring in both the economy and in the welfare state. The election itself was fought out in the midst of intensive class conflict. The Conservative campaign focused on the question of whether the government or the trade unions were going to run Britain. The manifesto talked of the dangers, both from outside, particularly oil prices, and from within, mainly from trade unions and extremists who controlled the Labour party. It talked about the need for a strong government 'able to take firm measures in defence of the national interest'.[40] The manifesto polarized the threatened miners' strike as either giving in to their demands or safeguarding the wider national interest against inflation and for fairness for all.[41] The question to the ruling class was who could best manage the capital–labour relation and which party was most likely to control the trade unions and restore 'normalcy' to the British economy.[42]

The Labour party during its period in opposition after its fight over trade union legislation had re-established firm links with the TUC. The outcome of this relationship was the Social Contract. The relation between the two was firmed up in opposition to Heath's policies, particularly the Industrial Relations Bill. A liaison committee was established to wage the struggle against this legislation. By 1973, Wilson and Victor Feather, chairperson of the TUC, had introduced a document called 'Economic Policy and the Cost of Living' which was a shopping list for the next Labour government. It included control of food prices through government subsidies, subsidization of public transit and rents with rent freezes, public ownership of land for building purposes, large-scale redistribution of income and wealth, phasing out of social service charges, large increases in pensions, and a re-evaluation of the conditions of entry into the EEC.[43] Also, Labour agreed to repeal the Industrial Relations Act, the Pay Board and the Housing Finance Act. For their part of the deal, the TUC agreed to voluntary wage restraint.[44] Wage agreements were not to be legislated, and the TUC would be the body to get individual unions to agree to wage restraint.

With the Social Contract, the Labour party shifted slightly leftward. Guttman suggests the reasons for this as the increased militancy of the

111

trade unions and the necessity of the Labour party to meet their demands in order to get in and to stay in power. There was also the need to represent themselves to the working class as having qualitatively different policies from the Conservatives; thus Labour attacked key elements of Tory policy, such as conditions of entry into the EEC, incomes policy, and cuts in the social services. Alternatives were formulated reflecting an understanding of the need for another strategy of state intervention in the economy besides demand management and incomes policy that might re-establish profitable accumulation. This included increased state control in private industry, planning agreements and industrial democracy as a way to integrate unions more effectively.[45] Both the conditions of the Social Contract and this leftward swing were present in the 1974 election manifesto. It was the most left-wing programme since the war and presented a clear-cut alternative to Tory policies. Underlying it, however, was the assumption that the trade unions would moderate wage demands and this would be the way out of the crisis, and possibly the way to moderate inflation and costs of production.[46] The goals once again were to re-establish profitable accumulation. The questions were under what conditions and at what costs would the government be able to establish industrial peace with more moderate wage demands.

Wilson's first period with a minority led to some reform. Politically, this was necessary in order to maintain working-class support for the next election, eight months later. Again, the first priority was to get production going again. The government had inherited the three-day week, the energy crisis, Heath's deflationary budgets, falling consumer demands, and a seriously stagnating economy.[47] The balance was tricky, as Labour had to maintain working-class support and at the same time restore accumulation. The first budget in March 1974 brought in some of the TUC's shopping list, such as food subsidies, higher pensions, changes in taxation to help the worst off. At the same time as the budget, the repeal of the Industrial Relations Board and the Housing Finance Act was announced and the Pay Board abolished. The budget was harder on corporations by increasing employers' national insurance contributions and corporation taxation, by toughening the price code, and raising prices of goods produced by nationalized industries, such as coal and steel. Healey announced extensive overseas borrowing to finance the balance of payments deficit.[48] The government did not restore the cuts in state expenditure brought in by Heath.[49] Further, Stage III of Heath's income policy remained in effect.[50] Inflation mounted; and the squeeze on profits worsened. The results were increased unemployment, low productivity and growth, and further economic stagnation. The balance of payments deficit did not improve. As well, even with the agreements with the TUC, large wage demands continued, and workers were successful in winning large increases above the Stage III guidelines. Inflation was accelerating, stagnation worsened, and large deficits in the public sector remained and grew.[51]

The second budget of July 1974 was an attempt modestly to reflate the economy. After Phase III, wage demands were left entirely in the hands of the TUC and the Social Contract. Wage gains continued to exceed productivity and inflation, adding to the financial deficits of many firms faced with increased unit labour costs. The crisis brought a continued decrease in production and rising unemployment.[52] Despite these economic difficulties, Wilson won re-election with a slim majority. The crisis continued with a deterioration in production, increased redundancies, and short-term work. Inflation was defined as the major problem. The key was helping the private sector to regenerate production and, at the same time, to keep wages down. The strategy was pursued in the third budget of that year in November. Major concessions were made to the private sector, with some social reforms benefiting the elderly and subsidies to nationalized industries were reduced.[53] Increases in public expenditures were to be held down below the average increase in national output at approximately 2.75 per cent for the next four years.[54] The budget tried to shift state expenditures in such a way as to get private accumulation going again, and restricted benefits with the exception of pensions. The consequence was that it undermined the basis of the Social Contract.[55] The budget did little to limit the already large public sector deficit. The crisis continued. This time it was expressed in terms of a crisis of confidence in the pound. The combination of large trade deficits, increasing public sector debt, and continuing inflation brought about the drop in value in the pound. This drop further endangered Britain's ability to finance rising overseas deficits. The solution to these problems became defined in terms of the necessity to restrain wage demands and increase productivity. The CBI and the government made it clear that unemployment would increase fast if the Social Contract did not have some effect on wage increases.[56]

The Labour government strategy to deal with the crisis involved acknowledging the necessity of continued unemployment and cuts in public expenditure. By April 1975 Healey claimed higher unemployment was part of the price that it was necessary to pay for high levels of inflation. He brought in a further cut of £1,100 million in public spending. From 1976-9 public spending would be reduced by a further £9,600 million.[57] In January 1975, the Industry Bill was passed by parliament, establishing the National Enterprise Board (NEB). Its functions were to assist in the establishment and development of particular industries, extend public ownership, and promote industrial democracy.[58] These changes represented an attempt to use the state to get accumulation going again. With Wilson's resignation, Callaghan was faced with the continuing problem of wages increasing faster than productivity and inflation. Unemployment was continuing to climb, surpassing 1.2 million in 1976. Further, the £6 wage increase limit negotiated in July 1975 was to end in July 1976. A new wage agreement was negotiated with the TUC limiting average wage increases to $4\frac{1}{2}$ per cent beginning in August 1976. By 1976, the government increased its attack on public expenditures. Further cuts were announced to prevent a fall in the value of sterling. These measures were insufficient. In order to prevent a collapse of the pound, the government was forced to seek a \$3,900 million loan from the IMF. The conditions of this loan were increased taxation and further cuts in public spending, amounting to £3,000 million over the next two years.[59] During this period, the resistance of the working class had diminished. The wage restraints of 1975–7 began to take their toll as for the first time since the war the living standards of the working class fell. Further, resistance to the cuts was fragmented and ineffective. The combination of the threats of unemployment, the ideological attack on the working class, and the acceptance of working-class and trade union leaders of the terms of the crisis as laid down by the government and the bourgeoisie led to this defeat.[60]

The attempt to resolve the crisis of British capitalism was made at the expense of the working class through an attack on its standard of living and its power. The Keynesian/Beveridge strategy of class rule was clearly abandoned. The working class could no longer be accommodated through it, and its techniques could not maintain a crisis-free capitalism. The period discussed here ends roughly in the years 1976–7. Some stability followed, with a slight recovery of the British economy, and improvements in the balance of payments were bolstered by revenues from North Sea oil. These improvements were at the expense of the working class. The question was would this stability and acquiescence of the class remain? This was shattered by the 'winter of discontent' in early 1979. The peace was short-lived. With the election of Thatcher, the question of her strategy emerges. With her election, the strategies of Keynes and Beveridge have been abandoned. It was unclear which way the Labour party would have gone if they had been re-elected, but what is certain is that the attacks by Thatcher on the working class are not only out of a 'new right' ideology, but follow in the path well cleared by her predecessor.

The welfare state 1964–76: introduction

This section will review some themes in the welfare state in the years 1964 to 1976. These will be integrated into the discussion of pensions that follows. The three governments pursued different strategies to get accumulation going and to limit and contain class struggle. The general orientation to the welfare state and changes in specific programmes in many ways mirror these strategies and orientations. These will be explored and, in many ways, set the framework in which the debate and pension reforms occurred. Also, as the limits of the welfare state became more obvious, it became more controversial. Criticisms of the welfare state increased from both the right and the left. The attacks, particularly from the right advocating greater market and less state provision, had important implications for Heath's strategy toward the welfare state. Criticism from the left demonstrated the profound failure of post-war welfare state activity to significantly alter poverty and social inequality. Finally, the welfare state became a battleground for the class war. Conflict surrounding welfare state activity increased as specific groups organized along with increasing feminist militancy and resisted state policy or demanded reform. Pressure group activity, particularly through the Child Poverty Action Group (CPAG), Shelter, Gingerbread and Claimants' Unions grew along with left criticism of the welfare state. These themes will be explored briefly, and then followed by a discussion of the approaches and welfare state strategies of the three governments.

Growth of the welfare state

The period after 1964 saw a very rapid growth of welfare state expenditure. From 1961 to 1975, all social services grew as a percentage of GNP at factor cost rose from 17.6 per cent to 28.8 per cent.[61]

Given the combination of the growth of social expenditures and the decline in accumulation, the question of financing the welfare state and how much it could or could not be expanded became an issue of public debate. Several important positions emerged in this debate. Increasingly, the welfare state was attacked by those advocating more market as opposed to state provision. This position was pushed by the Institute for Economic Affairs and increasingly influenced Conservative party policies.[62] Seldon, for instance, advocated more aid for the 'declining minority in need' and more freedom of choice for those able to buy benefits in the market.[63] The push was against universality, a principle that to varying degrees had been held by both Tories and Labour since the war.

The group most verbal in countering this position was the Fabian Society. For example, in responding to Seldon in *New Society*,[64] Abel-Smith advocated changes in Beveridge's principles, particularly flat rate contributions and benefits. He reasserted that the state is the preferable provider of benefits on a universal basis with wage-related benefits, along with increased family allowances to help to solve the problem of those most in need. In order to finance increased benefits, he sought wage-related contributions, but as well he raised the question of how much of 'their growing affluence people want to take in a state operated system of fringe benefits and how much are they willing to transfer to the existing aged'.[65]

Two Labour party ministers during the Wilson period contrast their perception of the financing of social services. Douglas Houghton questioned, with the crisis of the pound in the late 1960s, whether Britain could re-establish economic growth and at the same time expand the financing of the welfare state. His remedy to this problem was a shift away from universal provision and towards making social expenditure an acceptable and an increased part of personal expenditure.[66] The point here is that to Houghton growth of the welfare state was constrained by and competed with economic growth. Crossman, on the other hand, experiencing the same constraints on policy development, continued to insist on universal provision and financing services that would continue to expand through taxation on the working population.[67]

While the debate went on, the complacency of many observers was shattered as serious criticisms of the welfare state's solving the problems of poverty and inequality emerged. These criticisms were from the pens of those who most supported the concept of state intervention and provision.[68] As opposed to the positions held by the Institute of Economic Affairs, these critiques of the welfare state tended to put pressure on the Labour party. These harsh evaluations did *not* exist in isolation as debates among intellectuals, but popular mobilization of claimants and squatters made the welfare state an arena of conflict and confrontation.

The conflicts over the welfare state were diverse and involved differing ideologies and perspectives. These struggles occurred with a general increase in the class struggle and the feminist movement and confronted both the kinds of provision and the way that goods and services were provided. The most important groups were those of claimants themselves. These groups pressured local offices of the DHSS through direct action and confrontation, and acted as what can broadly be defined as trade union type representatives for their members, supporters, and followers. Similar direct action groups emerged in housing with organizations of council housing tenants and the development of the squatters movement.[69] Direct action put increasing pressure on the state. The weakness of these movements was their fragmented nature and isolation from the trade union movement and other groups and movements. This isolation is a reflection of the class relations produced by the capitalist

116

state which diffuse the totality of class relations and define problems in terms of the individual and citizenship rather than class and patriarchy. Further, these relations with the various groups and definitions were accepted by the groups themselves reflecting that the problem is not one of ideology but of the concrete operation of the state on a daily basis.[70]

In total, the period from 1965 to 1975 was one of intense activity and debate on the welfare state. The state, through various departments, attempted to quell and to co-opt much of this activity by establishing representative and consultative groups, and by modifying programmes to absorb this kind of activity.[71] Pressure from the Fabians, CPAG, the trade unions, and the more important direct action had the effect of keeping the Labour party committed to welfare progress in their traditions at least in their rhetoric and manifestos. The next section will review the general policy orientations of the governments to the welfare state.

Wilson's welfare programmes

The social welfare measures promised and those that were subsequently implemented were closely related to Wilson's broad economic strategy. As mentioned earlier, and as will be elaborated in the discussion of pension reform, the initial goals of social policy were severely limited by the crisis. With the abandonment of nationalization, Labour turned to the welfare state, and saw it as an instrument of establishing equality which became its major perspective on socialism. The commitment to large-scale expansion and development of the welfare state was central to Labour and one of the major ways that it could differentiate itself from the Tories. For example, in their 1964 election manifesto, the Labour party promised a shift of resources from the private sector to the welfare state through increased taxation on capital and labour. Also they assumed that economic expansion was the basis for growth of the welfare state.[72] Another theme of the Wilson welfare state was the emphasis on using various programmes of the welfare state to complement his strategy of industrial and technological modernization. This had particular relevance in the social security and education reforms. Social security provides a good example of his approach. The government was committed to major reorganization in this area, including a guaranteed minimum income for all. The other major reforms in social security[73] were closely related to the Labour government's economic strategy. This strategy was to implement technological innovation, modernization and rationalization of industry. In many cases, this would involve increases in redundancy and unemployment. In anticipation

117

of this, and as a way of minimizing labour resistance, the government introduced redundancy payments and earnings-related unemployment benefits.[74] Thus, those workers whose jobs were lost through the restructuring and industrial shake-out would supposedly be compensated. Crossman acknowledged the priority of changes in sickness, unemployment and redundancy programmes and linked these to government strategy for industrial development.[75] The government established the Ministry of Social Security and the Supplementary Benefits Commission in an attempt to make benefits more accessible, particularly for old people, who in many cases did not make claims. The Labour government, during this period of economic crisis, had to withdraw its proposals for a large-scale incomes guarantee. This reorganization of National Assistance was provided instead. As Crossman stated: [Supplementary Benefits are] a cheap substitute, a reformed national assistance which would be sold to the public under the new name of supplementary benefits.'[76]

In general, the approach to the welfare state was well within the traditions already established by post-war governments. Some innovation was introduced, while this was limited by the acceptance of the financial constraints imposed by the crisis. Principles of universality were maintained, particularly in health and education. Although the Wilson government made a lot of noise about welfare reform, it was not a period of major transformation and change in welfare provision but of small improvements within the Labourite and 'right progressive' traditions. These traditions were challenged by the Tories on assuming office in 1971.

Heath's welfare state

The shift in welfare policies pursued by the Heath government reflects the general change in orientation of the party described earlier. It expressed itself as how much state and how much private market provision there should be and, further, who or which group should be the major recipients of state services. Increasing market provision and 'individual choice' was the prominent strategy. They related their programme to reducing taxes, controlling state spending, and linking the growth of services to economic growth.[77] Resolutions adopted without controversy at the 1968 and 1969 Conservative party conferences demonstrated the increasing commitment to selectivity of benefits for specific groups – the most needy – and, along with this, making sure benefits were received by those who are deserving, and establishing 'freedom' to use market forms for social provision.[78] This orientation was integral with the rise of the right in the party who attacked the supposed decline in social discipline. A resolution, adopted a year later, supported increased market provision.

> That this conference calls for a policy that gives every encourage-ment to the many people in this country who wish to fend for themselves in education, health, housing and insurance . . . but at the same time when resources are limited, the greatest help may be to those in greatest need.[79]

This quotation is important as it formed the orientation for much of the social policy of the Heath government and represents a break from the policies of 'right progressives'.

In practice, the Conservatives carried through some of these policies. In social security this general policy expressed itself through the imple-mentation of income supplementation for specific groups. The 1970 Old Persons and Widow's Pension and Attendance Allowance provided a pension to those who were too old to join the National Insurance Scheme when it began in 1948. This entailed a modest extra pension without a means test for those over eighty years old. The widow's pension on a sliding scale gave a payment to women widowed between the ages of forty and fifty years. The attendance allowance was the payment of a regular amount to the severely disabled. These policies uphold a long tradition, of defining the 'deserving poor', those who are *not* expected to work, and increasing benefits for them. In other policies the government tied social security policies more closely to wage labour. It introduced the means-tested family income supplement to supplement low wages. The programme supported low wages and, like other means-tested benefits, had a low uptake.[80] The Conservatives used their time in office to attack those on supplementary benefits. It 'readjusted' supplementary benefits so that their rate of increase would be less than that of national insurance benefits.[81] As well, the govern-ment established a committee of inquiry to consider the question of social security abuse. Subsequently it increased the number of staff involved in investigation of claims, simplifying regulations, and starting new drives against fraud of the supplementary benefit scheme.[82] The government's policy was to minimize any disincentive to work and to keep people as dependent as possible on the labour market for their subsistence. Although the policies of the Heath government were part of a general shift from the state to market relations, they were not able to contain the growth of state expenditures.[83] Further, his strategy was closely linked to a general attack on the working class and a re-structuring of the conditions of wage labour established in the post-war period.

Back to Labour

The approach to the welfare state after 1974 used by the Labour government was shaped by the conditions of the Social Contract, on the one hand, and by the crisis, on the other. The approach was characteristically Labour. Grand plans but pragmatic policies dictated by the general conditions of accumulation. The Labour manifesto of February 1974 recognized the hardships caused by years of high inflation and it emphasized 'the claims of social justice'. It proposed 'urgent action . . . to strike at the roots of the worst poverty, to make the country demonstrably a much fairer place to live in'.[84] Many reforms were advocated including annual increases for national insurance proportional to increases in average national earnings and, as will be discussed in detail, a replacement of the Conservative retirement pension plan. The manifesto promised new help for the disabled, improvements in family allowances, price controls and food subsidies. As with other reforms, part of the approach to the welfare state was undoing changes made by Heath. Besides pensions, Labour committed itself to repeal the Housing Finance Act and to pass legislation to protect tenants. Finally, one major plank was to redistribute income and wealth through increased taxation of the rich.[85] This last pledge was related to the general leftward shift in the tone of the manifesto.

Once elected and re-elected, Labour's welfare state policies can be divided into two stages. The first brought some reforms in during the first year or so after election. The second stage was strongly influenced by cutbacks in state expenditure, culminating in the IMF crisis of 1976. As the crisis developed, programmes in the welfare state were reformulated to become more closely intertwined with the strategy of getting accumulation going again. Examples of this are plentiful and include such things as reorganization and rationalization of services and greater linking of social benefits with the labour market, for example, through the development of employment centres.[86] The general shift in orientation with the crisis can be seen in Table 4.3 on state expenditures. It is clear from this table that the most substantial cuts came about after 1975. Labour had to deliver some reforms early on as a way to maintain the loyalty of the trade unions and the working class. As the crisis increased, Labour quickly abandoned this strategy with cuts and rationalization quickly taking over.

Social security will now be used as an example of the kinds of reforms and changes pursued by Labour. In a general way, social security continued to grow irrespective of the cuts in other welfare state cutbacks. The reasons for this are not particularly surprising. As unemployment increased with the crisis, more and more people became dependent on either unemployment or supplementary benefits. Further,

TABLE 4.3
Rate of increase in expenditure (capital and current) at constant prices on the public social services (percentages)

	All social services	Social security	Education	Health	Personal social services	Housing
1974–5	9.0	6.9	0.4	1.0	8.3	44.1
1975–6	2.1	8.3	1.8	3.2	6.5	− 11.7
1976–7	1.0	2.9	− 0.3	0.8	− 1.3	− 1.0
1977–8	− 0.9	3.6	− 3.6	0.8	− 1.6	− 9.4

(Peter Townsend, 'Social Planning and the Treasury', in *Labour and Equality*, p. 11, edited by Nick Bosanquet and Peter Townsend, London, Heinemann, 1980.)

demographically the increase in the proportion of old people and retired people living longer put increased demands on pension payments particularly with annual increases.

The government was committed to maintaining a disciplined unemployed who would be ready to sell their labour power. This policy was enacted in several ways. With the increase in the number of long-term unemployed, more and more of them were forced to turn to supplementary benefits for their income.[87] These workers, regardless of unemployment conditions, were considered to be 'short term' claimants and, as such, were penalized with lower benefits than so-called long-term claimants, such as retired workers. As well, increases were fixed by increases in prices which were lower than the increases in national insurance that were linked to increases in earnings. The Labour government, following Heath and Joseph, increased the number of investigations and prosecutions for social security fraud, especially for those unemployed who were supposedly 'workshy'.[88] The unemployed were pushed back into the labour market to compete for jobs. The Labour government had become caught up in the assaults of the right against the 'scroungers' and the 'workshy' and did very little to resist these attacks. These attacks on the unemployed furthered the discipline and pressures on the reserve army of labour.[89] Finally, there was an administrative review of the Supplementary Benefits Commission, defined within a 'zero cost' condition laid down by the Treasury. The SBC response, led by David Donnison, was well within these conditions and involved attacks on various groups and cutbacks based on the principle of 'rough justice'.[90] The general orientation of social security in this period, even with the conditions of higher unemployment, was to attack those dependent on these benefits and increase the use of unemployment and supplementary benefits as a way of disciplining the reserve army of labour.

There were some improvements in social security, such as several new benefits for the disabled and, as will be discussed in detail, the major pension reform undertaken by the government. In total, Labour's welfare state reforms in this period were formed by a pragmatic approach accepting the conditions imposed by the crisis. The main aspect of this was extending the attack on the conditions of the working class to unemployed workers. On the other hand, the conditions of the Social Contract and the struggles of the working class necessitated some reform.

Occupational pensions

Before discussing the reform of state pensions, a short review of the development of occupational pensions will be presented. One of the central issues in each of the efforts at reform was the relationship of private to state pensions. This issue became more important as more and more workers became members of private occupational pension plans.

In the previous period, to approximately 1963, a general growth in occupational pensions was noted, particularly for manual and women workers in the private sector. In this period, to approximately 1975, a change occurs. The growth of private pensions peaked around the years 1967–70, and a gradual decline set in, particularly for manual workers in the private sector. This general trend is reflected in Table 4.4.

TABLE 4.4
Coverage by pensions (millions)

Year	Private sector Men	Women	Public sector Men	Women	Total
1967	6.8	1.3	3.1	1.0	12.2
1971	5.5	1.3	3.2	1.1	11.1
1975	5.0	1.1	3.7	1.7	11.5

(*Occupational Pension Schemes 1975*, fifth Survey by the Government Actuary, HMSO, 1978, p. 9.)

The decline in pension coverage in the private sector was mainly among manual workers, but also included non-manual workers.[91] The most striking aspect of this data is the decline in pensions in the private sector in general, and specifically for manual workers. The most dramatic drop took place between 1967 and 1971 when the number of manual workers enrolled in pension plans declined by approximately one million. This drop corresponds to the general shift in employment in this period discussed earlier, reflecting slowly rising unemployment, and restructuring of production. With the present crisis, it is probable that the decline in private pensions for manual workers will continue.

Two other factors are important to note. First, the taxation changes brought in by the Conservatives in 1970 and 1971 were designed to encourage the growth of private pensions. These remained unaltered by Labour. Taxation policies have been used traditionally to encourage these pensions.[92] Second, the level of benefits received from occupational pensions continued to be low. By 1975, a total of 3.4 million people were receiving some benefits from occupational pension plans.[93] Table 4.5 summarizes the level of benefits for occupational pensions and compares these levels with National Insurance and Supplementary Benefit levels.

TABLE 4.5
Benefit levels per week

		1971	*1975*
Occupational Pension		£	£
Weekly Amount Median (Males)		4.05	7.00
Females, including Widows (Median)		Not available	5.00
National Insurance			
Retirement Pension – Basic		6.00	13.30
Over 80 years		6.25	13.55
Married Women/Adult Dependant		3.70	7.90
Over 80 years		3.95	8.15
Supplementary Benefits	Couple	9.45	21.55
(excluding housing allowance)	Single	5.80	13.70

(*Family Expenditure Survey 1975*, cited in *Occupational Pension Schemes 1975*, fifth Survey by the Government Actuary; *Occupational Pension Schemes 1971*, fourth Survey by the Government Actuary, Social Security Statistics, DHSS, 1977.)

There are several interesting features that emerge with Table 4.5. The rate of growth of benefits of occupational pensions is much slower than the corresponding growth of state benefits. As well, the level of occupational pensions benefits, as defined by the median level, indicates that as a supplement to national insurance, these benefits may make an important contribution to the standard of living of retired workers. This benefit level is deceptive for two reasons. First, because of the structure of pensions, many retired workers are able to receive some supplementary benefits, particularly for housing expenses and other allowances. In these cases, the benefits from occupational pensions would have the effect of cancelling out supplementary benefits; thus gains which seem high are in fact less. Second, the benefits from occupational pensions calculated here are probably much higher than a working-class male or female worker ever received. There follow some examples of why this occurs. Public sector schemes tend to pay out larger benefits mainly because since 1971 they have been indexed to prices. In 1975, local authorities were paying an average of £16 per week to an employee and the central government, an average of about £12 per week.[94] At the same time, corporations employing manual workers with new pension schemes were averaging £6 per week. Further, in terms of benefits for widows and dependants, although the public sector provided them to more people the level of provision was lower — £4 as opposed to £8 per week for private sector pensions.[95] Finally and most important, is that none of the statistics of benefits in payment differentiate between manual and non-manual workers. The median, then, is probably much higher than a manual worker would receive and reflects the relatively disproportionately high number of white-collar workers receiving benefits. In 1971, 40 per cent of all pensions paid out by occupational pensions were less than £3.[96] Similarly, in 1975 slightly over 30 per cent of these benefits paid out £5 per week or less, and slightly over half of pensions paid out were less than £10 per week. For females and widows, approximately half of all benefits paid out were £5 per week or less, and around 70 per cent were under £10.[97] It is difficult to say, from these statistics, how much manual workers receive, but it is fairly clear that pensions reflect a combination of wage rates and years in a job, both of which will be less for manual workers and, therefore, the corresponding benefits will be less. What is striking is the complete disregard of this type of information in their support of private occupational pensions by both the Labour party and the trade unions in this period.

State pensions

The rest of this section will discuss the development of state pension reform, situated in the broader context of the conditions of class relations, and the particular government's strategy in relation to the balance of class forces and conditions of accumulation. The debate and strategies of Labour and Conservatives on the welfare state were played out very clearly through pension reform. Although there were basic differences between the two parties in power, it is important not to lose sight of commitment displayed in pension policy to the maintenance of the form of state provision which embodied the principle of work-tested benefits and links to wage labour. Thus, even in their diversity, wage labour as expressed through contribution conditions, earnings-related benefits and occupational pensions, was the basis of all pension reform. Finally, as described earlier, old people tend to be the poorest. The debate and reform of pensions has done little to change this except to hold out a promise that by 1998 earnings-related pensions will do something about this. The extensive tinkering with pension reform from Beveridge to Barbara Castle has done little to relieve the outrageous poverty of the elderly.

The Crossman plan

This section will discuss the Crossman Pension Plan from several perspectives. To begin, an analysis will be presented of those forces and pressures that were at least partially responsible for the development of the plan and those factors which delayed it until just prior to the election of Heath. The specific policies in the proposal will be presented, followed by some of the responses to the pension plan. Finally, the Crossman plan will be situated within the context of the general conditions of accumulation and class relations.

Pension and social security reforms played a central part in Labour's 1964 electoral campaign.[98] Labour had a clear commitment to major pension reform. Further, it already had a blueprint for pension reform prepared by Titmuss, Townsend and Abel-Smith.

Research on the failure of pensions to ameliorate poverty among old people was an important impetus to the debate on pension reform.

According to the Minister of Social Security at the time, Margaret Herbison, the research carried out in May and June 1965 by the government was in response to other research reports that showed a large number of old people with incomes less than the National Assistance Board (NAB) level.[99] The study revealed extensive poverty amongst old people. Besides the extensive poverty among the aged shown in this report, many people who were eligible for national assistance and not receiving it were identified.[100] Further, the combination of graduated pensions from the 1959 Act and existing flat rate benefits had 'no prospect of achieving the original objectives of the Beveridge Plan'.[101] The graduated pensions were inadequate because they were unprotected against inflation and were not adjusted for economic growth.[102] Clearly, the system as it had been constructed and modified in the post-war period had not come even close to solving the problem of

125

poverty in old age. These failures were understood by the government.[103]

The TUC during these years began to voice discontent about the government's slowness in bringing about pension reform. These pressures take on more significance in that the government was attempting to limit wage gains and trade union power. The welfare state was one place where the Wilson government appeared to be working for reform. The TUC had been pressuring the Conservative government for a review of both national insurance and national assistance levels,[104] and had endorsed the Labour party's proposals in 'New Frontiers for Social Security' that formed the basis for the manifesto proposals.[105] With the election of the Labour government, the TUC continued to pressure for a comprehensive review of social security and the national insurance system. They criticized the Labour government for the inadequate levels of national insurance, particularly in relation to the levels of supplementary benefits (national assistance) and the regressive nature of the system of contributions, and the relative burden placed on low-income workers.[106] The pressures from the TUC were presented in conventional ways through the channels of the Labour party and meetings with the government. Finally, one other pressure for reform came from the structure of the national insurance programme itself.

The 1959 Conservative reforms were not linked to inflation. The contributions provided by this plan, within a few years, had little effect on the increasing demands being made on the national insurance fund. Deficits were present every year except 1966 from the time Labour took over.[107] Even though the Labour government continued its policy of linking increased benefits with increased contributions, and raising funds with wage-related contributions, the deficits remained.[108] The deficit is of increased importance in the context of the government's fiscal strategy discussed earlier, to limit the growth of state expenditure programmes. Pension reform became one means of raising taxation. Further, in the context of the government's deflationary policies and policies to limit current consumption, pension restructuring fitted in as a way of delaying current spending with the promise of long-term spending in the future for increased retirement benefits.[109] These were, then, substantial reasons for the government to implement major pension reform; but at the same time several significant pressures delayed the reforms. Part of the delay in the implementation of the pension reform can be attributed to a lack of clarity or certainty about what to implement. The government quickly abandoned the earlier 1957 proposals. Kincaid suggests that these were too redistributive between rich and poor.[110]

The government's discussions of pension reform showed differing strategies. Between 1964 and 1966, Crossman wanted an immediate shift from flat rate contributions to a totally earnings-related contribution in order to pile up 'enormous sums' in the pension fund that could be used to dynamize the flat rate pension. Houghton and Herbison were pushing for an increased flat rate benefit financed by flat rate contributions.[111] However, more than the uncertainties and strategic debates, it was the crisis of accumulation and the limits the various manifestations of the crisis forced on state expenditures that were most important. Labour had established its priority as a total reorganization of all social security programmes, including pension reform expressed as half-pay on retirement. According to Crossman, by October 1965 the plan of total reorganization was dropped and the short-term benefits, particularly earnings-related unemployment and sickness benefits, were given priority. According to Houghton, priority was not accorded to a 'genuine half-pay pension scheme' for two reasons. First, the cost to industry would have been too high, particularly at a time when increasing exports was the highest priority. Second, for reasons which have been discussed earlier, priority was given to restructuring of unemployment and redundancy payments. But although these reforms also placed extra cost on industry, they were not nearly as high as those costs that would have resulted from pension reform.[112] Pension reform became secondary, as the priority of linking state programmes to the specific needs of the restructuring of capital was perceived by Labour as *the* priority.

The pension scheme proposed by Crossman was presented in a White Paper[113] in 1969. The scheme was based on pragmatism and attempted to form a compromise between traditional Fabian principles of universality and equality and the political and economic conditions. In this way it was a far more moderate plan than the 1957 plan. The conditions of class relations and accumulation had changed. The Labour party was in government in the context of an ongoing economic crisis; even small increases in pensions had serious repercussions.[114] Labour was to play the game within the prescribed boundaries and its policies of the period reinforced the narrow boundaries that existed. Pension policy was to be no different. The limits were defined yet improvements for those who would retire in the future, particularly the relatively lower paid, were attempted.

The actual plan began with the recognition of the poverty of old people and the failure of both the Beveridge reforms and the subsequent earnings-related pensions to solve these problems. Also, the problem of financing pensions was presented because of the large and growing number of retired workers in proportion to the rest of the population.[115] There were several basic goals for the pension reform. The principle of work-testing of benefits, that is, benefits can only be earned through contributions, and relating future benefits to present earnings remained. Benefits derived from this plan were to be sufficient to live on without other income. The pension plan promised equality of contributions and benefits for women. The scheme would not be funded but would be based on a 'pay-as-you-go' principle. Finally the scheme tried to work out a formal relationship with private schemes – a 'partnership'. In this partnership, occupational pension rights had to be preserved with changes in employment as a basic criterion for their recognition. The way the plan was to work will now be analysed in relation to these goals.

The first issue is that of contribution conditions. Long-established traditions were once again reasserted. The principles of combining contribution and exchequer financing was presented. The White Paper stated:

> Even if it were remotely realistic to consider a transfer of this order (necessary for total exchequer financing) from contributions to taxation, the Government would think it wrong for pensions to be wholly tax-financed. People do not want to be given rights to pensions and benefits; they want to earn them by contributions.[116]

The proposal states that a totally exchequer-financed scheme would inevitably provide lower benefits because people would be unwilling to contribute more through taxation than *via* contributions. As well, contributions guarantee pensions in the future, regardless of who holds political office.[117]

Changes in the system of contribution would be brought in. The total contribution would be paid through PAYE rather than having part of it being contributed with stamped cards. The existing scheme had three types of contributions: the old flat rate contributions; the earnings-related pension contribution; and contributions for short-term earnings-related unemployment and sickness benefits. These three contributions would be taken over by one contribution through PAYE. The contributions were to be a fixed percentage of earnings up to a ceiling of $1\frac{1}{2}$ times national average earnings. The total employee contribution rate was to be $6\frac{3}{4}$ per cent of earnings, of which $4\frac{3}{4}$ per cent would go to the superannuation scheme, and the remaining 2 per cent would be for other social insurance benefits, industrial injuries, and the National Health Service contribution. This aspect of the scheme was mildly redistributive compared to what existed. Lower paid workers would pay proportionately less contributions than higher paid workers. Employer contributions were to be $6\frac{3}{4}$ per cent of their total PAYE pay-roll with no earnings ceiling. Of that, $4\frac{1}{2}$ per cent would be for national superannuation which was to equal the total of employees' contribution to the national superannuation fund. The contribution of the exchequer was to remain the same as it was before at approximately 18 per cent of the combined national insurance contributions of insured persons and employers. In terms of total contributions, the plan did not bring about any major reform, but rather consolidated and rationalized contributions with minor shifts in redistribution from low to slightly above average wage earners. The sacredness of contributions remained with its emphasis on employer and employee contributions rather than increases from the exchequer.

A complicated system was proposed to calculate benefits. The retirement from work was assumed for eligibility for pensions. As opposed to Labour's implementation of the Beveridge plan, a build-up period was required before full benefits would be paid. Rights to full pensions would be built up over twenty years. A worker would only get his/her full pension after contributing for twenty years, with proportional levels paid in the interim period. The pensions themselves were to be fully earnings-related. The fully mature new pensions would be 60 per cent of earnings up to half of the national average, and 25 per cent of the remainder of earnings up to the scheme's ceiling. Calculation of earnings for pension entitlement was to take into account changes in the level of national average earnings; for example, if a worker earned wages at about the national average, these would be adjusted to reflect changes in the national average. Up until this proposal, review of the level of pension benefits had been left to whichever government was in office. The new plan brought with it reviews every two years as a matter of statute. The review would cover all state pensions, not only those in the new scheme, and increase pensions with the cost of living. In addition, the proposal saw pensions being increased with changes in the general standard of living as reflected through growth in wages. This aspect was the major improvement over what existed. Similarly, the pension provision for women and widows was improved.

One of the main issues of contestation on this proposal was the relation between state and private occupational pension plans. The question that Crossman faced was how much should those covered by occupational pensions be allowed to contract out of the state scheme. Given that the plan was based entirely on an earnings-related system, what proportion of a given wage would be deducted for contribution to the state scheme and what implications would this have for its financing? This issue involved prolonged negotiations between Crossman and representatives of pension organizations, over conditions of contracting out, and establishing conditions for the preservation of pension rights.[118] The principles laid out in the White Paper were based on the notion of partial contracting out and a greater integration of private and state pensions. Occupational pensions were viewed as a positive development, particularly because they represent savings of

129

workers. The compromise tried to strike a balance between the two forms of pensions so as to neither undermine the universality of the state scheme nor put excess demands on occupational pensions, such as inflation-proofing. In order to achieve this balance, a formula was worked out whereby the contribution paid by those contracting out would be reduced. There would be a deduction from the state pension that the worker would receive upon retirement. The corresponding occupational pension would have to guarantee a pension at least equivalent to that which would have been provided by the state; that is, that amount deducted from the state pension because of contracting out. The amount that could be contracted out would be limited. Partial contracting out was in the interest of the private pensions in that it preserved their freedom to sell the traditional non-dynamic type of pension, regardless of any improvements in the state scheme. Pensions could continue to offer benefits of fixed cash value without their being indexed for inflation. The state, in essence, would be paying the total pension minus that fixed amount paid out by the private pension plan, as well as benefits such as widows' pensions. The White Paper thought it unreasonable to demand that a private pension plan make an unknown commitment with rising prices.[119] The government did bring forward a policy that would force occupational pensions to be preserved for an employee changing his/her job. With these considerations and policies, the response to the proposals will be summarized briefly and some general comments will be presented.

Crossman's diaries open the door to some of the fights within the government and between the government and representatives of capital and labour in the process of pension negotiation. Crossman's own writing reflected how this moderate plan had to be 'sold' to the working class as a great reform. Pension increases were obviously a central issue with any pension reform, particularly in terms of high inflation. Crossman had pushed for increases to be linked to wage gains of the working class, but the Treasury prevailed and increases were biennial and linked only to increases in prices.[120] In either case, pension increases proposed in the plan only formalized what was already occurring. Crossman wrote:

> What the National Superannuation does is to ensure that instead of surrendering year by year to political pressure we have an escalator to carry the old-age pensioner up at the speed fixed in relation to the increase in national wages. We shall proclaim this as a great social advance but I know very well that John Boyd-Carpenter will be able to prove that the escalator will not be moving any faster than it has done by the jerks and jumps with which pensions have been upped in the last fifteen years. My pension plan is not wildly extravagant but unfortunately we dare not say so.[121]

Crossman initially was in favour of a funded pension plan but gave it up after pressure from the Treasury, whose representatives argued that even if the plan was funded, the contributions of workers and employers would still be paying for benefits of those in retirement.[122] In negotiating this position with the Treasury, Crossman wrote:

> To my mind national superannuation is a system of deferred pay and the essential thing is to convince the working class that it is a genuine pension scheme and not another Tory swindle. 'If it's simply a pay-as-you-go scheme,' I said, 'where each year you're just collecting enough money to pay out again that's another version of a Tory swindle and it's ridiculous to use thousands of officials for such a bogus pretence of a pensions scheme'.[123]

The pay-as-you-go scheme was in essence a tax scheme, but Crossman continued to sell it as a pension scheme. He had to convince the Treasury of the merits of his plan, and compromised aspects of it, mentioned above, because of their pressure. As well, the presentation of the White Paper was delayed because of bad trade deficits.[124] The Treasury thus continued to play an important role in mediating between social reform and its limits set up by the economic crisis. The second set of negotiations occurred with representatives of the CBI and of the pension and insurance business. Here Crossman showed himself to be accommodating and eager to carve out a place for occupational pensions. The government did not want to tamper with the funds amassed through occupational pensions.[125] Although the government attempted to collaborate with pension interests, it was this aspect that created the most controversy.

The TUC generally was very enthusiastic about the Crossman scheme and described it as 'the biggest advance in the field of social security since 1948'.[126] It was critical of certain aspects of the plan, particularly provision for existing pensioners, the level of the exchequer supplement which it thought should be increased, and the exclusion of the lowest paid from earnings-related benefits. It recommended that in the twenty-year build up period supplementary benefits be increased to keep up with prices, and that both the proposed plan for uprating of pensions and the existing flat rate benefits be increased to keep up with wages.[127] These were minor points, which was the main criticism raised by NALGO, who actively campaigned against the proposals. Some of the concerns they raised included whether or not members of NALGO's occupational pension plan would continue to be eligible for lump sum payments upon retirement, and whether the state pension, because it was indexed, would limit how much of a total pension they could receive. Eventually, their criticisms were assuaged by meetings between

131

the government and the TUC in which the government committed itself to yearly reviews of public service pensions in order to protect them against inflation. On this issue, the TUC was critical of the government's proposal on transferability of private pensions because it was not retro-active,[128] and they wanted the government to force the private sector pensions to be dynamized according to changes in the cost of living.[129] The support, however, was important to the government and the criticisms were relatively less so.

The response from other sources to the plan was mixed. Crossman summarized the response of the press as being positive, including the *Financial Times*. No one questioned the principle of providing earnings-related pensions. The major criticism, particularly from *The Daily Telegraph*, *Daily Express*, and *Daily Mail* was that the state was en-croaching on private pension plans.[130] *The Economist*, following on this theme, urged that all workers below middle age should be in private 'adequate, properly funded, savings generated transferable schemes', and for others, a properly funded state superannuation scheme with proper investments.[131]

One major criticism from an otherwise friendly source was on the issue of the lack of change for present pensioners. The *Guardian* wrote:

> There is a real danger of an ever widening gap between their (present and short term pensioners) pension standards and those of people coming into the wage related scheme.... Many thousands of these old people will still be alive when the rest of us are, hopefully drawing our wage related, inflation protected pensions in the 1990's. ... It is precisely the fact that no immediate increase in expenditure is promised that enabled Mr. Crossman to sell his scheme to the Treasury.[132]

The pension fund associations, such as the Life Officers' Association and the National Association of Pension Funds, were not too hostile to the state provision part. Although they were involved in negotiating the conditions of contracting out, particularly the percentage reduction in employee and employer contributions that would result with con-tracting out, this did not reduce their limited opposition.[133]

In contrast, Tony Lynes, writing in a Fabian tract, commented that in this respect the government proposals were too generous and would encourage large-scale contracting out.[134] This would result in a bad deal for the general contributors because private pensions tend to be over-cautious and tend to encourage higher contributions than they need. By contracting out at the commercial price, the amount reduced to state coffers would be higher than necessary.[135]

Finally, the Conservatives took two positions. In parliament, their criticisms were not extensive. They denounced the policies as 'a bogus pipe dream' and treated it as an electioneering policy. However, the Tories let the bill go through the House quite quickly as they supported the funds raised by the earnings-related contributions.[136] Crossman wrote that: 'they [Tories] know they need it themselves, because unless earnings-related contributions are enforced by 1972, they can't finance any pension'.[137] Several other criticisms were raised by the Conservatives. Many of these found their way into policy with Keith Joseph's pension plan. They criticized the vast complexity of the scheme and the difficulty most people and many experts had in understanding the plan. They raised the question of discrimination against those already retired, particularly people over eighty years. The pay-as-you-go scheme was challenged.[138] They argued that in the context of other Labour taxation policies, pension contributions, particularly from employers, would drive up prices at the same time that contributions would reduce take-home pay. More important than these criticisms was the attack on national superannuation because of the limits it placed on the growth of occupational pensions. Mr Paul Dean argued in the Commons that according to estimates of the National Association of Pension Funds, about 15,000 schemes covering one-half million people might be terminated.[139] Related to the scheme's complexity, the Conservatives argued that it would seriously damage occupational pension plans, particularly because of the difficulty employers would have in explaining the scheme and in justifying participation in these schemes to their employees.[140] Finally, as mentioned earlier, the Conservative party conference in 1969 pushed for policies that would be as advantageous as possible to occupational pensions. At the same conference Lord Balniel stated:

if the government curb occupational pension schemes . . . the Conservative government will alter the scheme. We will protect occupational pensions from damage which now seems likely to be the inevitable consequence of the Crossman plan.[141]

The Conservatives were determined to do all they could to support the growth and development of occupational pensions.

Before turning to the Joseph Plan, some final analytic comments will be made on the Crossman scheme. Much of the discussion of pensions, particularly on the left, has been on the theme of how much redistribution occurs through a given plan. In this plan, the redistribution was less than in the previous Labour proposal.[142] Further, once those in private pension plans are removed through contracting out, the amount of redistribution between high and low income is reduced, assuming those contracting out are earning more than those not contracting out. The exchequer contribution is another way to measure the amount of re-distribution. The second Crossman plan was less than the 1957 version. The positive redistribution feature of the plan was within those not contracting out and within a relatively narrower earning band than the previous Labour plan. It did provide some redistribution between higher and lower wage earners. The most obvious form of redistribution was from those working to those who are retired. Much of the same discussion on redistribution and regressive taxation mentioned in the discussion of the Beveridge reforms and the 1957 Labour plan applies and will not be repeated here.

The next issue of importance is the relation of state to market pro-vision of pensions. The tradition was well established and formalized by the Beveridge reforms that the state would have a clearly limited role in the provision of pensions, leaving room for the market and individual initiative. The characteristic differences between the two parties were on the questions of how much state and how much market provision should exist. Labour, following on the principle of universality, has supported an approach to pensions whereby all workers would be entitled to wage-related pensions at a level above the poverty line through state provision. The state plan would compete with private plans, particularly because the period of maximization was at twenty years as opposed to forty years for most private plans. This could force out inadequate private pensions that did not reach the same standards. This was one strategy of the Crossman plan. It cut off some of the market from occupational pensions by going into competition with them, particularly by making the state scheme more in the interest of manual workers than private plans. Along with the pension reform came increased state involvement in portability and vesting of pensions, thus again limiting the leeway of operations of occupational pensions. Also, this kind of legislation cut off a windfall that came from un-claimed pensions. For these reasons, and the general complexity of the contracting out procedures, it is not surprising that the private pension interests were to some extent against the reforms. Crossman's plan did give in quite a bit to them. It gave them a specific place to operate. In a formal way, they could provide a specific chunk of the pension with the state taking care of the rest of social security, particularly widows' benefits and inflation proofing *via* the state's pension. Implicit is the assumption that private pensions in fact can deliver the goods to retired workers, particularly manual workers. The assumption was not ques-tioned in any way and Labour proceeded as though they were balancing the interest of pension merchants and the state when the only thing that private pensions were doing, as has been pointed out, was bleeding the working class of part of their wages and delivering very little in return. There are several other issues in this plan but because the Joseph and Castle plan that follow raise similar issues, the discussion will be delayed. These include the question of contribution conditions, and their relation to taxation and the pension reform.

This ends the discussion of the Crossman plan — the second Labour pension plan that was not implemented. This time they got closer, but lost out because of the defeat of the Wilson government. The important point is the clear relation between the pension proposal and general state orientation. The continual financial crises placed important limits on expansion of the welfare state. Further, the government was committed to policies aimed at restructuring industry through modernization; thus, those programmes most functional to this process, particularly earnings-related unemployment and redundancy benefits, took priority. The general approach of Keynes/Beveridge still tended to dominate; however, increasingly the state entered into large-scale conflicts with trade unions about wages and the control of the working class through the unions. Social policy, particularly pension reform, tended to act as a counter-weight to the changing relations between the working class and the state which shifted from accommodation to increased conflict.

The Joseph plan

The plan for pensions brought in by Keith Joseph as an antidote to Labour's plan mirrors the general shift in the Conservative party's approach to the role of the state. The Heath government, particularly before the famous U-turn, broke with the traditions of Macmillan and Butler and attempted to restructure many state programmes. In pensions, this was expressed in a shift towards selectivity. The goal of their policies was that the state would provide for those most in need, and the rest would manage through the private pension market. The state would more actively encourage occupational pensions. This was part of a strategy to encourage savings.[143]

In the 1970 election manifesto the Conservatives promised to review pensions every two years and to provide non-means-tested pensions to those over eighty years who had none at all.[144] On pension reform they stated:

> We believe that everyone should have the opportunity of earning a pension related to their earnings. . . . For the great majority of people this can and should be achieved through the expansion and improvement of occupational schemes.[145]

For those who absolutely could not provide for themselves *via* private pensions,

135

there will be a reserve earning-related State scheme over and above the basic flat-rate scheme, and all approved occupational schemes will be enabled to contract out of it completely under simple conditions.[146]

The emphasis was clearly on occupational pensions for the majority and state, earnings-related pensions as a last resort. Total contracting out and reserve pensions was designed to avoid any competition between state and private pensions and to encourage the private sector. Finally, the shift from state to market emphasis as the major form of provision was related to the shift away from the Keynesian/Beveridge strategy of class relations towards one in which the free play of the market would be used to discipline labour. Although this strategy for wages and incomes was dropped in the middle of the Heath period, it was maintained in the welfare state.

The role of the state pension scheme was to change. The principle of contribution was to continue, but the government recognized that the state scheme was not and could not be an insurance scheme. The White Paper *Strategy for Pensions* stated:

It is a social scheme. . . . The contributions needed to pay for, and establish a right to, these benefits are a social obligation that can be recognized more clearly and accepted more readily if it is not confused with the principles of insurance.[147]

The contribution was to fulfil its traditional function without the illusion of insurance.[148] Again, work-testing, the willingness to labour was the central theme. The pension plan was stripped of it being an insurance scheme but the form, based on wage labour, remained central.

Another issue faced in this pension reform was the relation of benefit levels to the level of supplementary benefits. The government was concerned with the increasing number of pensioners receiving supplementary benefits. Further, the cost of increasing contributory pensions to a level to surpass substantially the supplementary benefit level would be too high. Yet the government did not want to raise supplementary benefits too high because:

To do that would sap the enterprise of|those who are in a position to do more for themselves. It would be damaging to the development of occupational pensions and other forms of savings for retirement if they did not offer the prospect of living standards in later life above the level of supplementary benefits.[149]

Contributory pensions increases were to be defined in relation to the

cost of living, but these increases would not be guaranteed indefinitely.[150] The plan, then, was oriented to restricting any competition
with private pension schemes *via* limiting improvements in the standard
of living for old people, either *via* supplementary benefits or contributory
benefits. The state earnings-related scheme was to be secondary, and
not substitute itself for private pensions. It was assumed that most
people could participate in occupational pension schemes. The plan did
suggest some improvements in private schemes, particularly in the
preservation of pension rights with job mobility. The government also
proposed and established the Occupational Pensions Board. Its mandate
was to supervise contracting out arrangements and preservation rights,
and to assist occupational pensions to change rules to adapt to new
situations.[151]

Given this general orientation, what were the specific mechanisms of
the operation of the scheme? The pension plan proposed by Joseph
closely paralleled and elaborated the 1959 reforms in some ways. The
separation between flat rate retirement benefits and earnings-related
benefits was formalized. The 'State Basic Scheme' was based on flat
rate benefits derived from earnings-related contributions. The benefits
were similar to what already existed. The reform in the contribution
conditions attempted to put the national insurance scheme on a sound
financial footing. This basic scheme was to be on a pay-as-you-go basis
and did not try to amass a fund. Income from contributions would be
linked to state obligations for pension payments. The Government
Actuary calculated that a combined employee/employer contribution of
12.5 per cent of reckonable earnings would be required to meet obligations by 1975.[152] Contributions would be fully earnings-related and
collected directly through PAYE. Those earning below one-quarter of the
average adult male manual worker wage would not be required to contribute. They would be covered for industrial injuries benefits only. Those
earning above this minimal level would pay 5.25 per cent on all wages
up to $1\frac{1}{2}$ times the average earnings. Employers would contribute 7.25
per cent based on the same earnings range. The exchequer contribution
would remain at 18 per cent.[153] In this respect, the plan was slightly
more redistributive from higher wage earners to lower than what
existed at the time.[154] The motivation was clearly not to redistribute
wages but to raise more money to finance national insurance.[155]

The benefits of married women and widows were to be linked to the
husband's benefits. A married woman could choose to contribute in
full, but she could only receive extra benefits beyond that of her
husband if her own contributions were sufficient to earn more than she
would through her husband's contribution record. The plan continued
to tie pension benefits to the traditional family structure and view
women as economically tied to husbands.[156] As discussed earlier, the

137

plan maintained contribution requirements, requiring contributions at a minimal level for nine-tenths of the years between entering the scheme and reaching pension age.[157] Pension contributions would continue to act as one more way to keep people at work.

The State Reserve Plan, or the earnings-related section, was entirely separate. It was to be an earnings-related pension for those who could not be part of a private pension plan and run along the same guidelines as any private pension. A Board of Management was to preside and invest the accumulated funds. A profit-sharing arrangement was to increase wage-related benefits and to offset increases in prices. Contributions of both employers and employees was to fund the plan. Employers would contribute 2.5 per cent of the same salary as the basic scheme, while workers would contribute 1.5 per cent. Pension benefits would vary according to contributions paid, the sex of the contributor and the age at which contributions were paid. The basis for sex discrimination according to the plan was that women retire earlier and live longer, and therefore the same contribution would provide less benefits. The obvious sexism of this approach was discussed in the previous chapter. Widows would receive pensions at half the rate the husband would have received. Finally, the Reserve Scheme Fund was supposed to be self-supporting; that is, it was to be financed solely by the contributions and income from its investments.[158]

The next important issue and the central point of this pension plan was the relationship between state and occupational pensions. The government wanted to restrict occupational pensions as little as possible, while at the same time setting out minimal conditions for these pensions. Contracting out was made as simple as possible and was from the State Reserve Scheme only. Related to the encouraging of private pensions, the white paper stated: 'This [pension scheme] should create a climate of opinion in which the normal job will be seen as providing not only a wage or salary but an earnings-related pension as well.'[159] The conditions for contracting out were both straightforward and relatively lenient for occupational pensions. In order to obtain recognition, the scheme was supposed to provide a personal pension for *men* at an annual rate of not less than 1 per cent of the PAYE earnings on what the reserve scheme will be payable, and a widow's benefit representing half her husband's pension rate paid either through a pension or a lump sum. For women, because of earlier retirement age and greater longevity, the amount was 0.7 per cent of defined earnings.[160] One of the following ways was to be incorporated into the scheme in order to protect the private pension and widow's benefits against increases in the cost of living. First, the actual pension could be linked to changes in the cost of living index. Second, a prescribed rate of increase could be provided after the pension was awarded. Third, the pension had to satisfy the Occupational Pensions Board that reasonable financial provision was being made to ensure increases could be made after the award, though without a commitment to a specific rate.[161] Finally, occupational benefits were to be preserved when a worker left his/her job. A deferred pension from that plan was the solution proposed with the option that an employer could transfer the value of contributions to another scheme. Preservation was to apply to all occupational pensions whether or not they had contracted out.[162]

With these regulations the government provided rational and fairly easy conditions for occupational pensions to operate. The actual pension provided hardly had to be greater than the State Reserve Scheme, and both contracting out and preservation conditions were straightforward and closely related to much of what was already common practice, so as not to upset it. Of course, the plan did imply a lot of administrative work for both pension managers and the government, but in total the plan would guarantee that whatever the maximum would be for occupational pension development in the market could be realized. State intervention, then, was oriented towards offering occupational pensions and providing conditions for their development with the state sector being limited to those for whom, for whatever reasons, it was not possible to be part of an occupational scheme, so that they could be part of at least a minimal earnings-related scheme.

There was one major change between the White Paper and its subsequent legislation. The biennial review of the basic pension scheme and related review of other national insurance benefits was to become an annual review. There were two related reasons for this change. First, inflation was so high during this period that old people fell very far behind everyone else. Second, and probably more important, was the protest activity of trade union and related anti-poverty groups against the low levels of pensions in the context of high and uncontrollable inflation.

In this period of rapid inflation wages increased as well. With the increase in wages, more money was raised for the national insurance fund. As well, the Tories shifted from increasing contributions from the flat rate pension contributions to increasing both the band on the earnings-related part as well as the percentage contribution. For example, in 1971 the ceiling on the band was raised from £30 to £42 and the percentage contribution on the band was raised from 3.25 per cent to 4.35 per cent.[163] This shift in contributions was supposed to finance most of the increase in pensions for that year.

In the period of the Heath government there were increases in many forms of direct political action on the issue of pensions. The TUC was involved in pressuring the Tory government and joined with other groups in demonstrations against the low level of pensions. The National Council of Labour (NCL) campaigned in March 1971 on behalf of retired workers. NCL demanded that the government double the amount of pensions for September 1971. A series of demonstrations and rallies were planned and carried out over the next few years.[164] Resolutions at the 1971 TUC annual meeting presented by Jack Jones demanded substantial increases in pension levels, an annual adjustment in pension levels linked to increases both in prices and in general standards of living. An amendment encouraged the use of industrial action to obtain these ends. This amendment, however, was defeated under pressure from the General Council.[165] This position is an example of the general caution of the trade union movement in pressing for welfare state reform. Traditional tactics that do not disrupt the day-to-day functioning of society, and demonstrations that can be orderly and controllable, and finally, parliamentary channels as the final basis of reform were the major strategies.

The TUC was critical of the Conservative party pension proposals. These criticisms reflected the general conservatism of the TUC on these matters. The General Council criticized the earnings-related contributions for flat rate benefits, arguing that this arrangement would destroy the link between an earnings-related contribution and an earnings-related benefit. They saw the earnings-related contributions as a social security tax.[166] Interestingly, they somehow assumed that any other form of contribution was not a tax. The traditional notion of contributory, work-tested benefits still prevailed in their ideology. They demanded increases in the exchequer contribution, as they had done in the past. Concern was raised about the indexing of occupational benefits, and how they only managed to move many workers to a point at which they would become ineligible for supplementary benefits.[167] They criticized the inequality for women in the plan, and recommended that occupational pensions should only be recognized if women were treated equally with men.[168] They wanted the level of benefits in the new plan at least to guarantee that the combined benefits from the basic and reserve scheme would be above the supplementary benefit level, and that the reserve scheme should be subject to an annual review.[169] Criticisms of occupational pensions focused on post-retirement increases, the calculation of the way in which benefits were based, and some of the conditions of preservation.[170] Many of the demands of the TUC were subsequently in the Castle scheme.

In summary, the Conservative pension plan raised several important points. The actual plan represented a substantial shift away from universalism. The market as the major way of pension provision was formally legislated. The state's role was limited to providing a minimal wage-related pension. Everything possible was done to increase the scope and potential growth of occupational pensions. Other traditional pension forms, particularly work-testing of benefits, were maintained. Two major shifts in this period were the movement of contributions from the flat rate to the earnings-related part of national insurance and the introduction of an annual review of pensions and other national insurance benefits. The pension reform was part of the change in Tory orientation to the welfare state and to the conditions of wage labour. In wage labour directly the Conservative strategy was initially to abandon incomes policy and to try to get wages restrained through the functioning of the labour market. In the context of high inflation and intensifying class conflict, this strategy failed and was dropped with a return to an incomes policy. The approach to the welfare state, and particularly pensions, was maintained. With the shift in pension strategy and rising inflation, increasing protests and campaigns mounted against the pension plan and for higher benefits, related to the general increasing militancy and class struggle of the period. Both the form of protest and the tactics used by the labour movement were kept within predictable channels such as lobbying and public rallies and protests. The call for the TUC to use its strongest weapon — the withdrawal of labour power — was defeated. The demands raised were for improvements but they implicitly accepted the general terrain and ground rules of the welfare state, particularly the links between contributions and benefits, and the system of occupational benefits. One consequence of the increased pressures and demands mounted by the TUC was that pensions were to play a central role in the Social Contract and the reforms brought in by Labour shortly after their election in 1974.

The Castle plan

Soon after their election, Labour, through the office of Barbara Castle, introduced a major reform of pensions which superseded the Conservative plan. As a reform it represented a compromise between the second Crossman and the Tory plan. Castle presented reforms which guaranteed a strong presence for occupational pensions for an indefinite period. Along with these concessions, the reforms were acceptable to the organized trade union leadership. The pension reform was an attempt at compromise and balance between state and market forms of provision, and succeeded in placating both labour and capital. The social policies of the newly elected government were influenced by the Social Contract. On their election, the Labour government's basic goal was to get workers back to work and re-establish conditions of exploitation. Part of the implicit bargain was that Labour would carry through on their promised reforms. One of the first and most important of these was an increase in pensions for those who were retired and a major redoing of the state pension plan. The reform, then, was mainly a response to the strength of the organized workers and the recent struggles of the working class, and was part of the conditions that the state provided in exchange for a return to work and, as well, an agreement of voluntary wage restraint on behalf of the trade unions. Further, during the Heath period, the organized Labour movement had campaigned for increases in pensions and for other improved conditions for retired workers and the elderly in general. Finally, in this period, as discussed earlier, there was a leftward shift of the ideology of the Labour party. One aspect of this was a commitment to redistribution of wealth and income, and a reassertion of the traditional Labour belief in universal provision of social benefits. Pensions, particularly after the Joseph plan, was an obvious area in which to act. Beside certain basic economic aspects of the actual plan itself, these conditions form the context and some of the pressures leading to the reform of pensions.

Many aspects of the Castle plan were part of the demands of the TUC. The principles proposed by the TUC were as follows: national insurance retirement pensions should provide an adequate retirement income sufficient to live on without other means; pension levels should be reviewed more frequently and these increases should be related to increases in average incomes and prices; pension levels in the future should be related to earnings, with a guaranteed minimum pension established. They pushed for better provision for widows, the chronically sick and disabled, with improved death grants. Equal treatment of women and recognition of the roles that women play in the home was another objective. In terms of occupational pensions, they pursued more simplified arrangements for contracting out of good occupational pensions, joint management of these pensions, and equality of women in them. The TUC pressed for what they called 'a proper distribution of the costs of pensions', implying shifting greater costs to employers and the exchequer, and finally, greater TUC participation in advising the government on national insurance matters.[171]

Although the government's proposals and subsequent legislation fell short of some of these principles, in many ways it embodied them. The TUC and Labour policy on this issue had come quite close during this period and the trade union leadership became part of the policy-making process. The moderation of policies, and the general broad consensus on social policy between Labour and the TUC is reflected not so much in the specifics but in their acceptance of the fundamental aspects of pensions, particularly the work-testing of benefits, the centrality of occupational pensions, and very limited redistribution.

The Castle plan was the third in a series of Labour pension reform packages and reflects the growing moderation of the party on social policy issues. The White Paper *Better Pensions*[172] begins by identifying some of the basic problems with both state and occupational pensions. The first problem was the large number of retired people forced to turn to supplementary benefits for at least part of their income, approximately 25 per cent of the eight million retired people. In addition, 60 per cent of all elderly widows were receiving these benefits and it was estimated that one million others who were eligible for supplementary benefits were still not receiving them. A second set of criticisms was directed at occupational pensions. Gaps in coverage for widows and the chronically ill were identified. The question of the difficulty in maintaining a pension upon changing jobs, the proportionately few manual to non-manual workers and men to women covered, and the lack of coverage for inflation were the main issues raised in the paper. Finally, the question of the impact of inflation for all retirement pensions was posed as a central issue. The government policy was not to legislate occupational pensions into line but to use state pensions as an example for the private sector.[173]

The basic approach to pensions, both private and state, varied little in fundamentals from what was already established. The orientation of the plan was to retain work-tested and earnings-related benefits. The major innovation was the insistence that all benefits, both state and occupational, would be protected by the state against inflation. Pensions would not be paid out in full until twenty years of contributions had been paid with interim partial pensions in proportion to contributions. Thus, even though the plan was not funded, a delay in full benefits was proposed and later passed. Clearly, this measure was introduced solely as a means of taxation, putting increased burdens on workers. Next, the formal equality of men and women was introduced. Again, the problem here is that the unequal position of women in the labour market and the fact that many women perform unwaged domestic labour leads to a fundamental inequality in pensions. Improvements were brought in for long-term sickness, invalidity, and widows' benefits, as well as improved death grants. Finally, the proposals foresaw more adequate tests for contracting out of occupational pension schemes.[174]

The specifics of the pension will now be presented. The final pension is based on two components, roughly equivalent to a basic and an earnings-related part. The major departure is that 'the value of earnings-related pension rights will be maintained during working life by revaluing past earnings in line with the growth in earnings generally'.[175] Thus, the pensioner would not be directly dependent on large-scale revaluation of pension increases at retirement, but his/her contribution will have been continually revalued. Further, on retirement, pensions would be revalued with increases in wages and prices. The actual pension formula divides pensions into two components. The basic pension is calculated on a basis of £1 pension for £1 of earnings up to basic level. This, then, formed the basic minimum pension for all fully paid-up contributors. The earnings component of the pension plan was to be calculated on an earnings band from the base and a ceiling equivalent to seven times that amount. The method of calculation is based on the following formula. For each year of contribution on this band, a contributor will receive $1\frac{1}{4}$ per cent of his/her average earnings. The maximum earnings-related pension is thus 25 per cent of these earnings, indexed to the equivalent in increased wages, after twenty years of contribution. The total pension is the total of the basic rate plus the earnings-related part. The pension totals were somewhat redistributive in so far as a lower paid worker could receive a higher proportion of final wages for a pension than a higher paid worker up to the ceiling.[176]

The contribution conditions followed along traditional lines. Contributions were to be earnings-related for all employees whose earnings fell within the earnings band. Those who earned less would be covered for industrial injuries and would be allowed − if they could afford it − to contribute on a voluntary basis to the pension fund. The total employee–employer contribution was to be $16\frac{1}{2}$ per cent of gross wages for those not contracted out. Of that, 10 per cent would be the employer's contribution and $6\frac{1}{2}$ per cent would be that of the employee. For those contracted out, the reduction in contributions would be between 6 per cent and 7 per cent of reckonable earnings. The employee's reduction would be 3 per cent and the employer's the balance. The Treasury Supplement to the national insurance fund would remain at 18 per cent of total contributions that would have been received if contracted out employees and employers had paid in their full amounts. Because the Treasury contribution was established in relation to total contributions, when contributions went up so did the Treasury contributions. The new plan, by increasing total contribution, would increase the amount of the Treasury contribution.[177]

A discussion of contributions as work-testing will not be repeated except for two points. First, Castle's defence of contributions shows how remarkably consistent the philosophy has been since 1911. She stated:

National Insurance has never been 'insurance' in the commercial sense of the word. None the less, there has been an enduring feeling in this country, particularly among the trade unions, that there is a kind of guarantee about a contributory scheme, a guarantee that would not obtain in the same way if the scheme were financed entirely out of taxation. It gives us some assurance that Governments will not use the lack of contributory principle as an excuse to economise in the important matters of pensions.[178]

Contributions, according to this argument, rest on the assumption that they protect future benefits. However, it is not future benefits that have been the issue for the elderly, but far more the level of benefits in the present and their relation to wages and the cost of living. This question has always been decided independently of contributions. Contributions have been raised in line with increases as a means of financing them, and not as a way of guaranteeing benefits.

Second, it might be argued that work-testing is only a formality, and that contribution conditions permit almost all workers to receive full national insurance benefits. This is far from the case. Large numbers have been excluded from pensions or some part of these benefits because they do not fulfil contribution requirements. This includes many women who are receiving supplementary benefits. They are excluded because many of them have not worked full-time or throughout their lives and, more important, because unwaged, domestic work has not counted as 'legitimate' work for pensions. Also, many others who do apply are turned away or receive lower benefits because they did not obtain adequate contribution levels. For pensions, the number of persons on a given day with a reduction of benefits because of an inadequate contribution record was as set out below.[179]

Date	No. of individuals
31 December 1970	404,000
31 December 1971	393,000
30 November 1972	403,000
30 November 1973	412,000
29 November 1974	439,999

With increasing levels of unemployment and the ongoing crisis, work-testing will have an ever increasing effect in denying pensions to many workers.

One of the more important aspects of Castle's pension reform was the establishment of the conditions of interaction between occupational and state pensions. The orientation of the plan was similar to that of the previous Labour plans which envisioned a partnership between state and occupational pensions. The conditions for contracting out of the earnings-related part of the state scheme — that is, the pension component above the base — were more demanding than those of the Joseph plan. The main reason for this is that the state plan, which formed the relevant mark of comparison, provided 'better' pensions so that an occupational pension in order to contract out had at least to match the level of the state scheme. The reduced contributions for

145

those contracting out still provided full coverage for the basic state pension short-term benefits – sickness and unemployment, invalidity pensions, and partial coverage for earnings-related widows' pensions.

There were several specific conditions for contracting out. First, pensions were to be based on the final salary of a worker or on the average salary revalued in relation to changes in the cost of living. Second, the pension must have an annual accrual rate of at least 1/80 of pensionable salary for every year in the scheme up to forty years. Third, a widow's pension must be available accruing at a rate of 1/160 of the spouse's pensionable salary. Fourth, increments in pensions had to be paid if retirement was deferred at a rate of $6\frac{1}{2}$ per cent per year. Fifth, on the question of early leavers from pension plans, the Castle scheme followed the Joseph arrangement which provided that pension rights of those over twenty-six years of age should be transferable to new employment or preserved until retirement, as long as that individual had completed five years of pensionable service. These rights cannot be renounced. The new plan required that preserved pension rights be revalued in line with the general increase in wages. The employer's obligation is up to a maximum of 8.5 per cent annually. The state pays the rest, and the employer is required to pay an additional amount to the state. If an employee had been in the occupational pension for less than five years, the employer is required to either buy the employee back into the state scheme through making up the reduced contributions paid or preserve the pension at the equivalent to the state pension. Finally, for those schemes either contracted in or out, women had to be treated equally. The decision for contracting out rested with the employer, and employees did not have the right *not* to join the scheme. An employer, upon deciding to contract out, must give at least three months' written notice to all employees and to trade unions, and the employer must consult the trade unions on these issues.[180] If the conditions are met, then an employer could contract out from the state scheme.

The specific interrelationship or partnership of state and occupational pensions was presented through the government accepting the responsibility of inflation proofing post-retirement benefits of occupational pensions. The state took on the responsibility of maintaining the purchasing power of occupational pensions up to a maximum level of what would be provided by the state scheme of someone with an equivalent contribution record. This last aspect of the pension scheme is of central importance. The pressures of inflation, coupled with relatively lower rates of return on occupational pensions, had begun to create a situation in which the occupational pension industry itself felt a squeeze.

A survey in the *Sunday Times* showed that the average rate of return on occupational pensions between 1970 and 1976 was 6 per cent per annum, while inflation had averaged around 14 per cent in that period.[181] Kincaid argues that between January 1974 and June 1975, the period during which the Castle plan was being prepared, inflation peaked at 37 per cent. Other related pressures on pensions were the dramatic decline of profitability in British industry, restrictions on dividends introduced in 1974, and the collapse in 1974 of the property boom in which pension funds had been heavily invested.[182] Some indication of the seriousness of the situation was expressed by a Conservative member of parliament who stated that the continuation of high inflation would mean 'the death knell of the private pension industry and that utter disaster will strike pension funds which will bankrupt themselves and their employers'.[183] The crisis was indeed serious and the government's options were to either press the occupational pension industry itself to inflation-proof their benefits, or to do it themselves. In essence, by admitting that the occupational pensions could not afford to provide benefits in line with increasing inflation demonstrates both the power and the limits of occupational pensions. Its power relates to the amount of investment capital, particularly during the crisis, and its limits relate to the problem of funded schemes getting adequate returns to meet future obligations. The failure of occupational pensions would have produced severe disruptions in investment and in retirement provision. Given the fact that the Labour government was not prepared to do battle with or to nationalize private pension interests, inflation-proofing them was the only option. The compromise was struck between state and private pensions, and this arrangement was widely accepted. The state would provide a pension accessible to many workers, inflation-proofed, and at the same time leave ample leeway for occupational pension development and bail them out at the point of their major weakness — inflation.

Other critical points that can be raised in relation to this proposal have been raised elsewhere in relation to other schemes. The most obvious is the fact that, in effect, contracting out provisions create two pension schemes. The bulk of the expenses for the state scheme will fall initially on the backs of those who are not contracted out, who tend to be those who receive lower wages, work in less stable sectors, and tend to be manual or women workers. Further, those contracting out receive additional benefits because their contributions, as well as those of their employers, count as a deduction against taxation. Thus, assuming an income tax rate of 35 per cent, it will cost £1.54 of gross income to make a £1 contribution to the state scheme, but only £1 to make the same contribution to an occupational pension. Further, occupational schemes themselves are protected against taxation. Kincaid estimates that this policy saves them approximately £2,000 million per year, compared to the £1,300 million exchequer contribution to the national insurance fund in 1976.[184] The various ways in which occupational pensions are protected from taxation reduce and eliminate any formal redistribution promised.

Finally, the very nature of the Castle plan furthers existing divisions between workers. Three basic groupings emerge: the first are those who are employed by a company with an occupational pension; the second are those who will be contracted into the state scheme and who, twenty years down the road, will expect to receive state, earnings-related pensions; the third consists of those men and women who work irregularly or women who provide unwaged domestic labour. This third group will tend to be dependent on a combination of small amounts from national insurance and supplementary benefits or supplementary benefits exclusively. Thus, basic divisions in the labour market will be reproduced in pension provision. Pension provision, then, becomes one way in which the working class is divided in our society and fundamental interests fragmented through the state. These divisions, however, cannot be analysed in static terms. As the crisis develops and unemployment increases, as well as rationalization and restructuring of industry, many workers in the first category may be pushed out of jobs with occupational pensions and many with long periods of unemployment will become more dependent on supplementary benefits at retirement age. The scheme presented here, then, must be understood in relation to these divisions and in the context of a labour market that is undergoing basic changes in the present crisis.

As mentioned earlier, the Castle scheme was an attempt at compromise on pension policy, and received wide support. The following quotation from *The Right Approach* illustrates the Conservatives' agreement:

> We have made it clear that we can accept the compromise reached last year. After years of chop and change, it is important to have a period of stability. Nevertheless, we reserve the right to improve the contracting-out arrangements so that the terms enable the pensions industry to operate as effectively as it can.[185]

The basic agreement was based on the crisis for pensions mentioned earlier and, with the previous attempts at reform, the occupational pension business had become destabilized with each new proposal. The Castle plan was acceptable because it promised adequate scope for private pensions without the consequences of having to guarantee pensions against unpredictable levels of inflation.

The Castle scheme was welcomed by representatives of the pension business. Mr Ronald Peet, chief executive of the Legal and General

Assurance Society said: 'I welcome the White Paper because it recognizes the value of good occupational schemes and shows a clear intention by the Government to establish a partnership between State and occupational schemes.'[186] He foresaw a period of pension stability and thought the contracting out arrangements were reasonably practical and would encourage the development of private pensions. Lord Byers, chairperson of the Company Pensions Information Centre, saw the Labour party proposals as recognizing the importance of private pensions and anticipated only technical problems, particularly with inflation arrangements.[187] After some modifications, which will be presented below, *The Times* thought the final bill 'attractive in many respects' but raised concern about some specifics of contracting out and the heavy Treasury commitment.[188] The TUC, not surprisingly, generally supported the pension plan.[189] The support from these sources indicate the degree to which the Castle plan was a compromise, an attempt to balance the positions of the Joseph and Crossman plans. Also, the high levels of inflation and the related instability for private pensions had changed their attitude towards 'partnership' that had led to some opposition to the Crossman scheme. In addition, although the Castle scheme was to improve the lot of the elderly, it was a plan for the future and, in the interim, was a form of taxation. The plan had an atmosphere of 'economic responsibility' about it, leaving it less vulnerable to attack. The plan for these reasons was politically skilful and could not be viewed by the financial community as irresponsible.

In its fairly quick passage, several modifications were made from the White Paper to the final Bill. Two of these changes came about in response to criticisms and pressures from the Conservatives and pension representatives. First, there was a $\frac{1}{2}$ per cent reduction in contribution for those in contracted out schemes.[190] This was more than was originally proposed and increased the financial burden on those not contracting out. Second, and perhaps more important, was a modification in how much liability an occupational pension plan would have to carry for those who were early leavers of that scheme. Under the initial proposals, the scheme would be responsible for keeping these partial pensions in line with inflation through indexing of the level of past contributions of those leaving. This was perceived by pension representatives as imposing too great a burden and risk, given the uncertain levels of inflation. The liability was modified from the indefinite level in the paper to a 5 per cent level per year with the state assuming the rest through final pension calculations. The third modification was on the upper tier or earnings-related component. The White Paper had proposed an earnings rule on this component but it was dropped to bring this part of the pension scheme into line with the practice of occupational pensions in which no earning rule exists.[191] These modifications, particularly the first two, helped make the legislation even more accept-able to the private sector.

The TUC was critical of the legislation, but the points raised did not alter their fundamental support. The major and most obvious criticism was that the legislation did not do anything for those already retired and those expecting to do so in the near future. This point was related to the continual demands of the TUC and the Labour party for in-creased pensions. This occurred particularly in the last few years of the Callaghan government in which pension increases did not grow as quickly as in 1974 and 1975. The TUC demanded as well with this that the base pension be raised from its very low level to half the average wages for a married couple.[192] Another critical point was the long maturity period of the scheme.[193] The TUC found the exchequer contribution of 18 per cent inadequate. Also, several points were raised in relation to occupational pensions. They expressed concern that contracting out arrangements result in an exceedingly heavy burden on the state scheme, and that the TUC and trade unions in general should be more formally involved in occupational pensions through the Occu-pational Pensions Board. The fundamental issues for the unions were the actual level of benefits and the failure of the Labour government to substantially increase benefits to those retired, and the very limited redistribution in this plan.

To summarize, the Castle plan represents a compromise between the Joseph and Crossman approaches. It provides a strong state pension with indexed earnings-related benefits and, at the same time, allows extensive scope for occupational pensions as well as underwriting the major instability of occupational pensions — inflation. In other respects, the Castle plan is fairly traditional, especially in relation to contribu-tions. The appearance of workers paying for their own pensions is maintained. Redistribution is limited because of the contracting out provision and the limited exchequer contribution. The position of women is made formally equal for state pensions but formal equality is not the same as real equality; it is limited because of the division of labour markets. The Castle plan does offer 'better pensions' than there had previously been, but in doing so the policies maintain the traditional forms of relations and the principle of work-testing.

The crisis of British class relations and accumulation had an import-ant effect on the development of this plan and the related changes in pension benefit increases during this period. The Social Contract formed the conditions under which the Labour party assumed office. Part of the Social Contract was increased pension levels. These were enacted quickly. After the crisis intensified and it was clear that limits were to be put on state spending, the rate of increase of pensions was reduced. Further, the way contributions were calculated was restruc-

tured to raise more funds for the state. The reform of the pension
scheme was promised in the Labour programme. Given the serious
crisis, how is it that a reform of this magnitude was brought in and
implemented in 1978? The scheme as implemented did a lot to help
capital out of its crisis, and did very little to upset the Labour government's strategy of attacking the living standard of the working class
through wage restraint. The proposed pension plan had a twenty-year
delay before full benefits were to be paid out, and the formula for the
benefits did not promise a life of affluence for retired workers. In the
meantime, the pension reform was in essence a tax reform, taking more
from workers with promise of future benefits. This increase in taxation,
through both the pension reform and ongoing pension policy, was in
the context of a tapering off of the class struggle, particularly between
1976 and 1978 before the 'Winter of Discontent' early in 1979. The
working class suffered a defeat in this period. This defeat, coupled with
increases in inflation, made increased contributions for national insurance more significant and, perhaps for the first time in the post-war
period, these contributions had an impact on workers by reducing their
standard of living. Thus, because the pension reform was based on
increases in contributions, the actual increases in state spending were
recovered and the national insurance fund continued to grow. Further,
the policy was certainly consistent with the general restructuring of
class relations. The other aspect of the reform was the interrelationship
of state and private occupational pensions. Clearly, the state's role here
was to establish stability and to buffer and protect occupational pensions against excessive obligations and the unpredictability resulting
from inflation. In total, although the Castle plan is a step 'forward' in
some ways from the Joseph plan in so far as it improved state pensions
in the long term, yet it is a traditional plan, a plan of compromise, and
like all aspects of the welfare state, has left workers and women sub-
ordinate and powerless.

Summary

This chapter has discussed three attempts at pension reform; the last
one, the Labour–Castle plan, finally succeeded, in so far as it was
implemented. The Castle plan will form the structure for an indefinite period. Even with the present attacks on the welfare state, the
Castle plan will most likely prevail because it allows the state to raise
large revenues with little payment of benefits at least until the end of
the 1990s, and it has temporarily solved the crisis of inflation and
private pensions. What will happen in 1990 is anyone's guess.

The actual plan remains close to previous efforts. The main change is that with wage-related benefits, theoretically those dependent on state pensions will be less poor in the future. As always, however, it is the government in power that defines pension levels so that even this improvement is not guaranteed. Otherwise, three central aspects of pensions remain. First, work-testing of benefits is central as both a way of taxing workers and defining future benefit levels. With wage-related benefits playing such an important role, a worker's long-term perform-ance in the labour market takes on even more importance. For those outside of the labour market either because of periods of unemploy-ment or redundancy, increasingly a shadow hanging over most workers, or because the labour performed is unwaged, poverty with retirement in later years is guaranteed. Further, with general attacks on wage levels the consequence for retirement income is obvious.

Second, because from now until 1990, and beyond, at least part of the retirement pension is determined by a basic, or flat rate component, the ghost of the principle of subsistence still remains to haunt many entering retirement. Even though some limited improvements have been made, the principle remains. Any gains have been made in relation to the first post-war poverty pensions defined by the Labour governments, and therefore, by definition remain inadequate. These low level benefits then have indirectly encouraged private pensions by guaranteeing that the state does not compete with private sector pensions.

Third, the Castle plan worked out a compromise, and a balance for private occupational pensions. It guaranteed a market for these pen-sions that had reached the maximum number of the working class that they could. As well, because of inflation-proofing of benefits by the state, private pensions have been guaranteed a long-term, relatively crisis-free existence. The principle, articulated in Beveridge, of allowing scope for the private sector has finally been maximized, with an in-tegration of private and state pensions. Further, a principle of universal-ism is undermined because for any higher wage worker it is more rational to be part of an occupational pension. The state plan is im-plicitly based on the principle of subsistence plus wage-related benefits, which guarantees low level benefits and therefore continues to encour-age contracting out for those with higher wages, thus reinforcing already existing divisions within the working class. In total, old principles have not changed. Pensions remain a form of domination based on wage labour and patriarchy with small possibilities of less poverty for some in 1990.

The process of pension reform discussed in this chapter has shown the close relation between general state strategy and particularly the response to crisis. The way in which class struggle influenced the formation of pensions was, in broad terms, by changing the broader conditions of accumulation and struggling against state attempts to attack the standard of living of the working class. It is these struggles that influenced state strategies, priorities; that limited, and shaped state efforts at reform. From Crossman's plan, restrained by the continual financial crisis to Joseph's attempt to return retirement pensions to the private market, to the Castle reform influenced by the Social Contract, each plan was part of a broader state response to restructure the social and class relations necessary to establish profitable accumulation. Although other factors such as pressures from trade unions, pension groups, and the distribution of private pensions influenced the final outcome of pension reform, without the link between broader relations of class struggle and state strategies for restructuring accumulation these forces give only a partial and limited and, by themselves, incorrect picture of pension reform.

5

Consequences and implications

Summary

This book has focused on the development of state retirement pensions
from the Second World War to the Castle reforms in 1975, implemented
through contracting out mechanisms and new contribution conditions
in 1978. Full earnings-related pensions will be payable in 1998. The
three major changes that occurred in this period have been the introduction of wage-related pensions, miserly in 1959 and less so in 1975;
the formal equality of women in state pensions, proposed with Crossman's plans but not passed until 1975; finally, the partnership of
private, occupational and state pensions which was consolidated with
the inflation-proofing agreements in 1975.

It has been argued that state pensions not only provide benefits to
those who have retired from work, but are a form of relations of
domination. These relations reflect the basic class and patriarchal
relations of contemporary capitalism. Further, the increasing technocratic and bureaucratic control of the daily lives of retired workers,
coupled with the way in which the state individualizes class relations,
isolates and increases the powerlessness of older workers and their
spouses to have any control over their lives and limits struggle against
the conditions of retirement imposed by the state. It is too simple
and inaccurate to argue that the welfare state embodies enhancing and
repressive tendencies that can be separated. It is argued here that these
tendencies are interwoven and are part of the domination experienced
in capitalist society. The development and reforms of state pensions
have been analysed in relation to the process of capital accumulation

and changing responses of the state to the struggles of workers and conditions of accumulation. State pension policy was linked to shifting orientations to the state. The methodology used here has demonstrated the connections between pension development and broader political, economic and social processes, and the limits imposed by the relations of capitalist society on their development and reform.

The elderly and the welfare state — consequences

One of the major consequences of state pension and supplementary benefit policies is the poverty and often related social and physical isolation of the elderly. A major transformation occurs with retirement; male and female workers become dependent on the state rather than wage labour for most of their basic needs. Two related changes occur, income falls significantly, and the ability to struggle against state-defined poverty decreases because of the social isolation imposed by retirement.

The question of poverty for older people begins with retirement. Even with low incomes in work, a worker and his/her spouse are better off financially than in retirement. For more and more workers in all capitalist nations there is a tendency towards earlier retirement.[1] This tendency began fairly early in the twentieth century and continued throughout the 1970s. In Britain, for example, of those males between the ages of 65 and 69, those *not* retired were 27 per cent in 1964, 16 per cent in 1971, and official predictions were for 7 per cent in the late 1970s.[2] There is a corresponding increase in those dependent on retirement pensions. Townsend's study reveals that 80 per cent of those of pensionable age were not employed and had not been employed during the preceding year. Eleven per cent of these depended on state retirement pensions exclusively for their income, and 16 per cent exclusively on state retirement, supplementary or other benefits. Two-thirds depended for more than half their incomes on state retirement pension and supplementary benefits. Of those who received some income from wage labour, 42 per cent had more than half of their income from state benefits.[3] For state pensions, at least as far as the basic pension is concerned, retirement from work is a prerequisite to receiving these benefits. Thus, increasingly, more and more of the elderly population are retiring from work and living on state-defined levels of benefits. As well, the number and proportion of elderly, and the length of time that they are living is increasing,[4] so that the way in which state pensions function is important to more and more people.

What can workers expect when they retire? As has been discussed, pensions have, in one way or another, reflected either wages in work or a subsistence minimum. The subsistence minimum was defined in miserly terms by Beveridge, and since then it has not increased substantially. From 1948 to 1976 rates of pensions as a percentage of average gross industrial earnings has fluctuated, from 18.8 per cent in 1948 to 19.9 per cent in 1976 for a single person and 30.4 per cent in 1948 to 31.7 per cent in 1976. Similar percentages exist for supplementary benefit levels.[5] If post-tax earnings are compared with these benefits, they are slightly higher in relation to the earnings of manual workers.[6] However, part of this apparent gain reflects high tax threshold levels faced by workers, reducing their take-home pay.[7] The point is that pension levels have increased only slightly, and as was discussed in Chapter 3, the base from which they increased was inadequate at best. Further, the earnings-related supplements introduced in 1961 have made little difference to the plight of the elderly.[8]

The low level of pensions has pushed many elderly into seeking additional assistance from means-tested supplementary benefits for part or all of their needs. Although these benefits are as high or higher than state retirement pensions because of housing and other allowances, they are means-tested, and therefore traditionally they have been lower in their uptake for retired workers. Although the proportion of those receiving national insurance plus supplementary benefits has fallen between 1968 and 1976 from 28.1 per cent to 22.0 per cent,[9] it still represents a sizeable proportion, and speaks of the inadequacies of national insurance benefits. Generally, the uptake of these benefits by older people has tended to increase, but still only 74 per cent of those eligible over pension age in 1976 took advantage of these benefits.[10] Clearly, the failure of state pensions has forced the kind of situation of means-testing that restricts benefits and therefore lowers the standard of living of many retired workers, and older women.

The consequence of the way in which pensions and supplementary benefits are defined is to create poverty among the elderly. This is generally true, but even more so for those in the working class, and for women performing unwaged domestic labour. Using state-defined levels of poverty – supplementary benefit levels – the results in Table 5.1 are presented in Townsend's recent study in 1979. The elderly comprise approximately one-sixth of the population, yet one-third of those in poverty by the state's definition were over retirement age.[11] Using Townsend's more realistic measurement of poverty, reflecting a relative approach, 54 per cent of the elderly fall below his deprivation standard, representing 4.4 million, and a further 37 per cent fall between 100 and 199 per cent of this standard.[12] Townsend's figures are the most recent and his measurement of deprivation perhaps most accurately reflects the hardship of the elderly in British society. For most, growing old means growing poor and, further, having most of

TABLE 5.1
Percentages and numbers of elderly in income units with incomes above and below state's standard of poverty

Net disposable income of income unit last year as % of supplementary benefit standard plus housing allowance	%	Estimated number in population (millions)
Under 100	20	1.7
100–39	44	3.7
140–99	17	1.4
200 +	19	1.6
Total	100	8.2

(Peter Townsend, *Poverty in the United Kingdom*, Harmondsworth, Penguin, 1979.)

their financial needs and the standard of living determined by the state.

The financial hardships are compounded by social isolation, and the deteriorating health that accompanies old age. For many workers, retirement from work deprives them of social contacts. For women, living longer than men usually means increasing difficulties. Because of the unequal relations in the labour market, many more older women rely on the lowest level of state benefits.[13] Thus the poorest of the poor are usually elderly women. The question of poverty among the elderly in Britain has been thoroughly documented since the first measurements of poverty; yet it persists, and there is little indication that it will change even with the 1975 Castle reforms, which promise a pension of 44 per cent of earnings for those with average earnings and a 3 per cent increase in total personal consumption for the elderly by 1998.[14] Given the levels of poverty that exist, and the fact that even 100 per cent of an average wage in Britain doesn't get a worker much more than basic needs, and with the present crisis, bringing with it unemployment and attacks on wages, the improvements promise little generosity.

The question remains, why is it that capitalism with its ability to produce tremendous wealth generates poverty alongside of it? This book has tried to answer part of this question by analysing the development of state retirement pensions. The failure of the welfare state to solve the problem of poverty among the aged is not simply an inadequate provision of resources or an anomaly, but much more in the nature of capitalism itself — its forms of domination and its social relations.

The post-Keynesian/Beveridge welfare state

This study ends with the passing of the 1975 Castle plan; however, it is important to comment at least briefly on more recent developments. In the period after 1960 the strategies of state implicit in the Keynesian/Beveridge mode of domination were gradually abandoned. This process was accelerated after 1976 and completed with Thatcher. The shift in the state represents a change in the form of class relations, and relations between women and the state. A new mode of domination is developing that can be broadly described as 'monetarist'.[15] It is not an anti-state approach, but as Gamble[16] points out, it is a different approach to the state, emphasizing a strong state and a free economy, implying less state intervention in some areas such as welfare state provision, and increased state activities in others such as police and other coercive forms. For example, the state response to the urban youth revolts of 1981 has emphasized repression and increasing the effectiveness of police action far more than using welfare state programmes to calm urban unrest. For workers, this has meant increasingly direct confrontations with the state around the conditions of wage labour and increasing attacks on living standards. As well, and deliberately under Thatcher, mounting unemployment has increased the reserve army of labour, and the competition for jobs between workers. The Tories have used the threat of job loss as a means of trying to discipline workers, trade unions and wage increases. Along with this, the welfare state has been used as a means of increasing the pressures of the reserve army of labour through the cutting of earnings-related unemployment benefits, and pressuring the unemployed actively to look for work even though none is available. In the welfare state, cutbacks of many services have been accelerated. The Conservatives have dropped any commitment to universal provision, and cutbacks have meant that people are forced to turn to either the market or unwaged domestic labour to compensate.[17] For example, in caring for the elderly, demands on the family, particularly women, will increase with cutbacks in state resources. It seems likely that options to state provision such as private health plans will be encouraged. What is more to the point is that the changes are continual, but a shift away from the policies of Keynes and Beveridge has been completed.

Accommodation with the trade unions and the working class has been abandoned, and government policies under Labour after 1975 and under the present Conservatives have attacked both the power of trade unions and working-class standards of living. Unemployment, rather than policies of full employment, has increased since the mid-1960s but dramatically, and as an anti-working-class weapon, under Thatcher. Finally, any commitment to an improved universal welfare state has been dropped, more dramatically with the Conservatives but the process was present under Labour. These major components of post-war policy have shifted, and although the final result is uncertain, the path for capital out of its present crisis will not be resolved by accommodation of the working class but at its expense, and probably with increasing conflict.

Even with the cutbacks and restructuring of the welfare state after the 1976 crisis, the Castle plan has remained intact and probably will do so until at least 1998. There are several reasons for this. Because full benefits will not be paid out for twenty years, during that period the reform is a tax scheme, one that will raise money for the state. What will happen after that is unclear. The government in each period has manipulated benefit rates by defining cost of living or indexing them by Treasury edict. Workers will probably receive a more substantial earnings-related pension after twenty years, assuming regular employment, but how much it will be and how it will change with either wages or prices will remain with the exchequer. Next, because any basic change in the structure of state pensions would alter the relationship with private pensions, and because the private pension business did well with the 1975 reforms and requires stability, any change in these arrangements would be troublesome, and disruptive to private pensions. Finally, it is unlikely but not impossible for the government in power to go against the tradition of contributions guaranteeing at least some earnings-related benefits, but with the cutting of earnings-related unemployment benefits who knows what can happen if the crisis continues unresolved.

The ways in which pension increases have been dealt with by both Labour and Conservatives since 1976 are important for the standard of living of the elderly. After the Social-Contract-related increases in pension benefits, Labour readjusted its method of calculation of pensions, reducing the value of national insurance pensions to those retired.[18] More recently, the Conservatives have cut the link between state pensions and wage increases, limiting pension increases to rises in prices only. Ironically, this shift occurred in a period in which prices were increasing faster than wages. As part of a Conservative strategy to shift taxation from income to other forms, such as VAT, national insurance contributions have been increased. For example, in Howe's economic package of November 1980, contributions were increased from $6\frac{3}{4}$ per cent to $7\frac{3}{4}$ per cent. Further, benefits were increased less than inflation by 1 per cent because of an overcalculation on the previous increase.[19] In the Cabinet discussion leading up to that economic package, Howe had proposed ending the link between pension increases and prices.[20] One other proposed change designed to save money is the gradual increasing of retirement age for women to 65 over several years.[21] It is ironic that women will be forced to labour five years longer in unequal, and usually the worst jobs in order to be equal in retirement age! Again, the changes involved here have not differed qualitatively from the way in which Labour had manipulated the balance between contributions and benefits and tried to restrain state expenditures, but in the context of high rates of inflation, increased VAT, and a decrease of those services used by old people, the life of retired workers and older men and women in Britain will be much harder with these changes.

Predicting the future of retirement pensions in Britain at this time of crisis is at best difficult. However, certain aspects are of particular importance. It is likely that with mounting demands on the national insurance fund because of a proportionately older population living longer, and with increasing unemployment, contribution conditions will play an important role. Because the relationship between benefits and contributions is non-existent in monetary terms, then the government will increase contributions to try to balance the increased demands on national insurance. The effect of this will be to attack the living standards of the working class. Along with attacks on wages and other tax increases, the result may provoke increased demands by workers for increased wages, thus intensifying class conflict. It is difficult to predict benefit levels, but with the current orientation of the Tories, increased standards of living of old people beyond the small increases in earnings-related benefits promised by the Castle plan are unlikely. There are limits to how much money can be raised by increasing the contributions of those working. This is the key to retirement pensions. If the crisis and low productivity continue, and the working class is able to defend its standard of living, then there is little prospect of increased retirement benefits and the old will remain poor. Further, the links between state and private retirement pensions will increase this dynamic and increase pressures on state funding as inflation-proofing agreements have to be paid off. With these pressures it is possible that the Castle plan will be abandoned after 1998 when full benefits have to be paid out, if the crisis is not resolved. On the bleak side, if the standard of living of workers falls as a way of resolving the crisis, then this will have severe consequences for the elderly whose benefits are so closely tied to wage labour.

Political implications and alternatives

In this period of cutbacks and restructuring of the welfare state, a discussion of the implications for political and social strategy is important. There are two interrelated questions. The first concerns the nature of the welfare state in capitalist societies, and how to defend against cutbacks if at all. The second is broader and poses the question of the nature of any future socialist society, and the related process of transformation. If the welfare state is understood as a relation of domination, and these relations are completely bound up with what the welfare state provides workers, then what are the implications for both of these questions.

From the perspective outlined here it is inadequate only to defend the state. Thus, in terms of defending the enhancing aspects of the welfare state, the position is impossible by itself. The benefits given out by the welfare state, because they are forms of relations of domination, cannot be separated from the repressive aspects. The consequence is that the expansion of the welfare state does not represent a simple improvement in the standard of living of workers, but a changing form of domination. As an aspect of social and class struggle, should the welfare state be ignored, and abandoned to be fought out between left social democrats, moderate social democrats, and conservatives? The other option is to struggle against the forms of relations of the state, and at the same time demand that social needs be met.[22] These two types of demands should be linked. Thus, in terms of pensions, it is not adequate simply to demand that the state increase pension benefits, but more important is the form of organization, and control by the working class in administering and controlling pensions, and further, a radical break with work-testing. In the previous chapters, it is striking how moderate the left has been in accepting the dominant terms of reference of the welfare state. Even in campaigns against the cuts, those who are committed to a position beyond left social democracy can use the occasion to pose basic questions of control, organization, and definition of welfare state activity. School and hospital closures can be struggled against not only with demands for re-opening but also for principles of worker/parent or worker/patient self-management. The struggles then pose new forms of organization and tactics such as occupations can put these into practice, albeit briefly. In this way, the struggles can become anti-state struggles aimed at gaining control of personal lives and redefining human needs. There is a danger involved, for those committed to socialist transformation, of confusing demands raised relating to standards of living and those that defend the post-war mode of domination implicit in the welfare state.

From the perspective argued here, it is inadequate for socialists only to raise demands for improved pension. Demands raised can be linked to the future society that socialists are struggling towards including principles of self-management, basic equality, collective ownership and control of productive property. For pensions, shorter term demands for increased benefits can be linked with a demand that the link between wage labour and benefits — work-testing — be abolished and that unwaged domestic labour constitute a precondition for pension eligibility. This implies a demand for guarantees for all for a decent standard

161

of living, irrespective of position in the labour market. This demand could be part of a left attack on the relations of the welfare state that embody wage labour and patriarchy. The working class should not be concerned about the balance of payments or whatever limit the ruling class puts up to them, but should fight for its needs. The stronger and the more militant the men and women of the working class, then the better the attacks against them can be resisted. The class nature of capitalism precludes any solution to the present crisis in the interest of workers, and only strength will win in the struggle.

The question of future socialist transformation poses the problem of power. The traditional left, social democratic, Euro-communist, and Leninist, accepts that at least some form of state is desirable or inevitable. Society is transformed from the top down either by parliamentary means or a revolutionary seizure of power. The end result must be an extension of domination of workers and women by the state. Is there any way that welfare state struggles can suggest another option? Two related questions can be asked — first, the process of revolutionary transformation, and second, future socialist society. If the state is rejected as the means to socialist revolution then organizations that prefigure a socialist society must be created as the option. There are limits, of course, to this, but as struggles emerge in capitalism, new forms of organization can develop from these struggles. Thus the principle of self-management in work and in welfare provision forms the basis of struggles against state forms, and becomes the principle for basic social transformation. It is here that the struggles about the welfare state can be linked to broader social struggles. They can raise ways of provision based on principles of local control and self-management, linked to other struggles for workers' councils in factories and neighbourhoods. Resistance against the forms of relation implicit in the welfare state can be linked to more general resistance and organization must be based on principles that can form the basis for a self-managed society. It is through these kinds of struggles that the possibilities of socialism from below can be built and in that sense the way the struggles about the welfare state are defined, and can lead to libertarian socialist options and not to new forms of state domination.

Given this position, how can workers control pensions? This is the central question — is there a form of organization that is anti-state and socialist in which workers would be able to control pensions, assuming a separation of those working and those retired from work. It is difficult to conceive of such a form within either western capitalist or so-called state socialist regimes, because in order to control things like pensions, workers must have control over the product and the process of their labour. Taxes are value, produced by workers, which is transferred through the state. For workers to control benefits in a collective way implies the control of both the process of labour and its products. It is only then that the resources can be appropriated that will allow distribution to retired workers based on the needs of older workers and their spouses without the forms of relations and limits imposed by patriarchy and capitalist class relations and accumulation.

In the present there are possible directions of action for pension reform that are prefigurative, and allow new forms of self-managed autonomous workers' organizations to develop. There are two approaches — one related to the workplace and one to community institutions. These are not exclusive and have larger implications than retirement pensions alone. Since in most places of work there are already occupational pension plans, then one orientation is for workers to take over and manage these plans and establish new ones. The money in the plans can be used as investment for projects such as the funding of production co-operatives, and workers' housing. Housing is of particular importance. Even if pension funds receive a lower rate of return than market value, workers could use these funds for self-managed housing co-operatives. Workers would benefit by cheaper housing before and during retirement. The goal, then, is not only the management of money by workers, but also the creation of autonomous working-class organizations, related to the workplace, that can control some of the product of their labour for collective needs.

This approach, based on workers controlling the products of their labour and using a portion of these for investment for retirement, is limited. One of the problems of retirement pensions or provision for those unable to work because of illness, unemployment or unwaged roles is precisely that they do not have any direct connection to the workplace. The question then becomes: what kind of organization is appropriate so that the relations implicit in a large bureaucratic state can be avoided? The organization of neighbourhood councils with co-operative banks is an option here. This can be a mechanism of redistribution in a socialist society. In these councils the wages of workers and social product can be distributed to the community on principles of need. Distribution at a local level can be effected, with forms of control and organization by men and women in their own neighbourhood. In the shorter term, the struggle for control of neighbourhoods and the establishment of locally controlled alternative institutions poses the question of funding. Clearly, the question involves demanding and fighting for money, raised by taxation, from the state without related strings. If these alternative services can be created then the basis for autonomous forms of social services becomes possible. Co-operative banks can be used as one aspect of this development, and can be involved in the establishment of pension funds to support those out of work and retired. Finally, links between workplace and neighbourhood organization are essential if these struggles are to overcome the fragmentation of class and to build longer-term solidarity. Alternative institutions can form the basis for redistribution of society's wealth in a post-revolutionary society and form some of the organization and strength necessary in the short term to build class strength, autonomy, and organization.

It can be argued that the two brief proposals are Utopian and idealistic, and do not pertain to the day-to-day struggles of the working class. The purpose here is not to present blueprints for a distant future in which all evils will be conquered. The argument is much more concrete. As the world stands, the options perceived by workers are capitalist society or various forms of Stalinist domination, both with their imperialist and repressive tendencies. The question for the left is whether or not concrete struggles against the increasingly menacing nature of capitalism can imply a vision of a society in which women and men of the working class can be liberated from both capital and the state. Concrete practice is a way forward, but practice that builds in the direction of greater control of one's life. The direction proposed here is that the struggles for control of production by workers at the factory level through organization of workers and neighbourhood councils is the first step in the process of transformation. Any activity that moves in this direction should be encouraged. One way is through the organization of worker-controlled pension funds which acts as a means to building a financial basis for increased worker autonomy. A second form of practice is the building of alternative community institutions such as co-operative banks which can be a democratic co-operative alternative that can both meet the daily needs of many workers and serve as an institution that can increase the autonomy of the working class in neighbourhoods. These two forms of organization provide a clear alternative to the options of capital and state or party and state, an alternative that can be part of socialist transformation. The welfare state, particularly pensions, must be part of this process and not ignored as a post-revolutionary question. The present attacks on the welfare state present an opportunity to pose clear options, as does the crisis of capitalist social relation. Responding with Beveridge-like solutions based on more state intervention is a social democratic option and should not be encouraged by those committed to socialist transformation. The link between concrete needs and prefigurative socialist forms needs to be made if a break from both orthodox Marxism and capitalist domination and their respective states can ever occur. This last section is an attempt to propose this alternative perspective.

Notes

1 The welfare state: a libertarian socialist critique

1 For discussions of the state that have influenced this perspective, see Simon
   Clarke, 'Marxism, Sociology and Poulantzas' Theory of the State', *Capital
   and Class*, No. 2, 1977; John Holloway and Sol Picciotto, 'Capital, Crisis, and
   the State', *Capital and Class*, No. 2, 1977; John Holloway and Sol Picciotto
   (eds) (1978), *State and Capital: A Marxist Debate*, London, Edward Arnold;
   Philip Corrigan (ed.) (1980), *Capitalism, State Formation and Marxist
   Theory*, London, Quartet; London Edinburgh Weekend Return Group,
   In and Against the State, London, Pluto, 1980. For a clear and useful
   application of these theories to the welfare state see Norman Ginsburg
   (1979), *Class, Capital and Social Policy*, London, Macmillan, chs 1 and 2.
2 There are many books that discuss a libertarian socialist perspective. Examples within a Marxist tradition include Paul Mattick, *Anti-Bolshevik
   Communism*, London, Merlin, 1978; D. A. Smart (ed.), *Pannekoek and
   Gorter's Marxism*, London, Pluto, 1978; and Michael Albert and Robin
   Hahnel, *Unorthodox Marxism*, Boston, South End Press, 1978. For an
   introduction to an anarchist perspective, see Daniel Guérin, *Anarchism*,
   London and New York, Monthly Review Press, 1970.
3 For a clear discussion of the differences between orthodox Marxist and
   libertarian perspectives, see Stephen Schecter, *The Politics of Urban Liberation*, Montreal, Black Rose, 1978, particularly ch. 3.
4 Ian Gough, *The Political Economy of the Welfare State*, London, Macmillan,
   1979, pp. 11–12.
5 Ibid., p. 153.
6 See *In and Against the State*, op. cit., for an elaboration of this critique.
7 See I. I. Rubin, *Essays on Marx's Theory of Value*, Detroit, Black and Red,
   1972.
8 Although the concepts of class and wage labour are different, and many who
   sell their labour power for a wage are clearly managers, the majority of those
   who sell labour power are subject to this form of domination and are

165

workers. There is an extensive, and often misleading, debate among Marxists on the concept of class starting from the point of view of position in a structure, for example Erik Olin Wright, *Class, Crisis and the State*, London, New Left Books, 1978. Here, a more general concept of class will be used and it will be assumed that most of those who are forced to turn to wage labour are workers. See Stanley Aronowitz, 'The Professional–Managerial Class or Middle Strata', in Pat Walker (ed.), *Between Capital and Labour*, Montreal, Black Rose, 1978.

9   See Philip Corrigan, Harvie Ramsay, and Derek Sayer, *Socialist Construction and Marxist Theory – Bolshevism and its Critique*, London, Macmillan, 1978, ch. 1, for a useful discussion of this issue.

10   See Stephen Yeo, 'State and Anti State: Reflections on Social Forms and Struggles from 1850' in Corrigan (ed.), op. cit., and Bentley Gilbert, *The Evolution of National Insurance in Great Britain – The Origins of the Welfare State*, London, Michael Joseph, 1966.

11   See Elizabeth Wilson, *Women and the Welfare State*, Tavistock, London, 1977, for a general discussion.

12   For a development of this argument see Holloway and Picciotto (1977), op. cit., p. 89.

13   See Yeo, op. cit., and Gilbert, op. cit.

14   For a discussion and explanation of the functions of the state in general see Ernest Mandel, *Late Capitalism*, Verso, London, 1978, ch. 15, and James O'Connor, *The Fiscal Crisis of the State*, St. Martin's Press, New York, 1973; for a left functionalist account of the welfare state, see Claus Offe, 'Advanced Capitalism and the Welfare State', *Politics and Society*, Summer 1972.

15   Gough, op. cit., pp. 45–6.

16   Ibid., p. 46.

17   See ibid., ch. 4.

18   See Holloway and Picciotto (1977), op. cit., p. 96, and J. Hirsch, 'The State Apparatus and Social Reproduction: Elements of a Theory of the Bourgeois State', in Holloway and Picciotto (1978), op. cit., p. 101.

19   Holloway and Picciotto (1977), op. cit., p. 95 and see Ben Fine and Laurence Harris, *Rereading Capital*, London, Macmillan, 1979, pp. 127–32, for a discussion of the issues.

20   Gough, op. cit., p. 51 and O'Connor, op. cit., ch. 4, for example.

21   This is based on Edinburgh CSE Group, 'The Crisis of the State and the Struggle Against Bourgeois Forms', mimeo, 1978, pp. 16–18.

22   Ibid., p. 16.

23   Ibid., p. 17.

24   Ginsburg, op. cit., p. 26.

25   See Gough, op. cit., ch. 4; Vic George and Paul Wilding, *Ideology and Social Welfare*, London, Routledge & Kegan Paul, 1976, ch. 1; John Saville, 'The Welfare State: An Historical Approach', *The New Reasoner*, Winter 1957/1958.

26   See Yeo, op. cit., and Ginsburg, op. cit., p. 7.

27   See Hirsch, op. cit., for a good discussion.

2   Beveridge and the post-war Labour government

1   See Ian Gough, *The Political Economy of the Welfare State*, London, Macmillan, 1979, pp. 69–74, for a summary, and Bob Jessop, 'The British State

Since 1945', Conference of Socialist Economists, State Apparatus Group, 1979, p. 9.

2 See London Edinburgh Weekend Return Group, *In and Against the State*, London, Pluto, 1980, pp. 65–70. This position is preferred because it focuses on the totality of relations between classes particularly the changes in broadly defined conditions of exploitation. As well, and perhaps more important, the post-war settlement implies that the Labour party and trade union leaders are the working class. Although a drop in class conflict took place, that does not imply that a settlement between classes actually occurred. The only possible settlement between classes will come with the abolition of class. Class struggle is from below and is not defined by the actions of class managers.

3 Ibid., p. 67.

4 See Jessop, op. cit., pp. 8–10; Henry Pelling, *Britain and the Second World War*, London, Collins Fontana, 1970, p. 317.

5 Henry Pelling, *A History of British Trade Unions*, 3rd edn, Harmondsworth, Penguin, 1976, pp. 214–19.

6 Quoted in Pelling (1970) op. cit., p. 317.

7 Ibid., pp. 16–17, 35, 113.

8 Paul Addison, *The Road to 1945 – British Politics and the Second World War*, London, Jonathan Cape, 1975, p. 131; and Arthur Marwick, *Britain in a Century of Total War – War, Peace and Social Change 1900–1967*, Harmondsworth, Penguin, 1968, p. 293.

9 Pelling (1976), op. cit., p. 222.

10 See Marwick, op. cit., p. 290; Pelling (1970), op. cit., p. 321; and Addison, op. cit., p. 130.

11 Pelling (1976), op. cit., pp. 219–22.

12 Marwick, op. cit., p. 290.

13 Ralph Miliband, *Parliamentary Socialism*, 2nd edn, London, Merlin, 1972, pp. 273–4.

14 Addison, op. cit., pp. 134–5.

15 Ibid., p. 162.

16 Ibid.

17 Cited in Marwick, op. cit., p. 298, and generally Richard M. Titmuss, 'War and Social Policy' in *Essays on the Welfare State*, London, George Allen & Unwin, 1958, pp. 75–87.

18 Marwick, op. cit., p. 298.

19 Ibid., p. 297.

20 Addison, op. cit., pp. 127–9.

21 Ibid., p. 116.

22 For a summary of the legislation, and White Papers, see ibid., p. 116; Marwick, op. cit., pp. 269–70; José Harris, *William Beveridge: A Biography*, Oxford, Clarendon Press, 1977, pp. 380–1, 438–9; R. C. Birch, *The Shaping of the Welfare State*, London, Longman, 1974, pp. 47–55; and Richard M. Titmuss, *Problems of Social Policy – A History of the Second World War*, Cabinet Office, ch. 25.

23 *Employment Policy*, Cmd 6527, London, HMSO, 1944, cited in J. Winternitz, *The Problem of Full Employment: A Marxist Analysis*, London, Laurence and Wishart, 1947, p. 19.

24 Ibid., pp. 19–20.

25 Addison, op. cit., pp. 170–1.

26 Eric Hobsbawm, *Industry and Empire*, Harmondsworth, Penguin, 1969, p. 245.

27 Ibid.
28 For a development of this theme, see Marwick, op. cit.
29 Cited in Addison, op. cit., pp. 185-6, and Marwick, op. cit., p. 305.
30 Miliband, op. cit., p. 275.
31 For a good discussion of the ideology of the coalition government, and the work of Keynes and Beveridge, see Vic George and Paul Wilding, *Ideology and Social Welfare*, London, Routledge & Kegan Paul, 1976, ch. 3, 'The Reluctant Collectivists', The importance of this perspective is the vision of a more humane capitalism with an active, interventionist state.
32 Addison, op. cit., pp. 168-9.
33 Harris, op. cit., pp. 379-83.
34 *Social Insurance and Allied Services*, Cmd 6404, London, HMSO, 1942, p. 6.
35 Ibid.
36 Ibid., pp. 7, 37, 120.
37 Ibid., p. 120.
38 Arthur Marwick, 'Labour Party and the Welfare State in Britain', *American Historical Review*, no. 73; and K. Jones, J.|Brown and J. Bradshaw (1978) *Issues in Social Policy*, London, Routledge & Kegan Paul, pp. 47-8.
39 *Social Insurance*, op. cit., p. 120.
40 Ibid., p. 121.
41 Ibid., p. 133.
42 For an elaboration of this argument, see Elizabeth Wilson, *Women and the Welfare State*, London, Tavistock, 1977, pp. 148-53.
43 Harris, op. cit., pp. 411-12.
44 *Social Insurance*, op. cit., p. 112.
45 Ibid., p. 171.
46 Ibid., p. 172.
47 *Social Insurance and Allied Services – Memoranda from Organizations*, Appendix G, Cmd 6405, London, HMSO, 1942, submission from Political and Economic Planning (PEP), p. 35.
48 Marwick (1967), op. cit., p. 398; Harris, op. cit., p. 424.
49 Quoted in Pauline Gregg, *The Welfare State – An Economic and Social History of Great Britain from 1945 to Present Day*, London, Harrap, 1967, p. 20.
50 Quoted in Aneurin Bevan (Celticus), *Why not Trust the Tories?*, London, Victor Gollancz, 1944, p. 33.
51 See Birch, op. cit., p. 52; Pelling (1970), op. cit., pp.|172-3; Marwick (1967), op. cit., pp. 398-9, and for a general discussion of the organized labour movement and family allowances, see Hilary Land, 'The Introduction of Family Allowances: An Act of Historic Justice', in Hall *et al*., op. cit., pp. 157-277.
52 Bevan, op. cit., p. 45.
53 Marwick (1968), op. cit., p. 312.
54 Harris, op. cit., p. 415.
55 See *Memoranda*, Cmd 6405, op. cit., pp. 16-17.
56 Ibid., p. 17.
57 Ibid., p. 6.
58 Addison, op. cit., p. 215; J. R. Hay, *The Development of the British Welfare State 1880-1975*, London, Edward Arnold, 1978, for a reprint of related documents, pp. 48-52, and Marwick (1968), op. cit., pp. 306-12.
59 Ibid., p. 310.
60 Ibid., p. 312; Addison, op. cit., p. 218.
61 Harris, op. cit., p. 240.

62 Addison, op. cit., pp. 220-3; Pelling (1970), op. cit., pp. 169-70; see Hay,
    op. cit., for a reprint of Churchill's response, pp. 77-8.
63 Addison, op. cit., p. 221.
64 Harris, op. cit., p. 425.
65 Addison, op. cit., pp. 227-8.
66 Ibid., p. 222; Marwick (1968), op. cit., p. 314.
67 *Social Insurance*, Part I, Cmd 6550, London, HMSO, September 1944.
68 Ibid., pp. 6-7.
69 Ibid.
70 Ibid., p. 5.
71 F. W. S. Craig, *British Election Manifestos 1918-1966*, London, Political
    Reference Publications, 1970, p. 91.
72 Ibid., p. 104.
73 Ibid.
74 Miliband, op. cit., p. 293.
75 Marwick (1968), op. cit., p. 332.
76 Miliband, op. cit., p. 287; and see Pelling (1976), op. cit., pp. 229-35,
    295-6.
77 Gregg, op. cit., pp. 38-9.
78 Marwick (1968), op. cit., pp. 262, 364; Alan Sked and Chris Cook, *Post War
    Britain – A Political History*, Harmondsworth, Penguin, 1979, pp 27-8.
79 Marwick (1968), op. cit., 334; Sked and Cook, op. cit., pp. 27-8; Gregg,
    op. cit., p. 39.
80 Sked and Cook, op. cit., p. 30; Marwick (1968), op. cit., pp. 334-5; for more
    detail, see J. C. R. Dow (1964), *The Management of the British Economy
    1945-1960*, Cambridge University Press, Part I.
81 Sked and Cook, op. cit., pp. 30-2; Marwick (1968), op. cit., pp. 335-7,
    and Dow, op. cit.
82 Sked and Cook, op. cit., pp. 34-5; Marwick (1968), op. cit., p. 341.
83 Sked and Cook, op. cit., pp. 36-7.
84 Miliband, op. cit., pp. 304-5; Sked and Cook, op. cit., pp. 37-9.
85 Dow, op. cit., pp. 45-6.
86 Gregg, op. cit., pp. 42-3; for a more\detailed discussion of some of the
    differences between Beveridge's recommendations, and the post-war legis-
    lation see Victor George, *Social Security: Beveridge and After*, London,
    Routledge & Kegan Paul, 1968.
87 For a general outline of the immediate post-war welfare state legislation,
    see Sked and Cook, op. cit., pp. 56-63; Marwick (1968), op. cit., pp. 347-50,
    Gregg, ibid., and George, op. cit., for social security.
88 Marwick (1968), op. cit., p. 308.
89 Ibid.
90 George, op. cit., ch. 2, for an elaboration.
91 J. C. Kincaid, *Poverty and Equality in Britain*, Harmondsworth, Penguin,
    1975, pp. 52-8.
92 See Peter Townsend, *Poverty in the United Kingdom*, Harmondsworth,
    Penguin, 1979, pp. 32-3, for the relationship of these measures of subsist-
    ence to the standard definitions of poverty.
93 Kincaid, op. cit., ch. 3.
94 George, op. cit., p. 34.
95 For a discussion of definitions of poverty, see Townsend, op. cit., ch. 2.
96 Kincaid, op. cit., p. 48.
97 G. D. Gilling-Smith, *The Complete Guide to Pensions and Superannuation*,
    Harmondsworth, Penguin, 1967, p. 21.

98   Dow, op. cit., p. 21.
99   George, op. cit., p. 209.
100 Ibid., p. 211, Table 57.
101 Kincaid, op. cit., p. 49.
102 Alan Peacock and Jack Wiseman, *The Growth of Public Expenditure in the United Kingdom*, Princeton University Press, 1961, pp. 176–77; see also Political and Economic Planning, 'The Cost of Social Services 1938–1952', *Planning* vol. XX, no. 354, 1953, pp. 1–12, 15 June.
103 Ibid.
104 George, op. cit., p. 62; DHSS, *Social Security Statistics 1976*, Table 44:02.
105 George, op. cit., p. 60.
106 Ibid.
107 Ibid., p. 224.
108 Ibid., p. 228, Table 65.
109 This summary is from Maurice Bruce, *The Coming of the Welfare State*, London, Batsford, 1961, pp. 250–4.

3 Pensions in prosperity

1   Arthur Marwick, *The Explosion of British Society 1914–1970*, London, Macmillan, 1971, p. 158; Hobsbawm, *Industry and Empire*, Harmondsworth, Penguin, 1968, pp. 262–3.
2   Ibid., p. 263.
3   M. C. Kennedy, 'The Economy as a Whole', in A. R. Prest and D. J. Coppock (eds), *The U.K. Economy: A Manual of Applied Economics*, London, Weidenfeld & Nicolson, 1976, p. 5.
4   Pauline Gregg, *The Welfare State: An Economic and Social History of Great Britain from 1945 to Present Day*, London, Harrap, p. 349.
5   Kennedy, op. cit., p. 38.
6   *Economic Progress Report*, Treasury Department, no. 112, October 1979.
7   Sidney Pollard, *The Development of the British Economy 1914–1967*, London, Edward Arnold, 1969, p. 442.
8   Gregg, op. cit., pp. 89–90.
9   Andrew Glyn and Bob Sutcliffe, *British Capitalism, Workers and the Profits Squeeze*, Harmondsworth, Penguin, 1972, pp. 41–3.
10   Hobsbawm, op. cit., pp. 258–9.
11   David Thompson, *England in the Twentieth Century (1914–1963)*, Harmondsworth, Penguin, 1965, p. 244; Alan Sked and Chris Cook, *Post-War Britain – A Political History*, Harmondsworth, Penguin, 1979, pp. 121–2.
12   Marwick, op. cit., p. 138.
13   A. J. Youngson, *Britain's Economic Growth 1920–1966*, London, George Allen & Unwin, 1967, pp. 177–8.
14   Pollard, op. cit., p. 473.
15   Ibid., p. 474.
16   Ibid.
17   Ibid., pp. 479–81.
18   Youngson, op. cit., p. 159.
19   Hobsbawm, op. cit., p. 267.
20   For example, see the election manifesto of the Conservative party of 1951 in F. W. S. Craig, *British Election Manifestos 1900–1974*, London, Macmillan, 1975, pp. 139–40, and Thompson, op. cit., p. 244.
21   Hobsbawm, op. cit., p. 283.

22 Marwick, op. cit., p. 139.
23 For a more detailed description, see Gregg, op. cit., 'The Affluent Society', ch. 16.
24 See manifestos of the Conservative party in this period in Craig, op. cit., and Thompson, op. cit., p. 247.
25 J. C. R. Dow, *The Management of the British Economy 1945–1960*, Cambridge University Press, 1964, pp. 342–3.
26 Youngson, op. cit., p. 247; Nicolas Davenport, *The Split Society*, London, Victor Gollancz, 1964, p. 54; Gregg, op. cit., pp. 88, 366; Marwick, op. cit., p. 138; Glyn and Sutcliffe, op. cit., p. 40.
27 Hobsbawm, op. cit., p. 284–5.
28 Cited in Henry Pelling, *A History of British Trade Unionism*, Harmondsworth, Penguin, 1976, p. 234.
29 Ibid., pp. 234–5.
30 Ibid., pp. 240–4.
31 Hobsbawm, op. cit., p. 267; Pelling, op. cit., p. 243.
32 Pelling, op. cit., pp. 243–4.
33 Ibid., pp. 257–9.
34 Ibid., Statistical Tables, pp. 295–6.
35 Ibid.
36 Andrew Gamble, *The Conservative Nation*, London, Routledge & Kegan Paul, 1974.
37 Ibid., p. 38.
38 See Craig, op. cit., pp. 140, 152 and 169.
39 Gamble, op. cit., p. 42.
40 Harold Macmillan, *The Middle Way*, London, Macmillan, 1938, p. 13.
41 Ibid., p. 15.
42 Gamble, op. cit., pp. 43–4; see also Nigel Harris, *Beliefs in Society: The Problem of Ideology*, Harmondsworth, Penguin, 1968, for a discussion of these beliefs under the concept of *étatisme*, pp. 109–10.
43 Macmillan, op. cit., p. 65.
44 Gamble, op. cit., pp. 62–3.
45 Ibid., p. 64; see also Macmillan, op. cit., pp. 37–8 for a discussion of this position.
46 Cited in Craig, op. cit., p. 86.
47 Ibid., p. 171.
48 Ibid., p. 195.
49 Ibid., pp. 146–7.
50 Ibid., p. 195.
51 Ibid., pp. 196–8.
52 Marwick, op. cit., pp. 134–5; Pollard, op. cit., p. 496; Gregg, op. cit., for a more detailed discussion.
53 See Pollard, op. cit., pp. 494–5; Youngson, op. cit., pp. 243–4; Marwick, op. cit., p. 136.
54 Pollard, op. cit., p. 498.
55 Ibid.,
56 Ibid., pp. 498–9; Sked and Cook, op. cit., pp. 210–11.
57 Youngson, op. cit., p. 242.
58 John Sleeman, *Resources for the Welfare State: An Economic Introduction*, London, Longmans, 1979, p. 47.
59 Ralph Miliband, *Parliamentary Socialism*, 2nd edn, London, Merlin, 1972, p. 318.
60 Cited in Craig, op. cit., p. 158.

61   Miliband, op. cit., p. 319.
62   Pelling, op. cit., p. 245.
63   Miliband, op. cit., p. 327; see also R. H. S. Crossman, *Planning for Freedom*, London, Hamish Hamilton, 1965, particularly the essay 'Towards a New Philosophy of Socialism' (1951) for an example of this unclear definition.
64   Pelling, op. cit., pp. 247–8.
65   Miliband, op. cit., p. 328.
66   Ibid., p. 331.
67   Ibid., p. 332.
68   C. A. R. Crosland, *The Future of Socialism*, London, Jonathan Cape, 1956.
69   Ibid., pp. 60–110.
70   See Fred Hirsh and Richard Fletcher (1977), *The CIA and the Labour Movement*, Nottingham, Spokesman Books, pp. 51–71.
71   Miliband, op. cit., pp. 333–4.
72   Ibid., pp. 344–6.
73   Craig, op. cit., p. 175; see also pp. 154–8.
74   Ibid., p. 204.
75   Ibid., pp. 205–7.
76   Ibid., p. 207
77   Ibid., p. 227.
78   *Social Security Statistics 1976*, DHSS, Table 44.02.
79   Ibid.
80   Ibid.
81   Seebohm B. Rowntree and G. R. Lavers, *Poverty and the Welfare State*, London, Longmans, 1951, p. 35; B. Abel-Smith and Peter Townsend, *The Poor and the Poorest*, London, Bell, 1965, relevant sections reprinted in A. B. Atkinson, *Wealth, Income and Inequality*, Harmondsworth, Penguin, 1973, pp. 353–72; see also Dorothy Cole with J. Utting, *The Economic Circumstances of Old People*, Welwyn, Codicote Press, 1962, particularly ch. 12.
82   See Victor George, *Social Security: Beveridge and After*, London, Routledge & Kegan Paul, 1968, p. 211 and ch. 8.
83   Ibid., p. 211.
84   Ibid., p. 228.
85   Ibid., pp. 214–15.
86   *Occupational Pension Schemes: A New Survey by the Government Actuary*, London, HMSO, 1966, p. 19.
87   Ibid., p. 7.
88   Ibid., p. 8.
89   Ibid., p. 10.
90   Michael Pilch and Victor Woods, *New Trends in Pensions*, London, Hutchinson, 1964, p. 75.
91   Ibid.
92   Ibid., p. 79.
93   *Occupational Pension Schemes*, op. cit., p. 13.
94   Ibid., p. 16.
95   For a discussion of taxation and occupational pensions, see G. D. Gilling-Smith, *The Complete Guide to Pensions and Superannuation*, Harmondsworth, Penguin, 1967.
96   National Insurance Act, 1946, Report by the Government Actuary on the First Quinquennial Review, House of Commons, 30 November 1954, pp. 5–6.

97   Ibid., p. 5.
98   Ibid., p. 6.
99   Ibid.
100   Ibid., p. 29.
101   Ibid., p. 30.
102   J. C. Kincaid, *Poverty and Equality in Britain*, Harmondsworth, Penguin, 1975, p. 31.
103   Samuel Brittan, *The Treasury Under the Tories*, Harmondsworth, Penguin, 1964, p. 256.
104   Ibid.
105   *Report of the Committee on the Economic and Financial Problems of the Provision of Old Age*, Cmd 9333, December 1954, p. 1.
106   Ibid., pp. 7–8, 11–13, 16–26.
107   Ibid., p. 31.
108   Ibid., pp. 31–3.
109   Ibid., p. 34.
110   Ibid., p. 36.
111   Ibid., p. 41.
112   Ibid., p. 44.
113   Ibid., p. 46.
114   Ibid., pp. 49–51. This recommendation on retirement age was the majority decision with two members of the committee dissenting.
115   Ibid., p. 57.
116   Ibid., p. 57.
117   Ibid., p. 81.
118   Ibid., pp. 11–13, 58–63.
119   *The Times*, 4 December 1954.
120   Enoch Powell, 'Providing for Old Age', *The Daily Telegraph*, 6 December 1954.
121   See, for example, Enoch Powell and Iain MacLeod, *The Social Services Needs and Means*, Conservative Political Centre, 1952.
122   Richard M. Titmuss, 'Pension Systems and Population Change' in *Essays on the Welfare State*, London, George Allen & Unwin, 1976, pp. 56–74.
123   Ibid., p. 65.
124   Ibid., p. 67.
125   Ibid., p. 68.
126   Craig, op. cit., p. 159.
127   Ibid.
128   The *Report of the Proceedings at the 86th Annual TUC*, 6 to 10 September 1954, pp. 139–43.
129   Ibid.
130   Ibid., p. 347.
131   The Labour party, *Report of the 53rd Annual Conference*, 27 September to 1 October 1954, p. 118.
132   Ibid., p. 114.
133   For example, see the speech by J. E. Goffen, p. 114.
134   *Report of the Proceedings at the 87th Annual TUC*, 5 September to 9 September 1955, pp. 154–5.
135   Ibid., pp. 367–8.
136   The Labour party, *Report of the 54th Annual Conference*, October 1955, see Resolution no. 38, p. 194.
137   Ibid., p. 195.
138   Ibid., p. 196.

139 Ibid., pp. 197–8.
140 Ibid., pp. 200–2.
141 Cited in Craig, op. cit., p. 205.
142 Ibid., p. 205.
143 *National Superannuation, Labour's Policy for Security in Old Age*, Labour Party, 1957.
144 Craig, op. cit., p. 224.
145 *National Superannuation*, op. cit., pp. 7–19, and pp. 60–4.
146 Ibid., pp. 72–3.
147 Ibid., pp. 55–60.
148 Kincaid, op. cit., pp. 117–20, for this point and a more general discussion.
149 *National Superannuation*, op. cit., pp. 54–5.
150 See Pilch and Wood, op. cit., for a general discussion of this issue. It should be noted that, according to Hugh Heclo, *Modern Social Politics in Britain and Sweden*, Yale University Press, 1974, the authors of the scheme originally opposed contracting out but had to compromise their position; p. 265.
151 *Report of the Proceedings of the 89th TUC*, 2–6 September 1957, pp. 138–9.
152 Ibid., p. 140.
153 Ibid., pp. 140–1.
154 Ibid., pp. 141–2.
155 Ibid., p. 142.
156 Ibid., p. 352.
157 Ibid., p. 353.
158 From the speech of Mr A. E. Sumbler, AEUW, ibid., p. 355.
159 Heclo, op. cit., p. 268.
160 The Labour Party, *Report of the 56th Annual Conference*, 30 September to 4 October 1957, Composite Motion no. 14, p. 109.
161 Ibid., Composite motion no. 15.
162 Ibid., p. 111, speech by Mr W. Burden.
163 Ibid., p. 115, speech by Mrs C. N. Scott.
164 Ibid., pp. 119–22.
165 Ibid., p. 121.
166 Ibid., p. 124.
167 Heclo, op. cit., p. 166.
168 Ibid., p. 267.
169 Ibid., p. 268.
170 Kincaid, op. cit., p. 123.
171 D. E. Butler and R. Rose, *The British General Election 1959* (1959), cited in Kincaid, op. cit.
172 *Guardian*, 22 September 1959, cited in Heclo, op. cit., p. 272.
173 *Provision for Old Age – The Future Development of the National Insurance Scheme*, Ministry of Pensions and National Insurance, October 1958, Cmd 538, London, HMSO, p. 13.
174 Ibid., pp. 5 and 11.
175 Ibid., pp. 6–7.
176 Ibid., p. 9.
177 Ibid., p. 9.
178 Ibid., p. 12.
179 Ibid., p. 16.
180 Ibid., pp. 14–17.
181 Ibid., p. 23.

182 *The Economist*, 18 October 1958, cited in *Hansard*, Parliamentary Debates, Commons, 1958-9, vol. 595, 10–21 November 1958.
183 *Provision for Old Age*, op. cit., p. 11.
184 Ibid., p. 16.
185 Ibid., p. 16.
186 *Hansard*, op. cit., 11 November 1958, p. 217.
187 Ibid., p. 221.
188 Ibid., pp. 233–4. For a more extensive Labour critique see Tony Lynes, *Pension Rights and Wrongs: A Critique of the Conservative Scheme*, Fabian Tract no. 348, London, Fabian Society, 1963.
189 Cited in *Hansard*, Parliamentary Debates, Commons 1958-9, vol. 598, 20–30 January 1959, pp. 888–9.
190 Kincaid, op. cit., p. 82.

4 Capitalism in crisis and pension reform

1 The theory of crisis used here draws on the work of Joachim Hirsch, 'The State Apparatus and Social Reproduction: Elements of a Theory of the Bourgeois State,' pp. 57–107 in *State and Capital: A Marxist Debate*, John Holloway and Sol Picciotto (eds), London, Edward Arnold, 1978; Ron Rothbart, 'The Limits of Mattick's Economics, Economic Law and Class Struggle', *Solidarity for Social Revolution*, no. 11, London, Jan.–Feb. 1980.
2 The CBI, *Economic Trends*, cited in *The Campaign Guide 1977*, The Conservative Party Research Department, p. 133; Department of Trade and Industry, 8 October 1976, cited in ibid., p. 144; and *Economic Progress Report*, Treasury no. 112, October 1979; OECD, *Economic Outlook*, no. 26, December 1979, p. 130; J. P. Cable, 'Industry and Commerce', p. 188 in *The U.K. Economy – A Manual of Applied Economics*, 6th edn, A. R. Prest and D. J. Coppock (eds), London, Weidenfeld and Nicolson, 1976; Andrew Glyn, *Key Economic Facts for Socialists*, Oxford, P & P, Oxford Militant Supporters, p. 3, Table 5, p. 4, Table 10, p. 5; R. Bacon and W. Eltis, *Britain's Economic Problem: Too Few Producers*, London, Macmillan, 1976, pp. 19, 161, 167; *The Economist*, 13 March 1976, p. 9, cited in 'The Recession: Capitalist Offensive and the Working Class', *Revolutionary Communist Papers*, no. 3, July 1978, p. 16; J. S. Metcalfe, 'Foreign Trade and the Balance of Payments', in Prest and Coppock, op. cit., p. 128; Nigel Harris, 'Deindustrialization', *International Socialism*, Series 2, no. 7, 1980, pp. 76, 77, 79; Department of Employment Gazette, cited in *The Campaign Guide 1977*, op. cit., p. 209; *A Study of UK Nationalized Industries*, appendix volume, NEDO, 1976, p. 47, cited in 'The Recession, Capitalist Offensive and the Working Class', op. cit., p. 17.
3 Glyn, op. cit., p. 7.
4 *Social Trends 1980*, p. 14, Fig. A.2. See also Bacon and Eltis, op. cit., pp. 164–5.
5 Harris, op. cit., p. 75; *Social Trends 1980*, p. 124, Table 5.7, p. 123, Table 5.4, p. 15, Fig. A.3, p. 16.
6 Ibid., p. 252, Table 12.17, p. 253, Table 12.19; Henry Pelling, *A History of British Trade Unionism*, Harmondsworth, Penguin, 1976, pp. 273–4.
7 Ibid., p. 274.
8 See Richard Hyman, 'British Trade Unionism in the 70's', in *Studies in Political Economy: A Socialist Review*, Spring 1979, pp. 93–112, for a general overview.

9   *Economic Trends Annual Supplement*, 1979 edn, p. 135; *National Income and Expenditures Blue Book* 1967–77, Table 1.1, cited in Tony Millwood, paper on State Expenditures, CSE state group, unpublished 1979.

10 Gough, op. cit., p. 77.

11 *Hansard*, vol. 910, 26 April to 7 May 1975/6, Written Answers, p. 479.

12 See John F. Sleeman, *Resources for the Welfare State– An Economic Introduction*, London, Longman, 1979, p. 67.

13 *Hansard*, vol. 910, op. cit.

14 Ralph Miliband, *Parliamentary Socialism*, 2nd edn, London, Merlin Press, 1972, p. 354.

15 Robert Rhodes James, *Ambitions and Realities: British Politics 1964–70*, London, Weidenfeld & Nicolson, 1972, p. 11.

16 See F. W. S. Craig, *British Election Manifestos 1900–1974*, London, Macmillan, 1975, pp. 256 and 258.

17 Quoted in Conservative Party Research Department, *Campaign Guide 1970*, p. 7.

18 Miliband, op. cit., p. 355.

19 Ibid., p. 357.

20 Ibid., p. 363.

21 This summary is based on Andrew Graham and Wilfred Beckerman, 'Introduction – Economic Performance and the Foreign Balance', in *The Labour Government's Economic Record 1964–1970*, by Wilfred Beckerman, London, Duckworth, 1972, pp. 13–21; See also Alan Sked and Chris Cook, *Post War Britain: A Political History*, Harmondsworth, Penguin, 1979, pp. 226–8.

22 See Pelling, op. cit., p. 262.

23 Sked and Cook, op. cit., p. 249.

24 Pelling, op. cit., p. 263.

25 Sked and Cook, op. cit., pp. 250–1.

26 Ibid., p. 252.

27 Graham and Beckerman, op. cit., p. 23.

28 Sked and Cook, op. cit., p. 256.

29 Pelling, op. cit., p. 266.

30 For an elaboration of these policies and their effect, see David Metcalf and Ray Richardson, 'Labour', in Prest and Coppock, op. cit., pp. 278–90.

31 See Pelling, op. cit., pp. 266–71.

32 Graham and Beckerman, op. cit., p. 24.

33 Andrew Gamble, *The Conservative Nation*, London, Routledge and Kegan Paul, 1976, pp. 89–101.

34 Ibid., for a description of this process, pp. 110–18 and 122–3.

35 Ibid., p. 123.

36 From Alfred Havinghurst, *Britain in Transition: The Twentieth Century*, University of Chicago Press, 1979, p. 547.

37 For a description and discussion, see Pelling, op. cit., pp. 276–7.

38 For descriptions of these events, see Havinghurst, op. cit., pp. 551–4; Pelling, op. cit., pp. 281–2; and Sked and Cook, op. cit., pp. 318–24.

39 Robbie Guttman, 'State Intervention and the Economic Crisis: The Labour Government's Economic Policy 1974–1975', *Kapitalistate*, 5–4, Summer 1976, pp. 231–9.

40 See Manifesto in Craig, op. cit., p. 373.

41 See ibid., pp. 376–7.

42 See Adamson, CBI leader, support of Labour cited in Sked and Cook, op. cit., p. 326.

43 Cited in Robert Taylor, 'Labour and the Social Contract', *Fabian Tract 458*, 1978, pp. 2-3.
44 Sked and Cook, op. cit., p. 334.
45 Guttman, op. cit., pp. 240-1.
46 Craig, op. cit., p. 398.
47 Guttman, op. cit., p. 241.
48 Ibid., p. 243.
49 Kevin McDonnell, 'Ideology, Crisis, and the Cuts', *Capital and Class*, no. 4, Spring 1978, p. 43.
50 Pelling, op. cit., p. 285.
51 Guttman, op. cit., pp. 244-6.
52 Ibid., pp. 247-8.
53 Ibid., p. 250.
54 McDonnell, op. cit., p. 43.
55 Guttman, op. cit., pp. 250-1.
56 Ibid., p. 252.
57 McDonnell, op. cit., p. 43.
58 Sked and Cook, op. cit., p. 344.
59 Sked and Cook, op. cit., pp. 357-9.
60 See McDonnell, op. cit., for an excellent general discussion of the cuts and restructuring in this period.
61 Gough, op. cit., p. 77.
62 See, for example, Arthur Seldon, 'Beveridge 20 Years Later', *New Society*, no. 20, 14 February 1963, p. 32.
63 Ibid., p. 32.
64 Brian Abel-Smith, 'Beveridge II – Another Viewpoint', *New Society*, no. 22, 28 February 1963, pp. 9-11.
65 Ibid., p. 11.
66 Douglas Houghton, *Paying for the Social Services*, Institute of Economic Affairs, Occasional Paper no. 16, 1967, pp. 17-23.
67 See R. H. S. Crossman, *Paying for the Social Services*, Fabian Tract 399, 1969, p. 1.
68 Many references can be listed that constitute part of the 'rediscovery of poverty'. Following are some: Brian Abel-Smith and Peter Townsend, *The Poor and the Poorest*, London, Bell, 1965; A. B. Atkinson, *Poverty in Britain and the Reform of Social Security*, Cambridge University Press, 1969, Ken Coates and Richard Silburn, *Poverty: The Forgotten Englishman*, Harmondsworth, Penguin, 1970; Dorothy Cole Wedderburn with J. Utting, *The Economic Circumstances of Old People*, Welwyn, Codicote Press, 1962; R. M. Titmuss, *Income Distribution and Social Change*, London, Allen & Unwin, 1962; Peter Townsend and Dorothy Wedderburn, *The Aged in the Welfare State*, London, Bell, 1965.
69 See Hilary Rose, 'Up Against the Welfare State: The Claimant Unions', *Socialist Register*, March, 1973; Norman Ginsburg, *Class, Capital and Social Policy*, London, Macmillan, 1979, pp. 104-7; Crescy Cannon, 'Welfare Rights and Wrongs', in *Radical Social Work*, Roy Bailey and Mike Brake (eds), New York, Pantheon, 1975, pp. 112-28, for discussions of claimant activity. See Ginsburg, op. cit., pp. 108-68; and Ron Bailey, *The Squatters*, Harmondsworth, Penguin, 1973, for discussion of housing struggles.
70 See *In and Against the State*, London Edinburgh Weekend Return Group, CSE, 1980, for an elaboration of this theme.
71 Cynthia Cockburn, *The Local State-Management of Cities and People*, London, Pluto Press, chs 3 and 4.

| 72   See Craig, op. cit., p. 263.
73   For a summary of the social security reforms during this period, see A. B. Atkinson, 'Inequality and Social Security', in *Labour and Inequality*, London, Fabian Society, 1972.
74   See Ginsburg, op. cit., pp. 71-2 and Victor George, *Social Security and Society*, London, Routledge & Kegan Paul, 1973, pp. 98-9.
75   Richard Crossman, *The Diaries of a Cabinet Minister: Volume One, Minister of Housing 1964-66*, London, Hamish Hamilton and Jonathan Cape, 1975, p. 361.
76   Ibid., pp. 410-11.
77   See Craig, op. cit., p. 336.
78   See a motion passed at Conservative Party Conference 1968. 86th Annual Conservative Party Conference, Blackpool, October 9-12, *Verbatim Report*, p. 84.
79   Motion passed at Conservative Party Conference 1969. 87th Annual Conservative Party Conference, Brighton, October 8-11, *Verbatim Report*, p. 52.
80   George, op. cit., pp. 67-9; J. C. Kincaid, *Poverty and Equality in Britain*, Harmondsworth, Penguin, 1975, pp. 109-10.
81   'Conservatives Keep Their Promises', *Notes on Current Politics*, Conservative Research Development, 14 June 1971, no. 12, p. 227.
82   *The Campaign Guide 1977*, op. cit., p. 429.
83   See Gough, op. cit., pp. 75-94; Sleeman, op. cit., pp. 45-8.
84   Quoted in Craig, op. cit., p. 402.
85   Ibid., p. 126.
86   For a more general discussion of this theme and a more detailed examination of specific programmes, see Conference of Socialist Economists, State Group, *Struggle Over the State*, London, CSE Books, 1979; and Gough, op. cit., pp. 136-41.
87   *Social Security Statistics 1977*, London, HMSO, p. 170; David Piachaud, 'Social Security', in *Labour and Equality: A Fabian Study of Labour in Power, 1974-79*, Nick Bosanquet and Peter Townsend (eds), London, Heinemann, 1980. For a detailed discussion of the relationship between unemployed and unemployment benefits and supplementary benefits, see Richard Disney (1980), 'Provision of Unemployment Insurance in Great Britain', in G. Creedy (ed.), *The Economics of Unemployment in Great Britain*, London, Butterworth, 1981.
88   Piachaud, op. cit., pp. 180-1.
89   See 'Social Security', in *Struggle over the State*, op. cit.
90   Social Assistance – A Review of the Supplementary Benefits Schemes in Great Britain, DHSS, July 1978.
91   *Occupational Pension Schemes 1975*, fifth survey of the Government Actuary, London, HMSO, 1978, p. 19.
92   See K. McKelvey Muir, A. E. G. Round, and T. G. Arthur, *Hosking's Pension Schemes and Retirement Benefits*, London, Sweet & Maxwell, 1977, p. 137, and Michael Pilch and Victor Wood, *Company Pension Schemes*, London, Gower Press, 1971, p. 59.
93   *Occupational Pension Schemes 1975*, 5th survey of the Government Actuary, London, HMSO, 1978, p. 19.
94   Ibid.
95   Ibid., p. 20
96   *Occupational Pension Schemes 1971*, fourth Survey of the Government Actuary, London, HMSO, 1974, Table 7.
97   *Occupational Pension Schemes 1975*, op. cit., p. 21.

98 Craig, op. cit., p. 265.
99 *Financial and Other Circumstances of Retirement Pensions*, Ministry of Pensions and National Insurance, London, HMSO, 1966, p. 1.
100 Ibid., pp. 35, 44–9.
101 A. B. Atkinson, *Poverty in Britain and the Reform of Social Security*, University of Cambridge, Department of Applied Economics, Occasional Papers 18, Cambridge University Press, 1969, p. 53.
102 Ibid., p. 54.
103 See *National Superannuation and Social Insurance – Proposals for Earnings-Related Social Security*, January 1969, Cmnd 3883, ch. 1, pp. 7–11.
104 See *Report of Proceedings* at the 92nd Annual TUC, 1960, especially the Report of the Social Insurance and Industrial Welfare Committee, p. 135.
105 *Report of the 95th Annual TUC* (1963), pp. 155–6.
106 See *Reports* of the Annual TUCs 1967, 1968, 1969, particularly Annual Reports of the Social Insurance and Industrial Welfare Committee.
107 *Social Security Statistics 1977*, DHSS, London, HMSO, Finance Table 44.02, p. 186.
108 For annual summaries of these policies, see TUC annual *Reports*, Social Insurance and Industrial Welfare Committees, op. cit.
109 Kincaid, op. cit., p. 118.
110 Ibid., p. 119.
111 Crossman, op. cit., p. 277.
112 Houghton, op. cit., p. 9.
113 *National Superannuation and Social Insurance*, Cmnd 3883, op. cit.
114 See Crossman, op. cit., p. 116 for a discussion of the political consequences of the first large pension increase after the government was elected.
115 *National Superannuation*, op. cit., pp. 7–11.
116 Ibid., p. 12.
117 Ibid.
118 R. H. S. Crossman, *The Diaries of a Cabinet Minister: Volume 3, Secretary of State for Social Services 1968–70*, London, Hamish Hamilton and Jonathan Cape, 1977, pp. 462–5; 481–2.
119 This critique is from Tony Lynes, *Labour's Pension Plan*, Fabian Tract 396, London, Fabian Society, 1969.
120 Crossman (1977), op. cit., p. 203.
121 Ibid., p. 137.
122 Ibid., p. 176.
123 Ibid., pp. 153–4.
124 Ibid., p. 314.
125 Ibid., pp. 616–43 *passim*.
126 *Report of the 102nd Annual TUC*, Brighton, 7–11 September 1970, p. 149.
127 Ibid., p. 251.
128 Ibid., p. 255.
129 Crossman (1977), op. cit., pp. 481–2.
130 Cited in Lynes, op. cit., p. 4.
131 *The Economist*, 1 February 1969, cited in Lynes, op. cit., p. 5.
132 *Guardian*, 29 January 1969, cited in Lynes, op. cit., p. 17.
133 See Crossman (1977), op. cit., p. 663.
134 Lynes, op. cit., p. 31.
135 Ibid.
136 Crossman (1977), op. cit., p. 399.

137   Ibid., p. 810.
138   See *The Campaign Guide 1970*, op. cit., pp. 427–9.
139   *Hansard*, 19 January 1970, cited in *The Campaign Guide 1970*, op. cit.,
       p. 427.
140   Ibid., p. 428.
141   Conservative Party Conference 1969, op. cit., p. 57.
142   See discussion in Kincaid, op. cit., pp. 111–21.
143   See Craig, op. cit., p. 330.
144   Ibid., p. 337.
145   Ibid., p. 338.
146   Ibid.
147   *Strategy for Pensions – The Future Development of State and Occu-
       pational Provision*, September 1971, Cmnd 4755, p. 4.
148   Ibid., p. 7.
149   Ibid., p. 6.
150   Ibid.
151   Ibid., p. 10.
152   Ibid., p. 12.
153   Ibid., pp. 12–14.
154   See Mike Reddin, 'National Insurance and Private Pensions', *Yearbook of
       Social Policy 1976*, London, Routledge & Kegan Paul, pp. 81–95 for this
       point and for a general discussion.
155   *Strategy for Pensions*, op. cit., p. 25.
156   Ibid., p. 15.
157   Ibid., p. 16.
158   Ibid., pp. 21–4.
159   Ibid., p. 17.
160   Ibid.
161   Ibid.
162   Ibid., p. 19.
163   National Insurance Act 1971, cited in Social Insurance and Industrial
       Welfare Report, *Report of the 103rd Annual TUC*, Blackpool, 6–10
       September 1971, p. 107.
164   Ibid., pp. 109–10, and *Report of the 104th Annual TUC*, Brighton, 4–8
       September 1972, p. 116; *Report of the 103rd Annual TUC*, op. cit.,
       p. 480.
165   Ibid., pp. 490–5.
166   Ibid., p. 115.
167   Ibid.
168   Ibid., p. 117.
169   Ibid., p. 116.
170   Ibid., p. 117.
171   *Report of the 107th Annual TUC*, Blackpool, 1–5 September 1975, pp.
       114–15.
172   *Better Pensions: Fully Protected Against Inflation*, Cmnd 5713, London,
       HMSO, 1974.
173   Ibid., pp. 1–2.
174   Ibid., p. 2.
175   Ibid., p. 5.
176   Ibid., p. 6.
177   Ibid., pp. 10–11.
178   *Hansard*, Parliamentary Debates, 1974–5, vol. 885, 28 January 1975, col.
       187.

179   Ibid., vol. 906, Written Answers, 23 February 1976, pp. 43–4.
180   See *Better Pensions*, op. cit., pp. 15–17.
181   John Bell, 'The Pension Crisis – Can they ever afford to let you retire?'
       Sunday Times, 23 March 1977.
182   Jim Kincaid, 'The Politics of Pensions', *New Society*, 16 February 1978,
       no. 802, pp. 369–70.
183   *Hansard*, 12 June 1975, cited in Kincaid, op. cit., p. 369.
184   Kincaid, op. cit., p. 370.
185   Quoted in *Campaign Guide 1977*, op. cit., p. 426.
186   Quoted in 'The White Paper on Pensions – Government Proposals for New
       Pension Schemes', *Post Magazine and Insurance Monitor*, vol. 135, pt. 39,
       26 September 1974, p. 2561.
187   Ibid.
188   *The Times*, 28 February 1975.
189   See *Report of the 107th Annual TUC*, op. cit., pp. 118–19.
190   Discussed in *The Times*, 28 February 1975, op. cit., and ibid., p. 119.
191   Ibid.
192   *Report of the 107th Annual TUC*, op. cit., p. 119; and *Report of the 76th
       Annual Conference of the Labour Party*, Brighton, 3–7 October 1977, pp.
       233–4; and *Report of the 77th Annual Conference of the Labour Party*,
       Blackpool, 2–6 October 1978, pp. 130 and 403.
193   See Harry Lucas, 'Pensions and the GMWU Role From Now On', *Pensions
       World*, July 1978, pp. 317–18.

5 Consequences and implications

1   Peter Townsend, *Poverty in the United Kingdom*, Penguin, Harmonds-
     worth, 1979, pp. 654–5.
2   Ibid., pp. 655–6.
3   Ibid., p. 789.
4   See *Social Trends 10*, 1980 edn, London, Central Statistical Office, Table
     1.2, p. 64 and 3.9 p. 98.
5   Townsend, op. cit., p. 789.
6   *Social Security Statistics, 1978*, DHSS, London, HMSO, p. 193.
7   Townsend, op. cit., p. 790.
8   Ibid., p. 789.
9   *Social Security Statistics 1978*, op. cit., p. 170.
10   Ibid., p. 138.
11   Townsend, op. cit., p. 788.
12   Ibid., p. 1061.
13   Ibid., p. 798 and Tables 23.8, 23.9.
14   David Piachaud, 'Social Security', in *Labour and Equality: A Fabian Study
     of Labour in Power 1974–79* edited by Nick Bosanquet and Peter Town-
     send (1980), editors, London, Heinemann.
15   See London Edinburgh Weekend Return Group, *In and Against the State*,
     London, Pluto, 1980, Postscript Section 2.
16   See Andrew Gamble, 'The Free Economy and the Strong State', in *The
     Socialist Register 1979*, Ralph Miliband and John Saville (eds), pp. 1–25.
17   London Edinburgh Weekend Return Group, op. cit., pp. 124–5.
18   See David Piachaud, 'Social Security', in *Labour and Equality: A Fabian
     Study of Labour in Power, 1974–1979*, Nick Bosanquet and Peter Town-
     send (eds), London, Heinemann, 1980, p. 173.

19   *Manchester Guardian Weekly*, vol. 123, no. 23, week ending 30 November 1980, p. 1.
20   Ibid., vol. 123, no. 22, week ending 23 November 1980, p. 3.
21   *Guardian*, 6 October 1979.
22   London Edinburgh Weekend Return Group, op. cit., ch. 6.

Bibliography

Books and articles

Abel-Smith, Brian, 'Beveridge II – Another Viewpoint', *New Society*, no. 22, 28 February 1963.

Abel-Smith, Brian, and Townsend, Peter, *The Poor and the Poorest*, London, Bell, 1965.

Addison, Paul, *The Road to 1945 – British Politics and the Second World War*, London, Jonathan Cape, 1975.

Albert, Michael, and Hahnel, Robin, *Unorthodox Marxism*, Boston, South End Press, 1978.

Aronowitz, 'The Professional–Managerial Class or Middle Strata', in Pat Walker (ed.), *Between Capital and Labour*, Montreal, Black Rose Books, 1978.

Atkinson, A. B., *Poverty in Britain and the Reform of Social Security*, Cambridge University Press, 1969.

Atkinson, A. B., 'Inequality and Social Security', in Peter Townsend and Nicolas Bosanquet (eds), *Labour and Inequality*, London, Fabian Society, 1972.

Atkinson, A. B., *Wealth, Income and Inequality*, Harmondsworth, Penguin, 1973.

Bacon, R., and Eltis, W., *Britain's Economic Problem: Too Few Producers*, London, Macmillan, 1976.

Bailey, Ron, *The Squatters*, Harmondsworth, Penguin, 1973.

Bell, John, 'The Pension Crisis – Can they ever afford to let you retire?, *The Sunday Times*, 23 March 1977.

Bevan, Aneurin, (Celticus), *Why Not Trust the Tories?*, London, Victor Gollancz, 1944.

Birch, R. C., *The Shaping of the Welfare State*, London, Longman.

Braverman, Harry, *Labour and Monopoly Capital – The Degradation of Work in the Twentieth Century*, New York, Monthly Review Press, 1974.

Brittan, Samuel, *The Treasury Under the Tories*, Harmondsworth, Penguin, 1964.

Bruce, Maurice, *The Coming of the Welfare State*, London, Batsford, 1961.

Cannon, Crescy, 'Welfare Rights and Wrongs', in Roy Bailey and Mike Brake (eds), *Radical Social Work*, New York, Pantheon, 1975.

183

Bibliography

Castles, Stephen, and Kosack, Godula, *Immigrant Workers and Class Structure in Western Europe*, Oxford University Press, 1973.

Castells, Manuel, 'Immigrant Workers and Class Struggle in Advanced Capitalism: The Western European Experience', *Politics and Society*, vol. 5, no. 1, 1975.

Clarke, Simon, 'Marxism, Sociology and Poulantzas' Theory of the State', *Capital and Class*, vol. 2, 1977.

Coates, Ken, and Silburn, Richard, *Poverty: The Forgotten Englishman*, Harmondsworth, Penguin, 1970.

Cockburn, Cynthia, *The Local State – Management of Cities and People*, London, Pluto, 1977.

Cole, Dorothy, with Utting, J., *The Economic Circumstances of Old People*, Welwyn, Codicote Press, 1962.

Conference of Socialist Economists, State Group, *Struggle Over the State*, London, Conference of Socialist Economists Books, 1979.

Conservative Party Research Department, *The Campaign Guide 1970*.

Conservative Party Research Department, *The Campaign Guide 1977*.

Corrigan, Philip, Ramsay, Harvie, and Sayer, Derek, *Socialist Construction and Marxist Theory – Bolshevism and its Critique*, London, Macmillan, 1978.

Corrigan, Philip (ed.), *Capitalism, State Formation and Marxist Theory*, London, Quartet, 1980.

Craig, F. W. S., *British Election Manifestos 1918-1966*, London, Political Reference Publications, 1970.

Craig, F. W. S., *British Election Manifestos 1900-1974*, London, Macmillan, 1975.

Crosland, C. A. R., *The Future of Socialism*, London, Jonathan Cape, 1956.

Crossman, R. H. S., *Planning for Freedom*, London, Hamish Hamilton, 1965.

Crossman, R. H. S., *Paying for the Social Services*, Fabian Tract 399, London, Fabian Society, 1969.

Crossman, R. H. S., *The Diaries of a Cabinet Minister: Volume One, Minister of Housing 1964-1966*, London, Hamish Hamilton and Jonathan Cape, 1975.

Crossman, R. H. S., *The Diaries of a Cabinet Minister: Volume Three, Secretary of State for Social Services 1968-1970*, London, Hamish Hamilton and Jonathan Cape, 1977.

Davenport, Nicolas, *The Split Society*, London, Victor Gollancz, 1964.

Disney, Richard (1980), 'Provision of Unemployment Insurance in Great Britain', in G. Creedy (ed.), *The Economics of Unemployment in Great Britain*, London, Butterworth, 1981.

Dow, J. C. R., *The Management of the British Economy 1945-1960*, Cambridge University Press, 1964.

Edinburgh CSE Group, 'The Crisis of the State and the Struggle Against Bourgeois Form', mimeo, 1978.

Fine, Ben, and Harris, Laurence, *Rereading Capital*, London, Macmillan, 1979.

Freyssenet, Michel, *La Division Capitaliste du Travail*, Paris, Savelli, 1977.

Gamble, Andrew, *The Conservative Nation*, London, Routledge & Kegan Paul, 1974.

Gamble, Andrew, 'The Free Economy and the Strong State', in Ralph Miliband and John Saville (eds), *The Socialist Register 1979*, London, Merlin, 1979.

George, Victor, *Social Security: Beveridge and After*, London, Routledge & Kegan Paul, 1968.

George, Victor, *Social Security and Society*, London, Routledge & Kegan Paul, 1973.

George, Victor, and Wilding, Paul, *Ideology and Social Welfare*, London, Routledge & Kegan Paul, 1976.

Gilbert, Bentley B., *The Evolution of National Insurance in Great Britain – The Origins of the Welfare State*, London, Michael Joseph, 1966.

Gilbert, Bentley B., *British Social Policy 1914–1939*, London, Batsford, 1974.

Gilling-Smith, G. P., *The Complete Guide to Pensions and Superannuation*, Harmondsworth, Penguin, 1967.

Ginsburg, Norman, *Class, Capital and Social Policy*, London, Macmillan, 1979.

Glyn, Andrew, *Key Economic Facts for Socialists*, Oxford, P & P Oxford Militant Supporters, 1979.

Glyn, Andrew, and Sutliffe, Bob, *British Capitalism, Workers and the Profit Squeeze*, Harmondsworth, Penguin, 1972.

Gough, Ian, *The Political Economy of the Welfare State*, London, Macmillan, 1979.

Graham, Andrew, and Beckerman, Wilfred, 'Introduction – Economic Performance and the Foreign Balance', in Wilfred Beckerman (ed.), *The Labour Government's Economic Record 1964–1970*, London, Duckworth, 1972.

Gregg, Pauline, *The Welfare State – An Economic and Social History of Great Britain from 1945 to Present Day*, London, Harrap, 1967.

Guérin, Daniel, *Anarchism*, London and New York, Monthly Review Press, 1970.

Guttman, Robbie, 'State Intervention and the Economic Crisis: The Labour Government's Economic Policy 1974–1975', *Kapitalistate*, 4–5, Summer 1976.

Harris, José, *William Beveridge: A Biography*, Oxford, Clarendon Press, 1977.

Harris, Nigel, *Beliefs in Society: The Problem of Ideology*, Harmondsworth, Penguin, 1968.

Harris, Nigel, 'Deindustrialization', *International Socialism*, Series 2, no. 7, 1980.

Havinghurst, Alfred, *Britain in Transition – The Twentieth Century*, Chicago University Press, 1979.

Hay, J. R. (ed.), *The Development of the British Welfare State 1880–1975*, London, Edward Arnold, 1978.

Heclo, Hugh, *Modern Social Politics in Britain and Sweden*, New Haven, Yale University Press, 1974.

Hemple, Bob, *Race, Jobs and the Law in Britain*, 2nd edn, Harmondsworth, Penguin, 1970.

Hirsch, Joachim, 'The State Apparatus and Social Reproduction: Elements of a Theory of the Bourgeois State', in John Holloway and Sol Picciotto (eds), *State and Capital: A Marxist Debate*, London, Edward Arnold, 1978.

Hirsh, Fred, and Fletcher, Richard, *The CIA and the Labour Movement*, Nottingham, Spokesman Books, 1977.

Hobsbawm, Eric, *Industry and Empire*, Harmondsworth, Penguin, 1969.

Holloway, John, and Picciotto, Sol, 'Capital Crisis and the State', in *Capital and Class*, no. 2, 1977.

Holloway, John, and Picciotto, Sol (eds), *State and Capital: A Marxist Debate*, London, Edward Arnold, 1978.

Houghton, Douglas, *Paying for the Social Services*, Institute of Economic Affairs, Occasional Paper no. 16, 1967.

Hyman, Richard, 'British Trade Unionism in the 70's', in *Studies in Political Economy: A Socialist Review*, no. 1, Spring 1979.

James, Robert Rhodes, *Ambitions and Realities: British Politics 1964–1970*, London, Weidenfeld & Nicolson, 1972.

Jessop, Bob, 'The British State Since 1945', Conference of Socialist Economists, State Apparatus Group, mimeo, 1979.

Jones, Kathleen, Brown, John, and Bradshaw, Jonathan, *Issues in Social Policy*, London, Routledge & Kegan Paul, 1978.

Kennedy, M. C., 'The Economy as a Whole', in A. R. Prest and D. J. Coppock (eds), *The U.K. Economy: A Manual of Applied Economics*, 6th edn, London,

Weidenfeld & Nicolson, 1976.

Kincaid, J. C., *Poverty and Equality in Britain*, revised edn, Harmondsworth, Penguin, 1975.

Kincaid, Jim, 'The Politics of Pensions', *New Society*, no. 802, 1978.

Lucas, Harry, 'Pensions and the GMWU Role from Now On', *Pensions World*, July 1978.

Lynes, Tony, *Pension Rights and Wrongs: A Critique of the Conservative Scheme*, Fabian Tract no. 348, London, Fabian Society, 1963.

Lynes, Tony, *Labour's Pension Plan*, Fabian Tract 396, London, Fabian Society, 1969.

London Edinburgh Weekend Return Group, *In and Against the State*, revised edn, London, Pluto, 1980.

McDonnell, Kevin, 'Ideology, Crisis, and the Cuts', *Capital and Class*, no. 4, 1978.

Macmillan, Harold, *The Middle Way*, London, Macmillan, 1938.

Mandel, Ernest, *Late Capitalism*, London, Verso Edition, New Left Books, 1978.

Marwick, Arthur, 'Labour Party and Welfare State in Britain', *American Historical Review*, no. 73, 1967.

Marwick, Arthur, *Britain in a Century of Total War – War, Peace and Social Change 1900-1967*, Harmondsworth, Penguin, 1968.

Marwick, Arthur, *The Explosion of British Society 1914-1970*, London, Macmillan, 1971.

Mattick, Paul, *Anti-Bolshevik Communism*, London, Merlin, 1978.

Mattick, Paul, *Economics, Politics and the Age of Inflation*, London, Merlin, 1980.

Metcalf, David, and Richardson, Ray, 'Labour', in A. R. Prest and D. J. Coppock (eds), *The U.K. Economy: A Manual of Applied Economics*, 6th edn, London, Weidenfeld & Nicolson, 1976.

Metcalfe, J. S., 'Foreign Trade and the Balance of Payments', in Prest and Coppock (eds), as above.

Miliband, Ralph, *Parliamentary Socialism*, London, Merlin, 1972.

Muir, K. McKelvey, Round, A. E. G., and Arthur, T. G., *Hosking's Pension Schemes and Retirement Benefits*, London, Sweet & Maxwell, 1977.

O'Connor, James, *The Fiscal Crisis of the State*, New York, St. Martin's Press, 1973.

Offe, Claus, 'Advanced Capitalism and the Welfare State', *Politics and Society*, Summer 1972.

Peacock, A., *The Economics of National Insurance*, Glasgow, William Hodge & Co. Ltd.

Peacock, A., and Wiseman, J., *The Growth of Public Expenditure in the United Kingdom*, Princeton University Press, 1961.

Pelling, Henry, *Britain and the Second World War*, London, Collins/Fontana, 1970.

Pelling, Henry, *A History of British Trade Unions*, 3rd edn, Harmondsworth, Penguin, 1976.

Piachaud, David, 'Social Security', in Nick Bosanquet and Peter Townsend (eds), *Labour and Equality: A Fabian Study of Labour in Power 1974-1979*, London, Heinemann, 1980.

Pilch, Michael, and Woods, Victor, *Pension Schemes*, London, Hutchinson, 1960.

Pilch, Michael, and Woods, Victor, *New Trends in Pensions*, London, Hutchinson, 1964.

Pilch, Michael, and Woods, Victor, *Company Pension Schemes*, London, Gower Press, 1971.

Political and Economic Planning, 'The Cost of Social Services 1938-1952',

Planning, vol. XX, no. 354, 15 June 1953.

Pollard, Sidney, *The Development of the British Economy 1914-1967*, 2nd edn, London, Edward Arnold, 1969.

Powell, Enoch, and MacLeod, Iain, *The Social Services Needs and Means*, Conservative Political Centre, 1952.

Powell, Enoch, 'Providing for Old Age', *Daily Telegraph*, 6 December 1954.

Reddin, Mike, 'National Insurance and Private Pensions', *Yearbook of Social Policy 1976*, London, Routledge & Kegan Paul, 1976.

Reid, G. L., and Robertson, D. J., *Fringe Benefits, Labour Costs, and Social Security*, London, George Allen & Unwin, 1965.

Revolutionary Communist Tendency, 'The Recession: Capitalist Offensive and the Working Class', *Revolutionary Communist Papers*, no. 3, 1978.

Rose, Hilary, 'Up Against the Welfare State: The Claimants' Unions', *Socialist Register 1973*, London, Merlin, 1973.

Rothbart, Ron, 'The Limits of Mattick's Economics, Economic Law and Class Struggle', *Solidarity for Social Revolution*, no. 11, London, January–February 1980.

Rowntree, Seebohm B., and Lavers, G. R., *Poverty and the Welfare State*, London, Longman, 1951.

Rubin, I. I., *Essays on Marx's Theory of Value*, Detroit, Black and Red, 1972.

Saville, John, 'The Welfare State – An Historical Approach', *The New Reasoner*, Winter 1957/8.

Schecter, Stephen, *The Politics of Urban Liberation*, Montreal, Black Rose, 1978.

Seldon, Arthur, 'Beveridge – 20 Years Later', *New Society*, no. 20, 14 February 1963.

Sked, Alan, and Cook, Chris, *Post War Britain – A Political History*, Harmondsworth, Penguin, 1979.

Smart, D. A. (ed.), *Pannekoek and Gorter's Marxism*, London, Pluto, 1978.

Taylor, Robert, *Labour and the Social Contract*, Fabian Tract 458, London, Fabian Society, 1978.

Thompson, David, *England in the Twentieth Century (1914-1963)*, Harmondsworth, Penguin, 1965.

The Times, The British Economy: Key Statistics 1900-1970.

Titmuss, Richard M., *Essays on the Welfare State*, London, George Allen & Unwin, 1958.

Townsend, Peter, and Wedderburn, Dorothy, *The Aged in the Welfare State*, London, Bell, 1965.

Townsend, Peter, *Poverty in the United Kingdom*, Harmondsworth, Penguin, 1979.

Wilson, Elizabeth, *Women and the Welfare State*, London, Tavistock, 1977.

Winternitz, J., *The Problem of Full Employment: A Marxist Analysis*, London, Lawrence & Wishart, 1947.

Wright, Erik Olin, *Class, Crisis and the State*, London, New Left Books, 1978.

Yeo, Stephen, 'State and Anti-State: Reflections on Social Forms and Struggles from 1850', in P. Corrigan (ed.), *Capitalism, State Formation and Marxist Theory*, London, Quartet, 1980.

Youngson, A. J., *Britain's Economic Growth 1920-1966*, London, George Allen & Unwin, 1967.

Government documents (in chronological order)

Social Insurance and Allied Services, Cmd 6404, London, HMSO, 1942.

Bibliography

Social Insurance and Allied Services – Memoranda from Organizations, Appendix G, Cmd 6405, London, HMSO, 1942.

Social Insurance, Part I, Cmd. 6550, London, HMSO, 1944.

Employment Policy, Cmd. 6527, London, HMSO, 1944.

National Insurance Act, 1946, Report by the Government Actuary on the First Quinquennial Review, House of Commons, 30 November 1954.

Report of the Committee on the Economic and Financial Problems of the Provision of Old Age, Cmd 9333, London, HMSO, December 1954.

Provision for Old Age – The Future Development of the National Insurance Scheme, Ministry of Pensions and National Insurance, Cmnd. 538, London, HMSO, October 1958.

Occupational Pension Schemes: A Survey by the Government Actuary, London, HMSO, 1959.

Financial and Other Circumstances of Retirement Pensions, Ministry of Pensions and National Insurance, London, HMSO, 1966.

Occupational Pension Schemes: A New Survey by the Government Actuary, London, HMSO, 1966.

National Superannuation and Social Insurance – Proposals for Earnings-Related Social Security, Cmnd 3883, London, HMSO, January 1969.

Strategy for Pensions – The Future Development of State and Occupational Pensions, Cmnd 4755, London, HMSO, September 1971.

Occupational Pension Schemes 1971, fourth Survey of the Government Actuary, London, HMSO, 1974.

Better Pensions: Fully Protected Against Inflation, Cmnd 5713, London, HMSO, 1974.

Department of Health and Social Security, *Social Security Statistics 1976*, London, HMSO, 1977.

Occupational Pension Schemes 1975, fifth Survey of the Government Actuary, London, HMSO, 1978.

Social Assistance – A Review of the Supplementary Benefit Schemes in Great Britain, DHSS, London, HMSO, July 1978.

Economic Progress Report, Treasury Department, no. 112, October 1979.

Social Trends 10, 1980, Central Statistics Office, London, HMSO.

Miscellaneous

Reports of the Proceedings of the Annual TUCs, 1954, 1955, 1957, 1960, 1963, 1970, 1971, 1972, and *1975*.

The Labour Party *Reports of Annual Conferences, 1954, 1955, 1957, 1978*.

Annual Conservative Party Conferences, *Verbatim Reports*, 1968, 1969.

'Conservatives Keep Their Promises', *Notes on Current Politics*, Conservative Party Research Department, 14, June 1971, no. 12.

Labour party, *National Superannuation – Labour's Policy for Security in Old Age*, 1957.

'The White Paper on Pensions – Government Proposals for New Pension Schemes', *Post Magazine and Insurance Monitor*, vol. 135, pt. 39, 26 September 1974.

Index

Index